The Origins of Neoliberalism

Neoliberalism is a doctrine that adopts a free market policy in a deregulated political framework. In recent years, neoliberalism has become increasingly prominent as a doctrine in Western society, and has been heavily discussed in both academia and the media.

In *The Origins of Neoliberalism*, the joint effort of an economist and a philosopher offers a theoretical overview of both neoliberalism's genesis within economic theory and social studies as well as its development outside academia. Tracing the sources of neoliberalism within the history of economic thought, the book explores the differences between neoliberalism and classical liberalism. This book's aim is to make clear that neoliberalism is not a natural development of the old classical liberalism, but rather that it represents a dramatic alteration of its original nature and meaning. Also, it fights against the current idea according to which neoliberalism would coincide with the triumph of free market economy.

In its use of both the history of economics and philosophy, this book takes a highly original approach to the concept of neoliberalism. The analysis presented here will be of great interest to scholars and students of history of economics, political economy, and philosophy of social science.

Giandomenica Becchio is Assistant Professor of Economics at the University of Turin, Italy.

Giovanni Leghissa is Assistant Professor of Philosophy at the University of Turin, Italy.

Routledge Studies in the History of Economics

The Origins of Neoliberalism
Insights from economics and philosophy

**Giandomenica Becchio and
Giovanni Leghissa**

Routledge
Taylor & Francis Group

LONDON AND NEW YORK

First published 2017 by Routledge

2 Park Square, Milton Park, Abingdon, Oxfordshire OX14 4RN
52 Vanderbilt Avenue, New York, NY 10017

Routledge is an imprint of the Taylor & Francis Group, an informa business

First issued in paperback 2019

British Library Cataloguing in Publication Data
A catalogue record for this book is available from the British Library

Library of Congress Cataloging in Publication Data
Names: Becchio, Giandomenica, author. | Leghissa, Giovanni, 1964- author.
Title: The origins of neoliberalism : insights from economics and philosophy
/ Giandomenica Becchio and Giovanni Leghissa.
Description: New York : Routledge, 2017. | Includes index.
Identifiers: LCCN 2016018993 | ISBN 9780415732246 (hardback) |
ISBN 9781315849263 (ebook)
Subjects: LCSH: Neoliberalism. | Economics--History. | Social
sciences--Philosophy.
Classification: LCC HB95 .B393 2017 | DDC 330.1--dc23
LC record available at https://lccn.loc.gov/2016018993

ISBN: 978-0-415-73224-6 (hbk)
ISBN: 978-0-367-86920-5 (pbk)

Typeset in Times New Roman
by Taylor & Francis Books

Contents

Tables

Introduction

The counter-revolution of neoliberalism

Neoliberalism has been defined as a political doctrine that basically adopts a free market in a deregulated political framework.[1] Lately many publications have been dealing with a rethinking of neoliberalism in a broader perspective as a 'collective' thought (Mirowski 2009; Dean 2014) following what Weber called 'political oriented action', i.e. the attempt to influence or seize power (Weber [1922] 1968) by organized groups.[2]

We consider neoliberalism as the *Weltanschauung* of the late twentieth century whose roots are deeply grounded in economic theory as it has been developing in the mid-twentieth century. Neoliberalism is not a 'vision' (according to Schumpeter's definition), which shapes the 'toolbox', like classical liberalism has been for political economy in the nineteenth century or socialism for Marxism (Schumpeter 1954). Neoliberalism is either the marketing of neoclassical economic theory or its propaganda. Neoliberalism is based on a relatively simple principle: the interaction between the maximization of expected results given scarce means and revealed preferences. In a society ruled by a neoliberal system, economic rationality has reached primacy.[3] This primacy has to be intended neither as a Marxian 'structure' nor as a mere pursuit of getting higher profits for capitalists. It is meant as the regular application of the logic of economics as the only rational way of organizing private lives as well as politics and the public sphere.

In this book both history of economics and philosophy will be used to help with a new interpretation of neoliberalism. This book's aim is to show the link between neoclassical economics (we will be using the terms 'neoclassical economics' and 'mainstream economics' as synonymous throughout the book) and neoliberalism as the most persuasive cultural doctrine of our time (Mirowski 2013).

Numerous publications have appeared lately on the nature of neoliberalism spreading from academia to the press, involving social scientists as well as journalists and opinion makers. The literature on the making of mainstream economics is also quite vast, especially amongst economists and historians of economics. This book represents a tentative approach to how to consider neoliberalism as deeply rooted and developed within the process of emergence of a particular way of thinking about political economy as a science (neoclassical economics) as well as human beings as neoclassical economic agents (maximizer individuals). Since this emergence, the neoclassical model of economic rationality has reached a hegemonic dimension not only within economics, but also within a more complex realm that involves society as a whole.[4]

Even though the term 'neoliberalism' appeared first in 1925 in the Swiss economist Hans Honegger's *Trends of Economic Ideas* (Plehwe 2009, 10), the origin of neoliberalism as a political and cultural doctrine has to be dated back to the late 1930s (Mirowski and Plehwe 2009). It rose within the Walter Lippman Colloquium, and it quickly became the economic philosophy of German ordoliberalism (Foucault 2008; Vanberg 2004). Since that initial stage, supporters and detractors have talked about whether there is a strong relation between the old classic liberalism and neoliberalism or are they basically different. This theme is a cross-disciplinary argument that has been involving political philosophers, economists, and social scientists since the interwar period.

Neoliberalism does not represent the ethical weakness of late capitalism; neither has it represented a new form of ideology. Our aim is to show the theoretical *strength* of neoliberalism, focused on its anthropological dimension: the most important trait of neoliberalism is the displacement of the economic rationality within the realm of government in order to manage the increasing complexity of Western society, and to reshape it on the sole efficiency paradigm, and to include *even* the performance of values and justice.

It would be tempting to consider neoliberalism as an ideology, the scope of which should be to support the evolution of the capitalistic system on a global scale after the fall of its main competitor in the 1990s.[5] However, it would be better not to term neoliberalism as an ideology, in order to avoid the trap in which the social scientist risks falling into when using this notion. Any discursive construction that the scholar – or the subject of science – decides to label as ideological is deemed to be substituted either with the truth, or with another discursive construction, which will be, however, as ideologically over-determined as the first one. The commitment to truth-seeking is an essential part of any scientific undertaking. There are circumstances, however, that make it very difficult to identify a description of the social world that can be defined as 'true' in opposition to another one, which, in contrast, deserves to be qualified as 'ideological' or simply false. Scientific theories rest on presuppositions for which it is not always possible to account. More specifically, the entire domain of the humanities is affected by the fact that the position of the subject that describes – or explains – human affairs is somehow intertwined with that realm of the life-world that needs to be described or explicated.

Many methodological devices can be deployed in order to account for this entanglement, but the fact that the operation of describing a collective is part of the collective itself lies at the core of the epistemological self-awareness one has to have if working within the humanities. And precisely this fact makes it very difficult to assume that the subject of science is able, first, to gain precedence over the social world and, second, relying on the supposed neutrality of its own position, to excerpt 'true' motivations from the 'ideological' biases that move the observed social agents. Conversely, those who accept this assumption tend to leave out their own ideological biases. In sum, the gesture which unmasks ideologies runs the risk of being itself ideological (Rossi-Landi 1990).

Furthermore, the broad spectrum of the use of the term 'ideology' induces one to be very cautious (Barth 1976). In the present case, it is tempting to consider the heuristic potential that Luhmann's concept of ideology still seems to have. According to Luhmann (1970), ideology is nothing but a set of shared assumptions – meant as a mixture of concepts and narratives – that guide the action of a collective. More precisely, an ideological construct helps the actors to achieve a common understanding of the relationship between goals and means. This construct reduces considerably the degree of infighting, in the sense that it offers a useful tool for legitimizing the course of action that has been chosen. Generally speaking, social actions need to be justified because not all the means can be valid, efficient, or morally acceptable. Ideologies frame the interpretation of social actions and thus constitute an essential part of any modern social technology. Instead of relying on the good will of actors, or on the mechanical reproduction of bequeathed styles of actions, modern institutions and organizations can find legitimation for collective behaviour only in the rational and mindful assessment of what is to be done, but the peculiar characteristic of ideologies, according to Luhmann, is that they are replaceable. When confronted with the necessity to justify the preference for this or that course of action, the collective can choose from different ideological options, and each of them can equally result in being either suitable or fungible. As long as an ideological construct provides a viable frame within which decisions can be taken in a consensual way, there is no need to abandon it; when it ceases to perform its function, it can be replaced.

Now, assuming that the Luhmannian way of conceiving ideology within modern organizations and institutions is plausible, neoliberalism will become the most diffuse and successful ideology at the present time. Although tempting, however, this assertion would not give a satisfactory account about the way that neoliberalism is able to shape collective and individual practices. Neoliberalism, in fact, presents itself neither as a set of guidelines for action nor as a useful narrative to frame the decision making process.

Neoliberalism is neither a set of guidelines nor a narrative able to be negotiated, chosen, and eventually changed when better alternatives come into the foreground. If the consensus about ideologies can never be definitive, because they are replaceable, a possible definition of neoliberalism as an ideology is uncomfortable: neoliberalism, in fact, does not seem to work as a freely chosen set of assumptions that can be compared with disposable alternatives. This does not mean that neoliberalism has shaped our social and political world in order to deprive democracy and freedom of any significance. Neoliberalism has worked as a political project that merges both organizational and institutional practices with systems of thought, whereas the latter take either the form of coherent scientific theories or everyday life mindsets. Hence, it would be more appropriate to compare the performative strength of neoliberalism with the capacity that myths have to shape practices and mentalities and, at the same time, to remain in the background.

Groups and individuals transversally share the core of neoliberalism, regardless of their position on the political spectrum or their cultural tradition.[6] In neoliberalism, the idea that there is a plain coincidence between what neo-classical economics considers as 'rational' and the most peculiar variants of human nature is taken for granted. This idea, which represents the core of the neoliberal narrative, induces one to compare it with narratives usually defined 'mythical' by anthropologists and historians of religions.[7]

This is a crucial point: within the neoliberal society it is not possible to pose fundamental questions about the origin of wealth and the mechanisms of its distribution. Only the cost an individual is willing to pay to have access to specific resources or services receives adequate attention within the neoliberal perspective. Neoliberalism, thus, erases the plausibility of the very question about social justice.

It would be misleading, however, to say that the neoliberal project does not take into account the possible emergence of social and political conflicts. Quite the opposite: the neoliberal stance intends to offer positive and concrete solutions for any question related to the government of a complex society. These solutions present themselves as 'technical', namely as solutions that are supposed to improve the welfare of (maximizing) individuals and, thus, can be evaluated only by considering the degree of efficiency of the obtained results. In this way, the ethical and political nature of neoliberalism remains in the background, hidden by the alleged apolitical character of economic rationality.

By suggesting that the economic model of rationality is able to provide the only conceivable framework for coping with *any* possible cause of social and political tension, neoliberalism assumes a mythical feature: it naturalizes that which belongs to the realm of history.[8] It has been already noticed that in order to make it universal, economic rationality has been presented as the quintessence of human nature (Dupré 2001). Neoliberalism does not simply entail this form of reductionism. Neoliberalism politicizes a specific concep-tion of human rationality: it presents economic rationality as the most coherent instantiation of human rationality considered in its evolutionary development.

Deconstructing neoliberalism does not mean to verify the validity of the mythical image of society provided by neoliberalism; in fact, myths are neither true nor false: they simply 'work' (Blumenberg 1985). It shows which requests they answer and which issues, on the contrary, they leave outstanding in order to ensure a stable equilibrium within the collective representations our contemporary society makes of itself.[9]

This 'mythical' way of looking at neoliberalism misunderstands and, con-sequently, hides, the fact that neoliberalism is a peculiar and innovative government of society, based on a certain organization of labour, and foremost, on an idiosyncratic way of applying the model of rationality that comes from neoclassical economics.[10]

Given this general premise, the focus of this book will involve the cultural dimension of neoliberalism, in opposition to any Marxist interpretation, and close to Foucault's representation of the performative character of neoliberalism.

When neoliberalism is regarded as a 'discourse' *à la* Foucault, it is neither true nor false: it is a powerful political project that has shown an outstanding resilience to criticism, and it is a discourse embedded in a vast array of practices. Last, but not least, it is part of an 'apparatus',[11] which encompasses governmental technologies, scientific disciplines, judicial systems, and normative assets that frame individual and collective behaviour within both institutions and organizations. This apparatus must be regarded in the broadest possible sense; otherwise, the link between discursive formations and institutional practices is bound to be lost.

The role played by economics as a scientific discipline in creating the core of the neoliberal narrative has been central. Neoliberalism would be unconceivable without the performative and rhetorical strength that only a scientific discipline can deploy – a scientific discipline, moreover, that abandoned its original domain within the humanities in order to be settled within the domain of the natural sciences. This shift was relevant for economists either to conceive their position within academia or to gain prestige and influence in a broader social context. Furthermore, it allowed neoclassical economics to play a decisive role within networks, institutions and agencies which influence individuals' lives.

Biopolitics is the notion Foucault coined during his Lectures at the Collège de France about the genesis of neoliberalism (Foucault 2008) in order to make clear the innovation introduced by neoliberalism itself. By offering a 'natural' explanation of how human beings behave as rational agents, neoclassical economics does not simply provide a guideline to govern them, but it builds up that cultural framework that enables institutions and organizations to 'nudge' individuals to choose a rational way of behaving – where 'rational' means in accordance with the prescriptions of the Rational Choice Theory.[12]

Foucault never stopped repeating that the subject whom the neoliberal discourse addresses is a free subject; it is important, thus, to bear in mind that the power exerted by the neoliberal discourse upon contemporary society is not a coercive power that stems from deploying disciplinary means of subjection.[13] It is rather a form of power that acts indirectly upon subjects whose freedom is never questioned: individuals' choices become the target of all biopolitical interventions inspired by neoliberalism.

Foucault made a great effort to clarify the distinction between classical liberalism and neoliberalism. To put it briefly, in classical liberalism economy and politics were independent, but related, and both based on the emancipation of free individuals. In neoliberalism, the distinction between the two realms is denied, because the model of economic rationality has reached an imperialistic position, and it shapes an individual's life, no matter whether they act as economic agents or citizens.

The substantial acceptance of Foucault's distinction between liberalism and neoliberalism explains why a definition of neoliberalism like the one offered by David Harvey could not be endorsed. But it is worth mentioning here because it vividly embodies a conception of neoliberalism, which is spread both inside and outside academia:

> Neoliberalism is in the first instance a theory of political economic practices that proposes that human well-being can best be advanced by liberating individual entrepreneurial freedoms and skills within an institutional framework characterized by strong property rights, free markets and free trade. The role of the state is to create and preserve an institutional framework appropriate to such practices. The state has to guarantee, for example, the quality and integrity of money. It must also set up military, defence, policy and legal structures and functions required to secure private property rights and guarantee, by force if need be, the proper functioning of markets. Furthermore, if markets do not exist (in areas such as land, water, education, health care, social security, or environmental pollution) then they must be created, by state action if necessary. But beyond these tasks the state should not venture. State interventions in markets (once created) must be kept to a bare minimum because, according to the theory, the state cannot possibly possess enough information to second-guess market signals (prices) and because powerful interest groups will inevitably distort and bias state interventions (particularly in democracies) for their own benefit.
>
> (Harvey 2005, 2)

In Harvey's thought, neoliberalism would be nothing but the continuation of liberalism in a different and more complex historical context, but neoliberalism is not about the restriction of state power to domains within which the logic of the market would be simply inappropriate, nor is it about the extension of this logic to domains that previously have been left untouched by it.[14] To make this point clearer, it is worth remembering the way in which the economist Henry Simons used to distinguish between domains regulated by the logic of the market and domains that are not subjected to it: hence, he was at the same time an advocate of laissez faire and a supporter of a progressive income taxation. Nowadays, the fact that the same author held these positions is simply unintelligible.[15]

Simons wrote:

> Turning now to a question of justice, of equitable distribution, we may suggest that equitable distribution is at least as important with respect to power as with reference to economic goods or income … Surely there is something *unlovely*, to modern as against medieval minds, about marked inequality of either kind. A substantial measure of inequality may be

unavoidable or essential for motivation; but it should be recognized as
evil and tolerated only so far as the dictates of expediency are clear.
(Simons 1938, 51–52; emphasis added)

If one is aware of the fact that for a classical liberal like Simons the concern
for social justice was obviously not included into economic issues, but it
belongs to ethics, then his attitude ceases to seem bizarre. The deep tie that
binds together economic inequality and the lack of individual agency (as it is
said today) was a typical feature of the way in which a classical liberal considered the question of social justice within a laissez-faire political economy.
The absence of this feature is what characterizes the neoliberal stance.

Foucault's insights about the difference between liberalism and neoliberalism
are also useful to avoid any kind of nostalgia for classical liberalism: what
really matters is to create a conceptual and narrative discourse that enables
the reader to understand to what extent neoliberalism continues and/or inter-
rupts the tradition of classical liberalism.[16] Despite some recent attempts to
enlist Foucault among the supporters of neoliberalism, he has never been a
partisan of liberalism nor a supporter of neoliberalism.[17]

Scholars who charge Foucault with a more or less explicit bent for neoliberalism are mostly leftist: Marxists, embedded in their tradition of the 'critique of
ideologies', feel uncomfortable with Foucault's critique of the ideological
apparatuses as well as of the hidden economic structure upon which these
apparatuses are supposed to rest. Furthermore, they arguably find it surprising that Foucault has never approached neoliberalism as a symptom of the
colonization of life-world by the economic sphere.[18] Finally, even though
Marxists, who intend to offer a critique of contemporary capitalism by interpreting it in terms of 'postfordism', have folded the Foucauldian notion of
'biopolitics' in their conceptual toolbox, biopolitics loses any meaning when it
has been forced to migrate from its original discursive field to the Marxist context. Yet, the issue does not seem to be the theoretical distance between the
Marxian tradition and Foucault's philosophy – a topic we will discuss in a more
detailed manner in Chapter 1. What is at stake here, rather, is a prosaic misread-
ing. Just a simple attentive reading of Foucault's texts should prevent one from
interpreting his attitude toward the political significance of neoliberalism which
he discussed both during his Lectures at the Collège de France and in further
essays as if he had succumbed in a sort of identification with the studied object.
A precise warning against any possible misunderstanding about this issue came
from Colin Gordon some years ago, precisely at the beginning of the reception
of Foucault's thought within the Anglo-Saxon academia (Gordon 1991).

Gordon wrote:

> One of the conspicuous attributes of Foucault's governmentality lectures
> is their serene and (in a Weberian sense) exemplary abstention from value
> judgements. In a pithy preamble he rejects the use of an academic dis-
> course as a vehicle of practical injunctions ('love this; hate that; do this;

refuse that ...') and dismisses the notion that practical political choices can be determined within the space of a theoretical text as trivializing the act of moral decision to the level of a merely aesthetic preference. (...) In a nutshell, he suggests that recent neo-liberalism, understood (as he proposes) as a novel set of notions about the art of government, is a considerably more original and challenging phenomenon than the left's critical culture has had the courage to acknowledge, and that its political challenge is one which the left is singularly ill equipped to respond to (...)

(Gordon 1991, 6)

Thus, in no way Foucault endorses the forms of biopolitical governmentality he analyses when attempting to make clear in which sense they are different from the classical liberal art of government.

Bearing that in mind, it is worth mentioning a certain affinity between this book's analysis of how neoliberalism has transformed the art of government and Davies's work (2014). In Davies's book, neoliberalism is challenged directly as a set of discourses and practices that have turned upside down the political landscape of contemporary societies.[19]

Davies defines neoliberalism as 'the pursuit of the disenchantment of politics by economics' (Davies 2014, 4), and this definition spans his whole book. His analysis is almost persuasive insofar as it shows the effects of an art of government that hides its own ethical and anthropological presuppositions by displaying a vast array of technical measures that, de facto, restrict the space of individual agency. But the veil that hides what can be well defined as the neoliberal political programme is rather thin, and it is not so complicated to elicit not only the idea of society, but also the idea of government that neoliberalism has forged.

Thus, it is hard to see in which sense neoliberal economic theories can be considered as deprived of any political significance. Instead of 'disenchanting' politics, the neoliberal programme supersedes both the economic and political programme of liberalism, by substituting a given set of values with another. Surely, what is definitely lost under neoliberalism is the possibility to appeal to the authority of a Weberian *Wertrationalität*, that can be *de iure* distinguished from a *Zweckrationalität*, whose function was to mark the boundary of the economic calculus. If neoliberalism has proved to be so successful, however, it seems hard to dismiss the way in which it fashioned the meaning of *Zweckrationalität* as simply 'cold', or 'disenchanting': the neoliberal economic discourse is imbued by a visionary *afflatus*; it thus possesses an attractiveness that makes it useless to search for an 'enchantment' that should compensate the ruthlessness of sheer *Zweckrationalität*.

Perhaps the metaphor of the veil should be abandoned: neoliberalism, as a network of governmental apparatuses that has its hub in neoclassical economics, does not conceal its willingness to offer the right tools that any Prince (in the Machiavellian sense of the term) needs in order to make a good job. The economic theory on which neoliberalism rests is able to encompass solutions for whatever the political problem. If, as Davies puts it, 'the liberal boundaries separating the "economic", "political" and "social" are dissolved by the distinctly neoliberal creation of networks and tools which extend a managerial-political calculus into all domains' (Davies 2014, 133), then what we need is a new insight into the political character of organizations. It is true that the shared discourse that permeates the managerial culture is – not surprisingly – far from giving room for the recognition that an organization is a political coalition.

Yet, firms exist not only because someone has decided to reduce transaction costs as explained by Coase (1937), but above all because the structure of modern societies takes advantage of the existence of hierarchically arranged forms of coordination of individual and collective goals, tasks and performances. As soon as those who investigate organizations became aware of this fact, it became possible to consider organizations as political coalitions whose overall activity does not depend uniquely on the goal of maximizing profits (March 1962). No differently from what happens within any other political coalition, the everyday life of an organization is deeply permeated by symbols and rituals whose function is precisely to provide an 'enchantment'. This enchantment contributes to the spread of cultural traits generally related to the capitalist worldview. It is less obvious, perhaps, to consider to what extent the organization is *per se* a sort of theatrical staging of neoclassical rationality, in the sense that it incorporates the model of rationality that neoclassical economics created.

The firm is to be seen as a 'school' where individuals are 'drilled' (in the Foucauldian sense of the term) to behave according to those precepts of the neoclassical economic rationality that are supposed to provide individuals with an unprecedented experience of freedom, as it has been recast by neoliberalism. Individuals are exposed to neoliberal forms of subjectivation; an entrepreneurial form of subjectivation constitutes a necessary premise for the construction of a free society. This formula is not simply the cultural framework of neoliberalism, it is neoliberalism as the most persuasive political project today.

It is common, among scholars who interpret neoliberalism as a form of 'economization' of the political, to claim that neoliberalism has to do with the extension of the logic of the market upon all the relevant spheres of human interaction. It is taken for granted that this logic entails a constitutive indifference towards ethics and the dimension of values in general. In this critique, neoliberalism exists in the cultural, social and political process along which everything has been transformed into an asset. The result would be the commodification of everything – not only of things that are usually not used as goods of exumptions, but also of human feelings, attitudes, desires, values and so on.[20] It is important to draw attention to the classical liberal argument about the positive effects that market behaviours have on the conduct of individuals. It would be fruitful to remember this argument, we suggest, if neoliberalism is ever going to undergo a critique for ethical reasons. If market-oriented behaviours, together with the values they help enforce, had the opportunity to spread and take root, then it is likely that they would be able to hinder, at least partially, the diffusion of the neoliberal worldview, which nurtures values like selfishness, greed, indifference.

The thesis that the simple fact of dedicating oneself to trade improves good personal qualities like open-mindedness, curiosity and, above all, trust, goes back to the period in which the elite of modern Europe began to appreciate the advantages brought by the spread of capitalism. Moreover, the extension of trade onto a global scale was seen as the necessary premise for a peaceful world. Starting from the nineteenth century, this conception – vividly rendered by the French expression '*doux commerce*' – began to be questioned. Once abandoned, it has been substituted by the concept – almost current, nowadays, within the Humanities – according to which individuals cannot find satisfaction or improve their happiness if involved in exchange and trade (Hirschman 1982). The result is that ethics and the market have been placed in two different and separate sides of social intercourse that do not communicate with one another any more. The moral subject, then, is requested to pursue virtue in a sort of 'economic vacuum'. In other words, all that the subject does when it acts according to its moral principles is not related to what it does when it seeks to maximize profit. This separation of ethics from market behaviour often rests on lack of appropriate information about the laws of the market. As a consequence, most of the reproaches to the market for being 'immoral' are flawed and ungrounded. A morally consistent behaviour, in fact, presupposes a specific learning ability, and the market experience offers patterns of learning that are relevant as regards not only the individual effort to improve oneself in general, but also the capability to engage oneself as a moral agent.

As Bruni and Sugden – among others – have rightly shown, people learn to behave virtuously when they are engaged either in market transactions or in other forms of interaction outside the market (Bruni and Sudgen 2013). Once acquired, a positive disposition towards virtue remains constant within the individual habitus. Thus, virtuous market participants do not cease to behave according to given moral principles and, moreover, do expect that other participants, whose virtue does not seem to be simulated for whatever reason, behave the same way. From this perspective, the virtues that can be attributed to a market participant are neither unrelated nor alien to the set of attitudes that she or he needs in order to pursue her or his goals within the market. In sum, the set of benefits that individuals expect to obtain by participation in a voluntary transaction entail – and not as a simple by-product – those mutual benefits that are proper to those forms of interaction that are not based on the pursuit of self-interest.

According to Bruni and Sugden, the most important virtues of a trustworthy trade partner are universality, enterprise, alertness, respect for the taste of one's trading partner, trust and trustworthiness, acceptance of competition, self-help, non-rivalry, and stoicism about reward. These virtues attest that trade exchange can be seen – better said, it should be seen – as a form of mutual assistance, which generates mutual benefits for those who are involved in a market transaction. They can plainly coexist with self-interest and the pursuit of profit. Of course, this coexistence becomes questionable if one thinks that self-interest and the willingness to increase one's wealth are in some way inferior, or deplorable, or contrary to morality and the general interest.[21] In other words, if an action is motivated by the aim to create a good that can be then used or exchanged, then this action is morally inferior to an action that has its end in itself. This distinction between actions as *per se* means to an extrinsic end, and actions that are done for the sake of themselves is deeply rooted in the western philosophical tradition: it goes back to the Aristotelian ranking of intrinsic value over instrumental value. This distinction is far from being obvious and universally accepted though. If seen from a historical perspective, the modern tradition within which there is no good justification for holding this distinction is surely no less important. It is more persuasive to hold that there is no contradiction between economic activity, which is merely useful, and the activities that are undertaken for the sake of themselves. If one follows this thread of thought, it becomes persuasive to hold that market transactions can be seen as valuable 'because individuals want to make them, because they satisfy individual's preferences, because they create wealth, and because the opportunity to make them is a form of freedom' (Bruni and Sugden 2013, 153). Within this perspective, the *telos* of the market is mutual benefit, and there is no reason to justify the existence of the market using arguments that infer their soundness from domains extrinsic to it.

The interpretation of the nature of the market belongs to the tradition of the history of classical political economy and its transformation into economics. The cultural transformation of classical political economy into economics took place in a historical period during which Western society was affected, in frantic succession, by the following: the First World War, totalitarian regimes, the Second World War, and the Cold War. Neoclassical economics had been developed within this framework, and it was intentionally adopted by those political movements that presented a society based on market economy as the only possible form of society that simultaneously is rationally organized and makes individuals free. The connection between the Mont Pèlerin Society (founded in 1947) and many economists of the Chicago School can be regarded as an example of the cultural influence of mainstream economics outside strict academic boundaries.

Although both neoclassical economics and neoliberalism have been presented as renewed forms of classical economy and classical liberalism, there are some crucial differences between them and the doctrines they are assumed to have originated: the nature of the market as well as the meaning of individual freedom are two examples of this idiosyncratic relation. Classical doctrines looked at the market as an institution that enabled a higher division of labour as a necessary condition to increase the wealth of a nation. Neoclassical economics and neoliberalism, instead, consider the market as the only *natural* institution that enables relations amongst rational agents. In classical doctrines, individuals are either *bourgeois* or *citoyens* whose degree of liberty had been measured against a benchmark produced by civil, political, and social rights.

Both neoclassical economics and neoliberalism have reduced individuals (and society) to rational (social) agents, whose goals are necessarily related to the maximization of their expected utility function.

Along the tradition of classical liberalism (from Locke to Hayek), the discourse on freedom has not been grounded in a specific rational theory based exclusively on the logic of economics; in neoliberalism (from Pareto-Robbins to the Chicago School), the logic of economics constitutes the only tool to define and to explain any rational choice, and, consequently, the meaning of freedom. It will be made clearer in the book about the crucial role, played by Hayek, whose position was different from neoliberalism (see Chapter 3).

In this big picture neoliberalism is not a natural development of the old classical liberalism; in fact, its nature and meaning has been dramatically changed during the past decades. Neoliberalism can be regarded as a set of practices going from the establishment of a specific economic rationality – based only on criteria of efficiency and accountability – within the departments of economics to the implementation of specific policies. This process has shaped the everyday lives of human beings, who have been gradually converted into rational agents, able to apply anytime the principle of maximization as the only rational way of behaving in any framework of scarcity.

After this transformation, the meaning of liberty within neoliberalism had been changed: for instance, the fight for economic freedom in classical liberalism was mainly intended as a struggle against any form of political limitations for trades; besides this, it was also related to the support of any form of entrepreneurial creativity. In neoliberalism, markets are supposed to be deregulated, and any form of political interference is banned, at least in principle. Classical liberalism brought formal and effective freedom to individuals as well as societies; in contrast, social and economic conditions under neoliberalism have been reducing the effective freedom of both. This is the counter-revolutionary aspect of neoliberalism, which, in a paradoxical way, led individuals far away from liberty.

There are two sources of neoliberalism when it is related to neoclassical economics: the shift from the classical notion of 'political economy' to the notion of 'economics', and the emergence of rational choice theory.

Keynes's contributions do not belong to this story: his approach to economic theory was not affected by the necessity to transform the discipline into a science; furthermore, his notion of individuality is far away from being reduced to an economic agent in neoclassical terms.[22] The Cambridge economist was outside the path of interconnections between economics as a science and neoliberalism as its cultural framework mainly for the following reasons: the central role of uncertainty in his system; the use of a concept like 'animal spirits' to present a possible explanation for fluctuations within the market; a macroeconomic approach as the focus of his economic analysis; the refusal to consider a general economic equilibrium as the aim, even temporal, of economics.[23] Part of this story was, on the contrary, the operation made by Hicks, in 1937, from which originates the so-called neoclassical synthesis: the reduction of Keynes' macroeconomics to a special case of the broader neoclassical theory that was emerging as the mainstream of the discipline. This historical reconstruction of the theoretical shift within economics implies a broader discourse on the methodological transformation of the discipline into a positive science.

In a discourse about the nature of neoclassical economics, on which neoliberalism is grounded, room for a debate around the epistemic status of economic models is not only important *per se*, but it is fundamental in order to understand the reasons for either the success or the fallacies of the discipline that has been forging present society.

This book's methodological premise is twofold: a. political economy is not a formal science (as it has been forged in neoclassical economics), but it is a human and social discipline able to describe the real word, hence 'model-building in economics has serious intent only if it is ultimately directed towards telling us something about the real world' (Sugden 2000, 3); b. human rationality has to be intended not in a constructive way (as has been used in neoclassical economics), but with an ecological meaning (Smith 2008; Gintis 2009).[24] This approach makes possible a critique of neoclassical economics *strictu sensu* (which is not our book's aim), as well as to point out how the transformation of political economy into neoclassical economics has been forging neoliberalism. The introduction of formalism and the quantitative approach in economics (1930s–1940s), as well as the process of the microfoundation of macroeconomics (1950s), was the starting point of the building of the present mainstream (Morgan 2012; Hausman 1998; Hoover 2001) upon which the neoliberal agenda has been grounded.

General assumptions developed by neoclassical economists are focused around the following: initial hypotheses (*ceteris paribus*[25]); the role of causality (economic relations usually depend on people's expectations[26]); methodology (individualism *versus* pluralism[27]); axiomatizations (axioms of preferences and general economic equilibrium prerequisites[28]); models (to describe the real world[29]); formalism (as a tool to express models[30]); microfoundation and aggregation (the use of microeconomics to explain aggregate phenomena[31]).

The building of neoclassical economics was mainly due to the adoption of the model of general economic equilibrium as well as econometrics.[32] In econometrics a model must be specified in an explicit linear function; data have to be included in the model; and statistics has to be considered as a bridge between theory and data to verify the theoretical model. Further statistics have to test the model to assess its performance.

The influence of logical positivism was deep either in general economic equilibrium economists or in econometricians: they both shared the belief that economic laws are able to reach an explanation as well as a prediction of economic phenomena.[33] The econometrics agenda followed through the National Bureau of Economic Research's manifesto.[34] In 1947 the NBER was involved by Koopmans in the so-called 'measurement without theory debate' (Rutherford 2011, Emmett 2016). According to Koopmans, experiments cannot be done in economics, because so many empirical relations are valid simultaneously and dynamics of economic variables make predictions unreliable. Furthermore, statistical analysis of data requires additional assumptions that cannot be subjected to statistical testing starting from the same data.

In the same year, Samuelson published his *Foundations*. Along with Friedman's *Essays,* published in 1953, these books represent the pillars of neoclassical economic theory from an epistemological point of view (see Chapter 3). Both Samuelson and Friedman explicitly claimed the necessity to go from physics to economics to found economic analysis as a science;[35] and Friedman clearly stated the urgency to free economics from any ethics and particular normativism and to establish it as a positive science.

A discourse around causality is particularly important in determining the epistemic nature of economics as a positive science.[36] In 1944 Haavelmo warned economists engaged in the building of the discipline as a science on this specific point: in a properly formulated stochastic model, where exogenous elements are considered fixed, hypotheses are able to determine which set of values are admissible to produce only a useful, not a specifically true, model (Haavelmo 1944). The microfoundation of macroeconomics was determinant in shaping economic theory in a neoclassical way and, consequently, in shaping society as a whole in a neoliberal pattern. The main tool that achieved this result (the microfoundation of macroeconomics) was the application of rational choice theory based on expected utility function.

Although detractors of general economic equilibrium cannot deny the fact that, in the recent debates, economists engaged in the general economic equilibrium model went far beyond Walras's unrealistic assumptions (Weintraub 1977), Haavelmo's critique still persists in a simpler formulation when economists wonder whether the model of representative agent is able to explain aggregates. Furthermore, it still difficult to admit that macro aggregates have emergent proprieties that cannot belong to agents' dynamics and cannot be wholly explained by the same causal relationships that connect them.[37] From the 1950s, division of labour between mathematicians who were engaged in the building of economic models and econometricians who specifically had been coping with statistical data determined a collapse of a truly synthetic economics (Baltagi 2008). Even though the introduction of models in economics has reduced the naturalism of the discipline (Sugden 2002; Morgan 2012), philosophers such as Cartwright defined economics' attitude of considering itself as a natural science, by following an 'imperialistic tendency', bound to fall into the trap of methodological fundamentalism (Cartwright 1999; Mäki 2013).[38] The lack of realism still seems to be the main fault of the discipline from a methodological point of view, in spite of the tentative efforts made by scholars like Blaug to introduce a normative methodology of economics (Blaug 1980, 1992; Mäki 2011).[39]

In such a context, more recent developments, especially some heterodox approaches (Lawson 1997; Hausman 1998; Lavoie 2014), consider the lack of realism in neoclassical economics as the most severe limitation within the discipline, and they introduced some alternative models, such as rhetoric, persuasion, metaphors, and heuristics (McCloskey 1983; Gigerenzer and

Todd 1999; Klamer and Leonard 1994; Lawson 2004). In McCloskey's works, for example, she considers the relevance of the social framework of a scientific community in terms of how it disseminates its ideas and arguments, as well as how individual economists are persuaded within the framework of those structures. Behavioural economics as well as experimental economics became very popular, at least since the attribution of the Nobel prize for economics to Kahneman for his and Tversky's *Prospect Theory* (Kahneman and Tversky 1979). Even though the introduction of psychology to explain economic behaviour has been regarded as a serious means to tentatively bridge the gap between economic theory and empirical evidence, and to problematize the neoclassical conception of economic rationality, their effective ability to reform the epistemological status of the discipline remains controversial. In fact, neoclassical economics was able to embed even uncertainty within the general explanation of how economic rationality works.

Prospect theory is an example of this internal development of the neoclassical approach. Even though expected utility theory has been criticized 'as a normative model of rational choice' and 'accepted as a descriptive model of economic behaviour', by Kahneman and Tversky, they presented bias and errors as deviation from standard behaviour, as well as violation of axioms of preferences. Their model is not an alternative to the neoclassical model of economic rationality (Kahneman and Tversky 1979).[40]

Heuristics *à la* Gigerenzer can offer a plausible alternative to the neoclassical model of rationality. Four concepts of rationality are involved in most recent debates within economics: 'as-if' theories of unbounded rationality, based on the maximization of expected utility for finding the optimal strategy (Bernoulli 1738; von Neumann and Morgenstern 1944); 'as-if' theories of optimization under constraints, based on a Bayesian model in predicting behaviour, given memory span and information costs (Wald 1947; Stigler 1961); the irrational cognitive illusions, based on the cognitive process that produces both valid and invalid judgements and on the fact that cognitive illusions are deviations from rationality (Kahneman and Tversky 1996); finally, the ecological approach, based on the relation between mind and social-physical environment and on the concept of bounded rationality as an adaptive toolbox that helps solve problems independent of whether an optimal solution exists (Gigerenzer 2008). Gigerenzer summarized that it is urgent to free heuristics from some misconceptions such as considering heuristics limited in producing just second-best results; to consider heuristics linked to cognitive limitations; to use heuristics just in unimportant or routine decisions; finally to think that more information is always better than less. Such a description of heuristics is biased by the implicit acceptance of the optimization model as the best one. Gigerenzer's heuristic is to be intended as 'fast and frugal' (Gigerenzer and Selten 2002): it is able to find good solutions independent of whether an optimal solution exists.[41] This represents a formidable heterodox approach to economics.

The use of the label *heterodoxy* in order to get a more precise definition for economic approaches that do not belong to the mainstream became clearer at the beginning of the 1980s. JEL codes provide boundaries within the discipline in a very official way: post-Keynesianism, Marxism, Austrians, feminists, even historians were outside the toolbox. Behavioural, experimental, ecological economists could belong either to mainstream economics or to heterodoxy (Davis 2006; Colander 2007). That was the period during which the neoliberal agenda was clearly defined.

This book's contents

Chapter 1 will provide a detailed survey of Foucault's interpretation of neoliberalism. Its reception began rather early, even before the English translation of his lectures at the Collège de France. Nevertheless, several misreadings and misinterpretations took place along with this reception. For this reason – and not for philological reasons, which would be misplaced in the present context – it seems to be important to highlight the major tenets of Foucault's position. The most relevant point is to decode how the rhetoric of neoliberalism has been able to globally spread rather quickly.

Foucault emphasized that there is a big difference between how liberals and neoliberals conceive of the origins and functions of the market. Despite their professed faith in the self-regulative capability of the market, the supporters of neoliberalism are well aware of the fact that the market needs to be not only protected and safeguarded, but literally built up by public institutions. By drawing attention to this point, Foucault showed neoliberalism as a new form of power, a new art of government, based on a specific form of rationality. This form of rationality is 'economic' in the sense that it has been arranged in order to give account of how human beings refer means to ends, but it is also thoroughly 'political' in the sense that it entails a specific normative vision of how human beings are to be governed for the sake of their happiness and realization.

This point has been systematically missed by the current Marxist interpretations of neoliberalism – even if these interpretations often tend to make use of some Foucauldian keywords like 'biopolitics' and 'governmentality'.[42] In order to offer a valid alternative to the Marxist way of describing the impact of neoliberalism, it is useful to consider how some authors, who work within the field of International Relations, have persuasively shown to what extent the post-Westphalian state still constitutes the basic institution whose behaviour one has to observe if one wants to understand how global frameworks of power come into existence and continue to exist. Thanks to this analysis the nation state stands out as an autonomous agent that pursues interests that are to enable it to be brought back principally to the position it occupies within the global arena – and this is true also when it deals with interests of an economic nature. The chapter concludes with a possible answer to the question of why neoliberalism has shown so much resilience and has demonstrated so much persuasive force in recent decades. The way neoliberal rhetoric is constructed gives the clue for a possible answer. In its core, neoliberalism offers very simple solutions to complex problems. It is this reduction of complexity, made possible by the assumption that agents – no matter whether dealing with individuals, organizations or institutions – always react rationally to external affordances, which makes neoliberalism so attractive. Both Luhmann's systemic approach and those theories stemming from Callon's insight about the performativity of the economic theory provide interesting explanations, we think, of how it has been possible for neoliberalism to become the reference framework that forms shared beliefs systems within public institutions as well as organizations.

Chapter 2 and Chapter 3 will describe – through the perspective of the history of economic thought – the genesis of economics as a science as well as the transformation of individuals into utility-maximizers through the building of the rational choice theory. Albeit neoliberalism and rational choice theory are different, they have been mixed up, and the result was a gradual transformation of Western society into a global mechanism ruled by the sole principle of the mere efficiency of governance.

The shift from the classical notion of 'political economy' (that fits classical political liberalism) to the notion of 'economics' (where neoliberalism is firmly rooted) is crucial to understand the transformation of the discipline into a science (Chapter 2). Hence, some considerations on this point will imply a study on the role of classical liberalism within the classical school of political economy.

Throughout the tradition of classical liberalism (from Locke to Hayek), the discourse on freedom was not grounded in a specific rational theory based exclusively on the logic of economics, rather it was rooted into the ethics of universal and natural rights, which allowed individuals to fight for their political, economic, and social rights within the legislation system. In neoclassical economics (from Pareto-Robbins to the Chicago School), debunking economics from ethics became the motto of the economists who considered themselves as scientists. The logic of economics constitutes the only tool to define and to explain any rational choice. Defining economics as the science of human choice under specific circumstances (given ends and scarce means) radically changed the meaning of freedom for individuals, who were gradually reduced to rational agents (Chapter 3). Freedom is no longer the outcome of the development of a complex discourse around liberty and justice, which includes material progress; it is the logical consequence of a rational behaviour, which implies a process of maximization and cut off of any moral premises.

Hence, Chapter 2 and Chapter 3 deal with the process of transformation of political economy into economics. To understand this process it is crucial to describe the history of the building of mainstream economics in Europe during the 1930s,[43] as well as the following exportation of economics to the American academia after the Second World War, as shown by the building of Chicago economics (Van Horn, Mirowski and Stapleford 2011).

It is relevant to understand the historical framework of the interwar period in Europe as a plausible correlation that led economists of that time to present economics as a value-free discipline: the formalization of the discipline within the general economic equilibrium theory as well as the introduction of econometrics were not only instruments to re-organize the scientific nature of the economic theory, they were also formidable tools used by European economists to avoid any relation with and commitment to totalitarian regimes in countries like Austria (Leonard 2010).

The gap between economic theory and politics sterilized the discipline from anything that was non-scientific, but, in a paradoxical way, the economics of freedom (as political economy was intended to be in classical liberalism) became the theory of efficiency without any regard to individual freedom. The case of Polanyi's prophecy, as described in Chapter 3, represented an example of the description of the process of debunking economics from individual liberty that led to a reduction of freedom. On this specific issue, the role of the Austrian school of economics in this transition will be reconsidered from a different perspective in order to show the differences between the Austrian school and the Chicago school on the nature of economics as a science, on the meaning of individual freedom, and on the nature of the market. The place of economists like von Mises and von Hayek is, in fact, not as clear as it appears in most of the secondary literature.

Chapter 4 deals with the existing relationship between corporate America and neoliberal doctrines about antitrust policies. Neoliberalism, on the one hand, owes part of its success to a narrative that exalts the moral, social, and political role of the freedom of enterprise, and, on the other, its fortune was due, in part, to coalition with those corporations after the end of the Second World War, following a clever restyling of their public image. American big business corporations succeeded in convincing their audience that 'big', referred to themselves, was not synonymous with soulless and ruthless and, furthermore, that their own prosperity and their achievements were not a matter regarding the portfolio of the shareholders, but were the keystone of the well-being of the entire nation.

The success of this propaganda machine served to hide the enormous power they had gained not only as economic, but above all, as political actors. This is not to be understood in the simple sense usually evoked by the image of the revolving door between the business and the political spheres. The constellation of mutual interests, which has made the relationship between institutional and organizational agencies, is to be intended as a win-win game. This state of affairs induces the formulation of the hypothesis that the network of power formed by corporate America can be seen as the cultural background from which the neoliberal discourse actually arose. Once again, this does not mean that neoliberalism provided a type of 'ideological justification' for the power big business corporations had acquired in the meantime. As a perfect embodiment of a rational agent, the corporation, in the eyes of the Chicago School, played the role of the sole force that could guarantee the good functioning of the market. From a liberal perspective it should be clear that a market cannot work properly if it is reduced to the stage on which only a few big corporations pretend to compete against each other. Nonetheless, the global world under the neoliberal rule is nothing but this stage, and the actors that play on it deliver performances praised for being 'efficient' by mainstream economics.

While it seems clear how it has been possible that CEOs of big corporations and also decision makers operating within state apparatuses found it convenient – to say the least – to espouse the major tenets of neoliberalism, what needs explaining is the emergence of those communicative channels, interaction sites and social environments that made it possible that neoliberalism became the standard view according to which contemporary subjectivity represents itself. The firm is to be seen, we suggest, as this site. This does not occur simply because the discourses that cross, vertically and horizontally, any given organization propagate those virtues that turn each agent into a calculating machine, whose scope is to resist environmental challenges and to survive even in a sea of troubles. The point is that the very structure of the organization, its hierarchy, even its physical arrangement, are able to convey specific images of the subject that forge not only an architecture of choice, but also an architecture of desire, within which each member of the organization is invited to find their own way toward self-representation, self-fulfilment and self-positioning.

This state of affairs is not new: organizations have always constituted a powerful framework that poses, both symbolically and physically, specific constraints on the processes of subjectivation. What seems to be new, in the neoliberal era, is that one and the same narrative is to be found within the communicational structure of firms and public institutions. If a totalitarian character may be ascribed to neoliberalism, this occurs because a very restrictive model of behaviour, stemming originally from the economic discourse and then spreading out through the code that compounds organizational settings, imposed itself almost universally.

Yet, it is precisely by starting from a critical study of organizations that it becomes possible to determine how an alternative narrative with respect to neoliberalism could look like. First, individuals are surely subject to constraints, but are also creative and able to find ways to express their freedom. Thus, forms of resistance are not only possible, but, as the ethnography of organizations shows, they develop spontaneously even within the most restrictive frame. Second, institutional and systemic approaches to the life-world of organizations, if combined together, offer theoretical tools that allow for a conception of human action that differ from that postulated by mainstream economic theory. This shift is important in order to build the theoretical space within which human freedom can be seen not as the expression of an individual preference, but as the capability to create common trajectories for collective action (see Postscript).

Notes

1 The contents of the neoliberal agenda, as it is usually perceived, are: deregulation of the market economy, liberalization of trade and industry, and privatization of state-owned enterprises (Steger and Roy 2010); a way of governance that considers the idea of the self-regulating free market, competition and self-interest as the models

for efficient government (Steger and Roy 2010); a prescriptive model for the labour market and capital, and for the role of the state (Boas and Gans-Morse 2009).

2   A massive literature on the Great Recession has lately been focused on the role of neoliberalism as a possible framework for either its origin or its persistence (Stein 2012; Mirowski 2013).

3   The use of rational choice analysis of political and economic institutions as a tool to explain institutional changes has been quite frequent to understand the rise of neoliberalism (Campbell and Pedersen 2001).

4   The definition of neoliberalism as a hegemonic mode of discourse is due to Harvey (Harvey 2005).

5   Emphasis on the definition of neoliberalism as an ideology has been central in a vast literature, especially amongst anthropologists (Ferguson 2010), and as reminded by Ganti (2014).

6   Widely shared, for example, is the idea that the rationality embedded in procedures of accountability can justify governmental practices that either reduce complexity or guarantee efficiency. This also applies to the idea that a good policy consists of coordinating the maximizing tendency of individuals, whereas the intrinsic rationality of this tendency does not need to be problematized, being self-evident.

7   Myths have the function to hinder the questioning of social habits and mentalities that are widely recognized as normal and obvious; in other words, they hide the historical nature of social processes and constellations. By doing so, myths help to simplify both the complicatedness of social relations and the mental schemas individuals use to orient themselves in the world. This simplification serves to inhibit the emergence of questions about the origins of both the contexts of action and the frames of reference needed to cope with the task of sense making.

8   By saying that neoliberalism works as if it were a myth, we are not interested in showing to what extent some influential economic theories could be compared with religious traditions of the past. Conversely, in Nelson (2001) the thoughts of some of the most important scholars among economists, like Samuelson, Knight, Becker, North, are seen as a sort of rebound of old religious themes, which are necessarily drawn from the Judaeo-Christian tradition. Nelson acknowledges that economic ideas do not compose a belief system that simply results in a Judeo-Christian heresy and he is prone to identify this system as a new secular religion (Nelson 2001, 23). Nevertheless, given the fact that the system of economic ideas offers an alternative vision of the 'ultimate value', he understands this system as another grand prophesy that *de facto* follows the biblical tradition. It is true that, by presenting neoliberalism as a secular religion, one gains fruitful insights into the mix of technical considerations and value elements that characterizes the economic discourse. Nevertheless, the idea of secular religion implies that the religious impulses of our times are necessarily the result of a secularization process, along which old concepts and narratives sprung from an originally theological context maintain their function within a broader cultural or political framework, even if deprived of their previous theological significance. By considering neoliberalism simply as a secular religion, one risks concealing that it has been conceived as a new way of governing the global society.

9   On a related topic, it is worth noting that the reference to the performativity of myth can be usefully evoked also to depict the way in which Marxists carry on their critique of neoliberalism. The image of neoliberalism that permeates Marxists scholars is mythical, and they do not make any subtle distinction between myths and ideologies. What counts, for them, is the concreteness of the economic structure, and every discursive construct must be understood as a sort of 'ideological translation' of this concreteness into the different languages and codes that characterize the cultural and symbolic exchange among humans. It is the whole reconstruction of modern capitalism offered by Marxism that should be understood as a myth – a

myth that culminates in the role played by neoliberalism meant as the acute phase of the illness that Marxism names 'capitalism'. According to this perspective, neoliberalism is nothing but the synonym for the apology of a society based on market values, which ends as the most refined and perverse version of capitalism.

10 The ghost of neoliberalism plays an essential role *chez* Marxist scholars, who conceive of a phantasmic post-capitalist society, which has the same nature as neoliberalism. In fact, neoliberalism is responsible for the propagation of the spirit of greed that pervades global finance and which corrodes the materiality of production and melts everything into the air of the 'virtual economy'. The phantasmic image of a post-capitalistic society should animate the 'multitude', that is the rhyzomatic and dispersed army composed of those whose manpower fills out the ranks of the knowledge workers who sustain the cognitive capitalism of our present (Negri and Hardt, 2000).

11 The notion of 'apparatus' (*'dispositif'* in French) is taken as well from the Foucauldian toolbox (Foucault 1980, 194).

12 Thaler and Sunstein (2008) illustrates rather clearly how to build an architecture of choice that enables individuals to take the best decision for the improvement of their lives. This book could be seen, in this respect, as a true manifesto for governmental interventions both in the private and public sector based on the neoliberal assumption that a happy and realized life can be achieved only by following the guidelines provided by neoclassical economic theory.

13 Neoliberalism does not represent the instantiation of a new form of totalitarianism – albeit the resistance neoliberalism shows toward any form of criticism could be interpreted as well as the symptom of a penchant for a totalitarian stance.

14 Even Mirowski fell into the trap of believing that Foucault was wrong 'about neoliberalism as fostering the autolimitation of state power' (Mirowski 2013, 101). Quite the opposite: Foucault has seen perfectly well that the state has become the most powerful tool to reinforce the maximization principle that rules society and institutions. Neoliberalism is about the political transformations that led to the foreclosure – in the Lacanian sense of the term – of the question of social justice.

15 Block (2002) offers a vivid example of this incomprehension. Instead, Shaviro (2013) offers a balanced effort to place correctly Simons' thought within the liberal tradition.

16 For the thesis of neoliberalism as a natural development of classical liberalism, see Coleman (2013).

17 Behrent (2009), for example, suggests that Foucault's interest in analysing neoliberalism was determined not only by epochal changes within the French political and cultural climate that occurred in the second half of the Seventies, but also by a personal and ideological kin to neoliberalism itself. See also Zamora (2014) and Pestaña (2011).

18 The notion of 'colonization of the life-word' plays a pivotal role within Habermas's critique of late capitalism in Western society (Habermas 1985). See Deetz (1992) for a more detailed interpretation of the late capitalism in Habermasian terms.

19 Davies focuses his attention on neoliberalism's capability to shape sovereignty in a new way: i.e. the way in which the neoliberal strategy aims at generating forms of government that find their ultimate justification both in the discourse of economics and in the discursive practices that are commonly shared by people who deal with organizations and enterprises. In this sense, Davies is well aware of the fact that neoliberalism does not mean to govern in the name of economy, or in the name of the market, as if it were still possible to maintain the distinction between the economical and the political sphere. Such a distinction is bound to get lost when public institutions treat those whom they are supposed to govern as 'clients' that pay a price for a service to be supplied, or when the governmental institutions raise no objection to the fact that they must be ready to give an account of their performances in terms of cost-benefit analysis.

20 Typically, this view is very common among those who do not see any significant difference between liberalism and neoliberalism, which are both reproached for

being responsible for the attempt to extend the logic of the market to the whole of society. This extension, so goes the argument, erases the possibility of building and defending those ethical values like justice, equality or solidarity that, being generated by affections like empathy, compassion and mutual understanding, encourage the construction of a good society.

21 The nurse, for example, who takes care of injured, ill or invalid persons receives a wage for her professional service, and the willingness to be paid for the latter is surely an important part of what motivates her professional engagement. But this does not prevent her from feeling compassion for the patients she takes care of. There seems to be no reason, thus, to consider the services she sells as 'commodified' and to deprive them of their moral worth. In order to assume that the nurse's service is somehow 'commodified' for the simple reason that she gets paid for it, one must assume as well that only those actions that have their goal in themselves are morally acceptable.

22 Hence, we do not agree with some theses according to which neoliberalism can be regarded either as a movement that emerged after the collapse of Keynes' system or as a transformation of original Keynesianism into a 'private Keynesianism' (Crouch 2008).

23 This interpretation is commonly accepted since Leijonhufvud contributed to Keynes' monetary theory (Leijonhufvud 1968).

24 The distinction between two orders of rationality is due to Hayek (Hayek 1945).

25 Examples of *ceteris paribus* are: Mill's absence of non-economic motives; Marshall's conditions for normal prices in the short run; Friedman's elimination of any variation of income.

26 Usually questions in economics related to causation are the following: are there any causal relations among dependent variables? Does controlling money supply limit inflation? Does deficit cause higher interest rates and increase inflation?

27 In an individualistic methodology, either atomistic or organicistic, social processes are completely determined by individual dynamics. In a pluralistic methodology, there is no hierarchical superiority to any methodology; economics as a science is regarded as an open-ended Darwinian process (Samuels 1977) by adopting Lakatos' reasearch programme (Lakatos 1980).

28 A theory has to be structured on a deductive system based on assumptions and axioms. Within a logical positivism, programme axiomatization requires a process of verification of axioms (axioms are tautologies in Hilbert's programme [1899] 1950). In economics, examples of axiomatization are the axioms of preferences (symmetry, completeness, transitivity), but also the consideration of utility as a quantity (Frisch 1926), and von Neumann and Morgenstern's notion of utility (1944) to describe an individual choice.

29 In economics models' quality depends on how much they can follow these five criteria: to measure theoretical laws (in economic theory); to explain and to describe the observed data (mainly in statistics and history); to be useful for policy; to develop theory; to verify or reject theory (Morgan 1999).

30 An example of formalism in economics is the analysis of the general economic equilibrium model as a Bourbakian approach (Debreu, 1952): an equilibrium exists if consumer preferences are convex; if it exists, it is unique, stable and determined. If it exists, it is Pareto-efficient, optimal (First Theorem of Welfare Economics), and every optimal allocation is an equilibrium (Second Theorem of Welfare Economics). This model can be translated into a perfect competitive market able to maximize social welfare, because resources are Pareto-optimal allocated.

31 It is intended as a method of making aggregations assuming that actions of individuals are the outcome of an optimization decision making processes, and that equilibrium is the final outcome (Hoover 2001).

32 From an historical perspective, as will be better explained in Chapter 2 and Chapter 3, this happened almost simultaneously in the 1930s when Wald on one

side and von Neumann on the other side gave a definite systematization to Walras' general economic equilibrium model, and Frisch founded the Econometric Society (1935).

33 In 1939 there was an important debate about the nature of economic laws between Keynes and Tinberger: Keynes claimed that multiple correlation analysis is useful only to measure phenomena, not to explain them, and mostly significant factors in economics cannot be measured, likewise animal spirits (Boumans and Davis 2016).

34 Established in 1920 in Cambridge MA, NBER's precepts were: research only on facts and connections amongst facts; use of quantitative knowledge; impartial and scientific knowledge; no recommendations about policy (Fabricant 1984).

35 Regarding the influence of physics on economics from an epistemological point of view, Mirowski presented a very critical perspective of mainstream economics (Mirowski 1990, 2002).

36 That means to understand what procedures of causal inference are able to explain macro events.

37 According to Hoover, the philosophical concept of supervenience can be usefully applied in a new and antireductionist way: any time the micro entities had exactly the same configuration, in the same context, the macro entities would be the same, otherwise the reduction of macroeconomics to microeconomics is not possible (Hoover 2001).

38 The opposite approach to fundamentalism is a so-called nomological pluralism: the idea according to which nature is governed in different domains by different systems of laws not related to each other in a uniform way. Hence economics cannot be performed as a natural science.

39 Robert Lucas, one of the most prominent neoclassical economists, claimed that the insistence of realism damages the scientific aspects of economics (Lucas 1981).

40 The role of uncertainty in explaining decision theory in social sciences has always been central in economics, particularly if the inclusion of realism is considered fundamental. The well-known Knight's distinction between risk and uncertainty (Knight 1921) could be seen in a double sense. Risk can be intended as randomness with knowable probabilities, and uncertainty as randomness with unknowable probabilities; thus uncertainty is regarded as a subset of conventional expected utility, either objective (von Neumann and Morgenstern 1944; Luce and Raiffa 1957) or subjective, and it can be treated as a branch of probabilities (Ramsey 1926; Savage 1954). Uncertainty could be also regarded as a state of non-knowledge (about decision makers or about environment), which derives not from a lack of information, but from the fact that human behaviour is unpredictable and outside of probability's domain. In such a scenario, Gigerenzer adopts the second meaning of uncertainty and better clarifies the place of uncertainty in the most recent debate on rationality as well as a real critique of the neoclassical model (Gigerenzer 2008).

41 The origin of fast-and-frugal heuristics is due to Herbert Simon's theory of boun-ded rationality (Simon 1991). Simon's analogy of bounded rationality is like a pair of scissors, where one blade is mind and the other is environment; it is to be con-sidered very close to ecological rationality, the sole model of rationality able to match mind and environment. His bounded rationality can be applied neither to optimization under constraints, nor to cognitive illusion approach, because they are both focused just on the cognitive side (the relation between mind and logical laws) without including analysis of the environment.

42 It is true that some scholars, relying on Gramsci's notion of hegemony, have drawn attention to the role played by nation states in constructing the international architecture that allowed neoliberalism to gain momentum up to the point in which it became the only normative narrative able to frame the shared vision of global issues. But, also in this case, the description of how global elites refer to

those neoliberal principles they share and contribute to propagate is not able to eschew the image of a global world governed by economic interests that 'colonize' the policy domain.

43 The development of economics as a formalized discipline was mainly due to the foundation of general economic equilibrium, as well as the introduction of econometrics, as in Weintraub (2002).

References

Baltagi, B. (2008) *Econometrics*. Berlin: Springer.

Barth, H. (1976) *Truth and Ideology*. Berkeley, Los Angeles, CA, London: University of California Press.

Behrent, M.C. (2009) 'Liberalism Without Humanism: Michel Foucault and the Free-Market Creed, 1976–1979', *Modern Intellectual History*, Vol. 6:3, pp. 539–568.

Bernoulli, D. [1738] (1954) 'Exposition of a new theory on the measurement of risk', *Econometrica*, Vol. 22:1, pp. 23–36.

Blaug, M. [1980] (1992) *The Methodology of Economics, or How Economists Explain*. Cambridge: Cambridge University Press.

Block, W. (2002) 'Henry Simons is Not a Supporter of Free Enterprise', *Journal of Libertarian Studies*, Vol. 16:4, pp. 3–36.

Blumenberg, H. (1985) *Work on Myth*. Cambridge, MA: MIT Press.

Boas, T. and Gans-Morse, J. (2009) 'Neoliberalism: From New Liberal Philosophy to Anti-Liberal Slogan', *Studies in Comparative International Development*, Vol. 44:2, pp. 137–161.

Boumans, M. and Davis, J. (2016) *Economic Methodology: Understanding Economics as a Science*. Second Edition, London: Palgrave and MacMillan.

Bruni, L. and Sugden, R. (2013) 'Reclaiming Virtue Ethics for Economics', *The Journal of Economic Perspectives*, Vol. 27:4, pp. 141–163.

Campbell, J. and Pedersen, O. (Eds) (2001) *The Rise of Neoliberalism and Institutional Analysis*. Princeton, NJ: Princeton University Press.

Cartwright, N. (1999) *The Dappled World*. Cambridge: Cambridge University Press.

Coase, R. (1937) 'The Nature of the Firm', *Economica*, Vol. 4:16, pp. 386–405.

Colander, D. (2007) *Pluralism and Heterodox Economics: Suggestions for an "Inside the Mainstream" Heterodoxy*, WP 7/24, Vermont: Middlebury College.

Coleman, W. (2013) 'What Was "New" about Neoliberalism?', *Economic Affairs*, Vol. 33:1, pp. 78–92.

Crouch, C. (2008) 'What Will Follow the Demise of Privatized Keynesianism?', *Political Quarterly*, Vol. 79:4, pp. 476–487.

Davis, J. (2006) 'The Nature of Heterodox Economics', *Post-Autistic Economics Review*, Vol. 40:1, pp. 23–30.

Davies, W. (2014) *The Limits of Neoliberalism: Authority, Sovereignty and the Logic of Competition*. London: Sage.

Dean, M. (2014) 'Rethinking Neoliberalism', *Journal of Sociology*, Vol. 50:2, pp. 150–163.

Debreu, G. (1952) *A Social Equilibrium Existence Theorem*. Santa Monica, California: Rand Corporation.

Deetz, S. (1992) *Democracy in an Age of Corporate Colonization: Development in Communication and the Politics of Everyday Life*. Albany, NY: State University of New York.

Dupré, J. (2001) *Human Nature and the Limits of Science*. Oxford, New York: Oxford University Press.

Emmett, R. (2016) 'Economics', in Mongomery, G. and Largent, M. (Eds) *A Companion to the History of American Science*. Chichester, UK: Wiley Blackwell, pp. 82–94.

Fabricant, S. (1984) *Towards a Firmer Basis of Economic Policy: The Founding of the National Bureau of Economic Research*. www.nber.org/nberhistory/sfabricantrev.pdf/.

Ferguson, J. (2010) 'The Uses of Neoliberalism', *Antipode*, Vol. 41:1s, pp. 166–184.

Foucault, M. (1980) *Power/Knowledge. Selected Interviews and Other Writings 1972–1977*. New York: Pantheon Books.

Foucault, M. (2008) *The Birth of Biopolitics: Lectures at the Collège de France, 1978–1979*. Basingstoke, UK, New York: Palgrave Macmillan.

Friedman, M. (1953) *Essays in Positive Economics*. Chicago, IL: University of Chicago Press.

Frisch, R. (1926) 'On a Problem in Pure Economics', *Norsk Matematisk Forenings Skrifter*, Vol. 1:16, pp. 1–40.

Ganti, T. (2014) 'Neoliberalism', *The Annual Review of Anthropology*, Vol. 43:1, pp. 89–104.

Gigerenzer, G. and Todd, P. (1999) *Simple Heuristics That Make Us Smart*. Oxford: Oxford University Press.

Gigerenzer, G. (2008) *Rationality for Mortals. How People Cope with Uncertainty*. New York: Oxford University Press.

Gigerenzer, G. and Selten, R. (Eds) (2002) *Bounded Rationality: The Adaptive Toolbox*. Cambridge, MA: MIT Press.

Gintis, H. (2009) *The Bounds of Reason: Game Theory and the Unification of Behavioral Science*. Princeton, NJ: Princeton University Press.

Gordon, C. (1991) 'Government Rationality: an Introduction', in Burchell, G., Gordon, C. and Miller, P. (Eds) *The Foucault Effect. Studies in Governmentality*. Chicago: The University of Chicago Press.

Haavelmo, T. (1944) 'The Probability Approach in Econometrics', *Econometrica*, Vol. 12:1, pp. 477–490.

Habermas, J. (1985) *The Theory of Communicative Action. Volume 2: Lifeworld and System*. Boston: Beacon Press.

Harvey, D. (2005) *A Brief History of Neoliberalism*. Oxford: Oxford University Press.

Hausman, D.M. (1998) 'Problems with Realism in Economics', *Economics and Philosophy*, Vol. 14:2, pp. 185–213.

Hayek, F. (1945) 'The Use of Knowledge in Society', *American Economic Review*, Vol. 35:4, pp. 519–530.

Hilbert, D. [1899] (1950) *Foundations of Geometry [Grundlagen der Geometrie]*. La Salle, IL: The Open Court Publishing Company.

Hirschman, A.O. (1982) 'Rival Interpretations of Market Society: Civilizing, Destructive, or Feeble?', *Journal of Economic Literature*, Vol. 20:4, pp. 1463–1484.

Hoover, K. (2001) *Causality in Macroeconomics*. Cambridge: Cambridge University Press.

Kahneman, D. and Tversky, A. (1979) 'Prospect Theory: an Analysis of Decision under Risk', *Econometrica*, Vol. 47:2, pp. 263–293.

Kahneman, D. and Tversky, A. (1996) 'On the Reality of Cognitive Illusion', *Psychological Review*, Vol. 103:3, pp. 582–591.

Klamer, A. and Leonard, T. (1994) 'So What's an Economic Metaphor?', in Mirowski, P. (Ed.) *Natural Images in Economics: Markets Read in Tooth and Claw*. Cambridge: Cambridge University Press, pp. 20–51.

Knight, F. (1921) *Risk, Uncertainty, and Profit*. Boston: Hart, Schaffner & Marx; Houghton Mifflin Co.

Lakatos, I. (1980) *The Methodology of Scientific Research Programmes, Volume I: Philosophical Papers*. Cambridge: Cambridge University Press.

Lavoie, M. (2014) *Post Keynesian Economics: New Foundations*. Cheltenham, UK: Edward Elgar Publishing Limited.

Lawson, T. (1997) *Economics and Reality*. London: Routledge.

Lawson, T. (2004) 'Reorienting Economics: on Heterodox Economics, Themata and the Use of Mathematics in Economics', *Journal of Economic Methodology*, Vol. 11:3, pp. 329–340.

Leijonhufvud, A. (1968) *On Keynesian Economics and the Economics of Keynes: A Study of Monetary Economics*. London: Oxford University Press.

Leonard, R. (2010) *Von Neumann, Morgenstern and the Creation of Game Theory*. Cambridge: Cambridge University Press.

Lucas, R. (1981) *Studies in Business-Cycle Theory*. Cambridge, MA: MIT Press.

Luce, D.R. and Raiffa, H. (1957) *Games and Decisions*. New York: John Wiley and Sons.

Luhmann, N. (1970) *Soziologische Aufklärung. Aufsätze zur Theorie sozialer Systeme*. Opladen: Westdeutscher Verlag.

Mäki, U. (2011) 'Scientific Realism as a Challenge to Economics (and Vice Versa)', *Journal of Economic Methodology*, Vol. 18:1, pp. 1–12.

Mäki, U. (2013) 'Scientific Imperialism: Difficulties in Definition, Identification, and Assessment', *International Studies in the Philosophy of Science*, Vol. 27:3, pp. 325–339.

March, J.G. (1962) 'The Business Firm as a Political Coalition', *Journal of Politics*, Vol. 24:4, pp. 662–678.

McCloskey, D. (1983) 'The Rhetoric of Economics', *Journal of Economic Literature*, Vol. 21:2, pp. 481–517.

Mirowski, P. (1990) *More Heat Than Light. Economics as Social Physics, Physics as Nature's Economics*. Cambridge: Cambridge University Press.

Mirowski, P. (2002) *Machine Dreams: Economics Becomes a Cyborg Science*. Cambridge: Cambridge University Press.

Mirowski, P. (2009) 'Postface', in Mirowski, P. and Plehwe, D. (Eds) *The Road from Mont Pèlerin: the Making of the Neoliberal Thought Collective*. Cambridge, MA: Harvard University Press, pp. 417–455.

Mirowski, P. (2013) *Never Let A Serious Crisis Go to Waste: How Neoliberalism Survived the Financial Meltdown*. London: Verso.

Mirowski, P. and Plehwe, D. (Eds) (2009) *The Road from Mont Pèlerin: the Making of the Neoliberal Thought Collective*. Cambridge, MA: Harvard University Press.

Morgan, M. (1999) 'Models as Mediating Instruments', in Morgan, M. and Morrison, M. (Eds) *Model as Mediators*. Cambridge: Cambridge University Press, pp. 10–37.

Morgan, M. (2012) *The World in the Model: How Economists Work and Think*. Cambridge: Cambridge University Press.

Negri, A. and Hardt, M. (2000) *Empire*. Cambridge, MA: Harvard University Press.

Nelson, R.H. (2001) *Economics as Religion. From Samuelson to Chicago and Beyond*. University Park, PA: Pennsylvania State University Press.

von Neumann, J. and Morgenstern, O. (1944) *Theory of Games and Economic Behavior*. Princeton, NJ: Princeton University Press.

Pestaña, J.L.M. (2011) *Foucault y la Politica*. Madrid: Tierradenadie Ediciones.

Plehwe, D. (2009) 'Introduction' in Mirowski, P. and Plehwe, D. (Eds) *The Road from Mont Pélerin: the Making of the Neoliberal Thought Collective.* Cambridge, MA: Harvard University Press, pp. 1–42.

Ramsey, F.P. (1926) 'Truth and Probability', in Braithwaite, R.B. (Ed.) *The Foundations of Mathematics and Other Logical Essays.* London: Trubner & Co.

Rossi-Landi, F. (1990) *Marxism and Ideology.* Oxford: Clarendon Press.

Rutherford, M. (2011) *The Institutionalist Movement in American Economics, 1918–1947: Science and Social Control.* Cambridge: Cambridge University Press.

Samuels, W. (1977) 'Ideology in Economics', in Weintraub, S. (Ed.) *Modern Economic Thought*, Pittsburg, PA: The University of Pennsylvania Press, pp. 467–484.

Samuelson, P. (1947) *Foundations of Economic Analysis.* Cambridge, MA: Harvard University Press.

Savage, L.J. (1954) *The Foundation of Statistics.* New York: John Wiley & Sons.

Schumpeter, J. (1954) *History of Economic Analysis.* Oxford: Oxford University Press.

Shaviro, D. (2013) 'The Forgotten Henry Simons', *Florida State University Law Review*, Vol. 41:1, pp. 1–38.

Simon, H. (1991) 'Bounded Rationality and Organizational Learning', *Organization Science*, Vol. 2:1, pp. 125–134.

Simons, H. (1938) *Personal Income Taxation. The Definition of Income as a Problem of Fiscal Policy.* Chicago, IL: The University of Chicago Press.

Smith, V. (2008) *Rationality in Economics. Constructivism and Ecological Forms.* Cambridge: Cambridge University Press.

Steger, M.B., and Roy, R.K. (2010) *Neoliberalism: A Very Short Introduction.* New York: Oxford.

Stein, H. (2012) 'The Neoliberal Policy Paradigm and the Great Recession', *Panoeconomicus*, Vol. 59:4, pp. 421–440.

Stigler, G. (1961) 'The Economics of Information', *Journal of Political Economy*, Vol. 69:3, pp. 213–225.

Sugden, R. (2000) 'Credible Worlds: the Status of Theoretical Models in Economics', *Journal of Economic Methodology*, Vol. 7:1, pp. 1–31.

Sugden, R. (2002) 'Credible Worlds: The Status of Theoretical Models in Economics', in Mäki, U. (Ed.) *Facts and Fictions in Economics: Models, Realism, and Social Contruction.* Cambridge: Cambridge University Press, pp. 107–136.

Thaler, R.H. and Sunstein, C.R. (2008) *Nudge. Improving Decisions about Health, Wealth and Happiness.* New Haven, CT: Yale University Press.

Vanberg, V. (2004) *The Freiburg School: Walter Eucken and Ordoliberalism*, WP. http://hdl.handle.net/10419/4343/.

Van Horn, R., Mirowski, P. and Stapleford, T. (2011) *Building Chicago Economics.* Cambridge: Cambridge University Press.

Wald, A. (1947) *Sequential Analysis.* New York: John Wiley & Sons.

Weber, M. [1922] (1968) *Economy and Society: An Outline of Interpretative Sociology.* New York: Bedminster Press.

Weintraub, R. (1977) 'The Microfoundation of Macroeconomics: A Critical Survey', *Journal of Economic Literature*, Vol. 15:1, pp. 1–23.

Weintraub, R. (2002) *How Economics Became a Mathematical Science.* Durham, NC: Duke University Press.

Zamora, D. (Ed.) (2014) *Critiquer Foucault. Les années 1980 et la temptation néolibérale.* Saint-Gilles, Belgium: Les Editions Aden.

1 Foucault and beyond

Although Foucault was not a scholar who worked within the history of economic thought, his insights in the revolution that led to the emergence of neoliberalism seem to be persuasive. In the present chapter Foucault's analysis is to be seen as a starting point, in the sense that other authors and other strains of contemporary critical theory will be considered in order to achieve a deeper comprehension of neoliberalism – or, better, in order to posit neoliberalism as a research object that can be defined and grasped in its autonomy and self-consistency.

Before offering an outline of what Foucault understands by neoliberalism, it is important to pay attention to the reasons that led him to shift his research to this subject. Then, the difference between his interpretation and the one provided by neo-Marxist or neo-Gramscian authors will emerge more clearly. The autonomy of the domain where the sovereign state acts will be outlined starting from some insights coming from the disciplinary domain of international relations. Finally, the global reach of neoliberal governmentality will be explained as a form of reduction of systemic complexity that draws its efficacy from the rude simplicity of its assumptions.

1.1 Foucault's distinction between liberalism and neoliberalism

The difference between classical liberalism and neoliberalism is the object of the lectures he held at the Collège de France during the year 1978–79. Within these lectures he introduces the term biopolitics in his philosophical vocabulary – *Birth of Biopolitics* is in fact the title of the lecture (Foucault 2008). This notion is strictly intertwined with another important element we find in Foucault's toolbox starting from the second half of the 1970s, namely the notion of governmentality. Asking rhetorically to his audience why an analysis of some scholars of the twentieth century who belong to the discipline of economics should provide an explanation of what biopolitics and governmentality are, Foucault answers that methodological reasons induced him to take that step. These reasons are strictly related to the question of how power structures arise and propagate within society. To better understand that point, a step back is necessary, namely to the lectures of the year before. The topics of the lectures Foucault held during the year 1977–78, *Security, Territory, Population* (Foucault 2007), was the birth of modern state. The reason for this detour becomes clear if we consider that Foucault's aim was not only to provide a historical reconstruction of the shift from liberalism to neoliberalism through the grid of intelligibility offered by the notions of biopolitics and governmentality, but, above all, to show how the process of subjectivation that characterizes the rise of contemporary subjectivity depends on the performativity of a given set of discourses. What makes Foucault's reconstruction so interesting for us is the fact that economics plays an essential role being the discipline that, more than others, has contributed – and is still contributing – to shape the frame within which individual paths of life cross the multifaceted trajectories of modern – and contemporary – power.

First of all, Foucault's aim was to contest the idea that the state acts as a monolithic agency of power, as a source of interventions that governs the conduct of subjects – or citizens – through specific measures of control. Surely, not only the enforcement of law, but also the more general set of interventions whose aim is to guarantee the ordered development of societal intercourses requires the presence of the public hand – it requires, in other words, those kinds of intervention that Foucault designates through the notion of discipline. But what Foucault deeply contests is the idea that the state action can be always and mainly recognized and represented as a bundle of forces coming from 'above' and floating 'down' to the social structure taken as a whole. More precisely, what Foucault contests is the idea that it is possible to identify and isolate a clear line dividing the public sphere and society itself, whereas the latter is meant as the sphere within which individuals negotiate their own position in the face of the pervasiveness of public interference in order to preserve their freedom of action. In opposition to this way of conceiving state action, which reduces the latter to disciplinary power, Foucault suggests that the state – and this since its inception at the beginning of the modern era – should be seen as the central node of a broader network that includes a vast array of agencies the scope of which is the government of individual life. Politics being, according to Foucault, nothing but the art of governing people, the modern form of politics is peculiar not because the sovereign state imposed itself as the only institution that was allowed to make use of legitimate force within a given territory, but because the state succeeded in creating an interconnected and interrelated chain of local powers, distributed among the population in order to supervise and control each aspect of that which made the population grow and thrive or, conversely, fail and degenerate. The term 'governmentality' reveals its heuristic efficacy precisely by capturing the multifaceted and dispersed character of state action: it invites us to shift our attention from the traditional view of the latter, which rests on a top-down scheme, to a conception of power that underscores the autonomous creativity of those institutional agencies that take care of individual needs, prevent disruptive conflicts, ensure against collective risks. Further: Foucault points his – and our – attention to the ongoing character of governmental intervention, which he describes as flexible, changing, and always attentive to the corresponding features of collective needs and individual interests, which are fluctuating and varying as well. Thus, the effectiveness of governmental action cannot be measured by simply evaluating the long term results of each intervention, but it must be monitored step by step along the interdependency of governmental interventions and the manifold ways in which their target – it being the population taken as a whole or a specific set of individuals – reacts to them. In conformity with his more general pattern of analysis of power relations, Foucault confers great importance on the fact that governmentality cannot be understood simply as a practice, but must be considered as a dispositive – or 'apparatus' – that encompasses a set of practices and a set of theoretical devices.

> By the word 'governmentality' I mean three things. First, by 'governmentality' I understand the ensemble formed by institutions, procedures, analyses and reflections, calculations, and tactics that allow the exercise of this very specific, albeit very complex, power that has the population as its target, political economy as its major form of knowledge, and apparatuses of security as its essential technical instrument. Second, by 'governmentality' I understand the tendency, the line of force, that for a long time, and throughout the West, has constantly led towards the pre-eminence over all types of power – sovereignty, discipline and so on – of the type of power that we can call 'government' and which has led to the development of a series of specific governmental apparatuses (*appareils*) on the one hand, [and, on the other] to the development of a series of knowledges (*savoirs*). Finally, by 'governmentality' I think we should understand the process, or rather, the result of the process by which the state of justice of the Middle Ages became the administrative state in the fifteenth and sixteenth centuries and was gradually 'governamentalized'.
>
> (Foucault 2007, 108ff.)

The subject that governs (in this case the state, but what is at stake here affects every governing agency) needs, in order to govern, a specific knowledge, needs, better, a set of scientific devices that allows them not only to understand how members of a population settled within the state boundary live, think, work and so on, but also to mould the architecture of choice within which each individual is supposed to shape their personal life project. This is the reason why the term 'biopolitics' is strictly tied with that of 'governmentality': the action of governing individuals is supposed to affect not only those aspects of individual conduct that are expression of the *persona*, meant from a juridical point of view, but also those that are related to the individual project of life. And the latter needs to be captured by a specific knowledge.

To understand why knowledge and the exercise of power are such important elements of any modern governmental action we must bear in mind that the peculiar kind of intervention pursued by governmental agencies is not supposed to be brought about predominantly through the direct or indirect influence that the rule of law exercises onto the conduct of individuals. It is true that the understanding of such influence is important in order to construct a persuasive view of the way in which a given social formation – or collective, as we would prefer to say – decides to frame the space of liberty possibly granted to each of its members. Foucault himself has never denied that. Truly, his analysis of the disciplinary aspect of governmental intervention, explored in his previous works, attributes great importance to the role played by the legal system meant as a tool that can be used not only to bring an end to social conflicts, but also to shape the form that the different types of conflict within society can assume. But what the mere focus on the rule of law leaves out is the fact that collectives undergo practices of control and government whose effectiveness rests not on the law, but on a set of local norms. The latter are neither in contrast to the law, nor can substitute it. Local norms can simply better insert themselves into those tiny spaces of social interaction where the appeal to the law is not requested, or does not seem appropriate, because what is at stake is rather the definition of the frame within which the interplay between those who govern and those who are governed takes place. The organizational space that encompasses firms or public institutions provides a good example of the interplay we are talking about: here, internal rules and guidelines, customs, shared habits, different leadership styles determine each time what is to be the range of the bargaining power each actor is supposed to have – and effectively has. But the government of individuals within a collective goes far beyond the abstract and impersonal form provided by the law as it rests on the knowledge of what constitutes the different individual features. This is the reason why it is important to focus on the disciplines that allow those who govern to understand what motivates the individual action, what enables individuals to behave this or that way. According to Foucault, it is not possible to analyse a given power relationship if we do not understand through which discourses those who rule can represent the conditions of possibility of collective action. Here we meet one of the most recurring topics of Foucault's philosophy, namely the intertwining of power and knowledge. He conceives of this intertwining not in the sense that a given set of scientific discourses helps legitimize a given set of power practices; the point is, rather, that those who govern shape their action by constantly referring its results to what they know about its target. To a certain extent, knowledge itself is supposed to have a performative power: in fact, it frames the range within which any single act of government takes place not only by defining its own scope, but above all by constructing the subject that must be governed – or imprisoned, disciplined, nursed, educated, sustained, helped, looked after, promoted, stimulated, and so on. More specifically, the birth of the modern state led to the parallel development of those disciplines that made available an insight into what could have improved the welfare of a given population – the creation of the concept of 'population' was in itself the secondary effect of the interest the state had in considering the improvement of the welfare of those who were under its rule as a main goal to be pursued. Among these disciplines, economics played a pivotal role since the beginning of the modern era. Economics defines what must be done – or avoided – by those who govern in order to let the subjects or citizens pursue their objectives within the market. The boundary of the latter can be regulated, of course. It must even be subdued to the law. But this regulation is supposed to produce the freedom individuals enjoy when pursuing their goals. This production of freedom has become part of the art of government during the modern age, at least since the second half of the eighteenth century. Thus, the modern state has legitimized its own action both by granting freedom to those who are able to partake in the market, and by imposing the rule of law on each member of society. And the mutual relationship between these two aspects determines, according to Foucault, the model – or the models – of rationality upon which the action of government rests. If the main goal of the governmental action taken as a whole consists in creating those spaces of freedom within which individuals are supposed to pursue their own project of life, it is clear that economics is likely to increase its importance as a source of knowledge that can – and must – offer to those who govern both guidelines and inspiration. Of course, other disciplines like psychiatry or statistics – just to mention two examples – have also been revealed to be important for the modern art of government: the first supplies the 'adjustment' of individuals that are at odds with their own self-positioning within society, individuals whose behaviour cannot be therefore considered as 'normal'; the second, on the other hand, supplies the monitoring of what individuals do and desire. But the discourse about human action offered by economics shapes the abstract reference of what individuals do when attaining their goals as free actors. As economics succeeded in constructing a theoretical frame according to which it was possible to both describe the deep structure of human action and recognize what makes it to be self consistent, it became easier to forge the art of government in accordance with the model of man postulated by economics itself. In a certain way, as the discipline aims at investigating what improves the wellbeing of individuals, economics became not surprisingly the presupposition for governmental interventions of a biopolitical kind. Not the abstract subject meant as an individual entitled to specific rights, but the concrete desiring subject that economics describes and investigates becomes more and more the target of governmental interventions. The latter can acquire a biopolitical character, as their role is to take care of human life as such. In this context, 'human life' becomes nothing more than the epitome of the raw material each individual needs to build her own welfare. What Foucault describes, thus, is the historical process along which the model of rationality created by the economic discourse has become part of a broader governmental dispositive.

It is not worth exposing the historical reconstruction Foucault provided within his lectures of the year 1977–78 on the emergence of state power in a detailed manner. But the core of his arguments is of chief importance here, namely the relationship between individual life and politics meant as an art of government. Not life in general, not the various forms of life that give rise to the complexity of a given societal asset, but the bodily experience of the world that marks the presence of a single individual and makes out its uniqueness constitutes the focus of governmental intervention. Thanks to our individual body – better: through it and in the force of it – we both become part of the human species and receive those entitlements that make us *personae*, namely physical entities upon which the state exercises its legal power. In this sense, each individual is the instantiation of the human species and, at the same time, the collector of those proprieties that define the realm of human agency in its broader extent. If the goal of governing individuals coincides with the implementation of a collective space within which human life as such is to be protected, reproduced and enhanced, then it becomes impossible to ignore what moves individuals and leads them to take this or that decision as regards their conduct of life. Moreover, since economics has become the science that studies human behaviour as a relationship between ends and scarce means which have alternative uses, according to the universally known definition given by Lionel Robbins in 1932, it is not surprising that the disciplinary discourse of economics advocated for itself a leading role with regard to what every decision maker needs to know in order to shape the context within which human beings make their choices. What confers a deep significance to Foucault's analysis of neoliberalism is precisely the fact that the latter stands out as the most successful attempt to conflate a given set of hypotheses about human behaviour into an art of government.

Now, if we take the term of comparison that allows to consider neoliberalism as a successful case of government based on a specific model of rationality, we gain the opportunity to elucidate the distinction between liberalism and neoliberalism. In our view, this is one of the most important moments of Foucault's argument, and one of the most misunderstood as well. Foucault builds a narrative for the rise of neoliberalism that underscores both the continuity and the rupture with the liberal form of government. The fact that knowing how people live (and die) is a necessary premise for governing them is not a recent discovery, peculiar to the second half of the twentieth century. Since its inception during the age of the Enlightenment, the discipline of economics offered its services to the rulers of the modern state in order to make the space where market interactions take place visible, recognizable and thus governable. In a sense, the rise of economics as an independent science and the rise of the modern state are two elements that belong to the same historical process. Here it is worth mentioning the fact that Foucault has been very careful in describing the way in which economics burgeoned from *Polizeywissenschaft*, which, during the first half of the eighteenth century, embedded into one bundle of knowledge different scientific approaches to the social reality in order to better govern it. As a typical result of the attention paid by the sovereign to the welfare of his subjects, *Polizeywissenschaft* encompassed not only what we would call political economy, but also public law, administrative science, public health concerns, urban planning and statistics. Those who have been trained in the *Polizeywissenschaft* and acted as devoted public managers could make the sovereign sure that the availability of a continuous source of money would not have been interrupted by an inappropriate or malfunctioning administration of the state as long as their skills proved to be appropriate to monitoring and measuring the welfare of the population. The birth of autonomous disciplines and their specific domains took place in step with the growing complexity of the relationship between state apparatuses and modern society. The latter can reflect upon itself only by observing the way in which each discipline describes what human beings do and how they account for their actions. It is in this context that economics became the discourse that provided the art of government with those tools according to which the nation state could limit its own action in front of – and in relation to – the individuals who acted within the market during the age of classical liberalism. According to Foucault, liberalism was not simply the ideology of rising capitalism; it was rather the result of the awareness that the sphere within which economically relevant actions took place is separate from the sphere within which individuals act in the name of principles that do not coincide with the preservation of self-interest. The first sphere has been the object of the analysis we can still read in Smith's *Inquiry into the Nature and Causes of the Wealth of Nations*, while he devoted his *Theory of Moral Sentiments* to the second. Taking the views expressed in Smith's two masterpieces as paramount examples of the classical liberal thought, we see how the latter held that selfishness, on the one hand, was to be seen as a good virtue as long as it remains a constitutive element of the behaviour of individuals whose thirst for profit is the main motivating factor, while sympathy, on the other, was supposed to take the place of selfishness as soon as human action is triggered by the desire to build a collective in which it is possible to give expression to those feelings that improve mutual respect and solidarity. It is important to notice that both selfishness and sympathy were to be considered as 'natural' forces that animate human behaviour. The liberal art of government aimed at leaving these natural forces to grow and expand by themselves. The self-limitation of the power that state rulers were ready to exert during the liberal era was, according to Foucault, nothing but a sign of the acknowledgement that the mutual encounter of individuals would have led to a reconciliation of their interests. Despite the overwhelming differences that characterize human interests in general, what drives their emergence was supposed to rest on a natural tendency toward socialization, which could find its expression even in market-oriented behaviour. What Foucault is interested in pointing out is not so much the self-restriction of public intervention in the economy *per se*, but rather the fact that the defence of this self-restriction was part of a broader argument according to which the realm of the economy constituted the ultimate truth of any political intervention. If we assume that individuals that are driven by the thirst for profit, or success, give expression to one of the highest forms of human freedom precisely when they can pursue their objectives within market-oriented interactions, then it becomes more than reasonable to fashion the art of government in such a way as to guarantee the minimum of interference in these interactions. But the rational justification for such a reduction of interference came from the arguments of economics, namely from the only discipline that could demonstrate why the pursuit of individual interests was not at odds with the self-establishment of a harmonic interplay among individuals. Here we face a clear continuity between liberalism and neoliberalism: in both cases, the discipline of economics constitutes the discursive domain by virtue of which the art of government can discover and perceive the truth of its own action. More precisely, Foucault defines the market as the 'site of veridiction' of any governmental performance.

> The market now means that to be a good government, government has to function according to truth. (...) Political economy does not therefore owe its privileged role to the fact that it will dictate a good type of conduct of government. Political economy was important (...) inasmuch as (...) it pointed out to government where it had to go to find the principle of truth of its governmental practice.
>
> (Foucault 2008, 32)

The social and political landscape that neoliberalism has been marking worldwide in recent decades is not different: the neoliberal art of government rests on the idea that the model of rationality developed by economics can provide the frame within which governmental practice can be assessed and evaluated. Of course, both methods and contents of what characterizes contemporary economics as a discipline are hardly to be compared with the core elements that authors like Smith, Ricardo or Marx recognized as being constitutive of political economy. But what counts more than this difference is the fact that neoliberalism coincides with a way of governing, the legitimacy of which depends on the pervasiveness of an economic grid that makes it 'possible to test governmental action' and 'gauge its validity' (Foucault 2008, 246).

Further, Foucault seems to identify a second line of continuity between liberalism and neoliberalism as regards the persistence of the biopolitical power apparatuses. By exhibiting this continuity, however, Foucault seizes the opportunity to show where the main rupture between liberalism and neoliberalism can be perceived more clearly. As we have already seen, biopolitics is not appropriate to the way in which institutions have been taking care of individual life during the last century; on the contrary, biopolitical forms of government are as old as the modern state.[1] However, the nearer we come to the contemporary world, the more pervasive they become. In recent years biopolitics has affected the circumstances of individual and collective experiences and cross projects of life in a way that was not conceivable in the age of the Enlightenment, nor during the nineteenth century. In other words, the growing spread of biopolitics, which seems to have reached each corner of the social network, goes with the growth of social complexity itself, being part of the institutional and organizational management of the latter. But in the increase of biopolitical arrangements, in their refinement, or in their gradual becoming part of the institutional land-scape that forms the backdrop of our everyday life, it is not correct to see what makes the difference between the liberal and the neoliberal government. This difference is rather to be seen in the role that economic rationality plays in shaping the practice of a biopolitically oriented government. The liberal gov-ernment was focused on those aspects of human conduct that assume a social or a political relevance, namely on forms of behaviour in which individuals are engaged when they do not pursue market objectives. This means that the range of governmental intervention was mainly confined to a sphere within which the competence of physicians, teachers, and judges was essential. The power structure that this intervention produced was sustained by the use of local norms, but it met a possible limit in the rule of law, whereas the type of rationality that informed the law and its meaning for the social construction of an ordered and just society owed nothing to the type of rationality that informed the economic thought. Albeit only in theory, the liberal state had to account for its actions in the eye of the law: the legitimacy of its own exis-tence, after all, stemmed from the fact that it would have been always possible to appeal to the law in order to obtain justice not only in the cases in which somebody affected a citizen's rights, but also in the case in which the infrin-gement on the citizen's rights came from representatives of the state itself. Many examples taken from modern history show how frequently the com-mitment of the liberal state to its own function as a regulator of an ordered society that acts in the name of the law has been neglected. In this sense, Foucault is right in defining what he calls the governmentalization of the state as the process along which a set of institutional interventions, which may be different in scope and range, attains the goal of controlling specific compo-nent parts of the social structure by applying norms and procedures the validity of which is restricted to their field of application. Nevertheless, the law that the state was supposed to safeguard and in the name of which it acted could be clearly distinguished from any local norm by virtue of its claim of universality. The presence, or the absence, of this claim is what makes the difference here: what has disappeared from the neoliberal art of government is precisely the sheer possibility of considering the domain of law in such a way that it may represent, at least ideally, the embodiment of justice. Any idea, or conception, of justice is certainly the result of a historical and cultural process if we take into consideration its genealogy; as soon as this idea becomes what a legal system rests on, nonetheless, it loses its character as a product floating in the flux of history. It is thus reasonable to maintain, on the one hand, that a legal system contains, in its core, a specific set of arguments concerning what is right and what is wrong and, on the other, that this set exposes itself to the judgment of a universal audience. The latter is not supposed to arrive at a conclusion that puts an end to any possible controversy, but it is clear that at least a partial consensus can be reached.[2] The point here is not the degree of irrefutability that can be reached by this or that idea of justice; what counts, rather, is the ideal-typical relation that is supposed to exist between a given legal system and a given set of arguments about what justice is or should be. Such an ideal-typical character, which derives from postulating a universal audience, provides for the appeal to universality. Within the cultural and political frame that characterized the liberal era it was still possible to uncover the relation that links a legal system to the underlying idea of justice that informs it. On the contrary, within the cultural and political context that Foucault characterizes as neoliberal, even the system of law obeys a model of rationality that stems from economics. What becomes problematic, thus, is not the vanishing of the political; if that were the case, than neoliberalism should be understood as the generalized condition under which the realm of the economy absorbs into itself all forms of associated life. Foucault, rather, terms neoliberalism as a political project that aims at governing institutions and organizations, no matter whether private or public, according to a model of rationality that has been shaped by a very peculiar and idiosyncratic form of economic thought. The latter is peculiar in its claim to be a natural science, and idiosyncratic in its attempt to explain human behaviour starting from a very short number of assumptions and categories the extension of which is virtually endless.

Put in this way – and, of course, properly understood – Foucault's narrative concerning the difference between liberalism and neoliberalism is a very simple one, but at the same time very powerful from a heuristic point of view. Both within the liberal and the neoliberal power structure governing agencies are part of a broader dispositive that includes economics, whereas the latter is the discipline that, more clearly than others, provides the truth needed to govern. In spite of that, the science of economics that informs the neoliberal practice of government is not the same discipline that helped those who governed during the liberal era put the boundary between the domain of economy and that of policy. Under the rule of neoliberalism, on the contrary, the function of this boundary has simply become inoperative because what informs the art of government responds to one model of rationality that is supposed to be the same on both sides of it.

Within Foucault's narrative the transformation that economics underwent during the last century coincides not so much with the rise of rational choice theory, but rather with the attempt to extend its explanatory range to all forms of behaviour. In other words, with the attempt to explain macro economy thanks to conceptual tools whose main function was to explain micro economy. Foucault does not go very deeply in the analysis of this issue, to say the least. As a matter of fact, he provides useful insights with regard to the political meaning of this extension. He pays most of his attention to what he defines as the formalization of society on the model of the enterprise.

> In other words, what is involved is the generalization of forms of 'enterprise' by diffusing and multiplying them as much as possible, enterprises which must not be focused on the form of big national or international enterprises or the type of big enterprises of state. I think this multiplication of the 'enterprise' from within the social body is what is at stake in neo-liberal policy.
>
> (Foucault 2008, 148)

At this point, one could expect that Foucault would undertake an analysis of how the enterprise works and it allows for the establishment of specific power relationships, how individuals attempt to negotiate their positioning within the latter, how the organizational structures of the enterprise enact specific architectures of choice and, in more general terms, processes of subjectivation take place within the enterprise. Yet, Foucault seems not be acquainted with the sources concerning the theory of organizations. Nevertheless, he chooses to analyse the thoughts of an economist who contributed more than others to shape the economic discourse in such a way that it became possible for the latter to explain all human behaviours as if they would coincide with those of an enterprise. The economist here in question is Gary Becker, an author who was not yet well known outside the circles of economic thought in the period Foucault gave his lectures. Foucault's analysis focuses in particular on Becker's theory of human capital, to be seen as the very core of the neoliberal theory of human action. The classical liberal theory aims at describing to what extent actions conducted in the name of self-interest can lead to positive results if their enactment takes place within a market oriented context, while assuming that individual behaviour could be motivated in a different way as soon as the context is not that of a market exchange. Foucault is right in stating that, from a neoliberal point of view, the very distinction between the two contexts of action loses any significance. This does not happen as neoliberalism is about blurring the boundary between market oriented interactions and those forms of social intercourse that are not ruled by the norm of self-interest; this happens, rather, because the neoliberal discourse is about shifting the attention from the question of exchange to the question of choice. What individuals do when buying or selling goods constitutes only one among many possibilities to exercise the capability to choose. In this sense, human existence, taken as a whole, is nothing but a series of choices, and each one of them is oriented to achieve something that the subject judges as an instantiation of a utility. Becker pays no attention to how individual preferences emerge and are related to peculiar contexts of choice, and thus he assumes their exogeneity, but, strictly in this way, he succeeds in building an economic theory able to capture the utility value that each individual associates to objects of choice that can be consistently different in nature and significance. Foucault, here, is interested in showing how deep is the shift, within the economic theory, that an approach to human behaviour like Becker's one is able to perform. The *homo oeconomicus* the neoliberal theory talks about is not any more the main character of a narrative that takes place within the market; the stage where *homo oeconomicus* performs his script now coincides with each situation in which a decision is enacted, no matter what is the goal that is to be pursued.

> *Homo oeconomicus* is an entrepreneur, an entrepreneur of himself. This is true to the extent that, in practice, the stake in all neoliberal analyses is the replacement every time of *homo oeconomicus* as partner of exchange with a *homo oeconomicus* as entrepreneur of himself, being for himself his

own capital, being for himself his own producer, being for himself the source of his earnings.

(Foucault 2008, 226)

Within a neoliberal frame, the question about what constitutes a subject can be answered in a very simple way: one needs to gauge the circumstances within which one acts, and then one takes an appropriate decision as regards the means that lead to the pursued goal using the least time, money, effort, energy, and so on. In other words, the subject envisaged by the economic discourse is nothing but a maximizing subject, whereas the act of maximizing something – or, better, the process that allows for maximization – is considered as the only act to which rationality can be ascribed. Here the adjective 'economic' before the substantive 'rationality' would be out of place: maximizing is, in fact, the economic behaviour *par excellence*. Foucault focuses precisely on this coincidence between rationality and economic behaviour, both understood as properties of a maximizing subject, and he does it in order to explain how the enterprise could become the general paradigm for subjectivity during the neoliberal age. If each course of action is nothing less than a series of choices made in order to maximize utility, then the courses of action undertaken by a human being and those undertaken by an enterprise are not substantially different from each other. However, it is important to understand that Foucault's analysis of neoliberal discourse does not aim at debunking the alleged ideological significance of the latter, as if Becker's discourse on human capital were nothing but the transposition of an ideological stance to the terrain of economics. Foucault is not saying that the view of the individual as a computing device that tries to maximize utility is false – and thus ideological. His issue is, rather, to highlight the transformations modern subjectivity undergoes when contemporary processes of subjectivation are informed by a unique model of rationality according to which the maximization of utility is the only conceivable fate of human beings.

It is worth remembering that Foucault has always maintained a distance toward the idea that a critical discourse on present society should necessarily assume the feature of a critique of ideologies. The subject that carries on the act of unveiling a stance that is supposed to embody an ideology does not conceal his detachment from the object of its critique – and it is precisely this detachment that allows for the unmasking of the ideologically biased position. Nevertheless, this means that the subject that acts in the name of the truth – whereas the latter is meant as the opposite of ideology – is not able to give any account of its own self-positioning. According to Foucault, it is methodologically incorrect to assume a position of absolute exteriority with regard to the domain that the critique envisages. Still, there is another, and more important point that helps clarify the distance between Foucault's position and the one of the critique of ideologies. Foucault is interested here in the relationship between the manifestation of truth and the art of government. What counts more, for him, is how the truth becomes part of the process that constitutes the subject and informs its self-understanding. If one considers economics as the discourse supposed to provide a true account of human behaviour, then it is out of place to reject economics as a mere ideology. A critique that envisages neoliberalism as a political project should consider, on the one hand, how the truth of economic discourse forges the architecture of choice within which the subject acts and, on the other, which strategies the subject adopts to free itself from power. It is the movement of freeing oneself from power that reveals how the truth affects the subject; at the same time, this movement reveals the contingency of any given structure of power. A critical discourse centred on the notion of ideology, on the contrary, runs the risk of crystallizing power relationships: the legitimacy that power takes from ideology, in fact, is supposed to be steadfast and solid, so that it becomes difficult to think of the mobility and fluidity that characterize any given power relationship. As Foucault insists, the latter presuppose both the freedom of the subject, and the contingency of power structures.

Thus, the problem Foucault invites us to take into consideration does not consist of the relationship between a theory and the set of practices it serves to legitimize. The point is rather to understand the performativity of a theory, or, better, the performativity of the model of rationality that a given theory embodies. Models of rationality are broader than theories, as they include those conceptions of man that disciplines generally presuppose in order to articulate their inquiry on specific aspects of human behaviour. If one pays attention to the argumentative structure of any inquiry of this kind, it is not difficult to find that there are, more or less explicitly, some points where description and prescription end up being strictly intertwined. Nevertheless, the issue we are confronted with when we analyse the neoliberal economic theory is not the fact that it makes it impossible to separate between descriptions and prescriptions with regard to what individuals do when they make a choice. What makes the neoliberal stance problematic is that it presents itself both as the only conceivable model of rationality, and as the only conceivable model of government. If *all* the choices individuals make in order to organize their lives are nothing but the expression of a behaviour based on maximization, then it becomes difficult to appeal to models of rationality different from the economic one when one deals with questions concerning justice or freedom. But this does not mean that the economic model of man has absorbed the political one, in order to nullify any possible discussion about values or ethics. This means, rather, that the model of rationality on which the neoliberal stance rests is understood so broadly in its application that it becomes able to prescribe its own conception of what is to be the most desirable asset of society. Reductionism, consequently, is not the main problem posed by the neoliberal economic theory. The fact that rationality coincides with maximization is problematic in the moment where this model of rationality is supposed to find an application as a general guideline regarding the most efficient government of every possible interaction occurring between individuals. The *homo oeconomicus* outlined by neoliberal reasoning is not only a calculating machine that is able to achieve efficient outputs; the efficiency of maximizing behaviour is always coupled with self-responsibility, so that it is not necessary to look for those aspects of human action that are relevant from an ethical point of view outside the realm of economics. The commitment to efficiency, in fact, coalesces into the commitment to self-responsibility. But what makes Foucault think of neoliberalism as an art of government is not only the capacity the latter has demonstrated to develop an ethical perspective, which ends up in articulating a political stance. What characterizes neoliberalism at most, according to Foucault, is its claim to offer appropriate technologies of government that do not draw upon coercion, or any form of disciplinary devices, but simply rest on the individual capability to regulate its own behaviour in compliance with reality. An efficient individual – as well as an efficient enterprise – never loses sight of the environment within which the act of maximizing utility takes place. The result is that neoliberal policies, on the one hand, leave room for the desire to fashion one's life in a fully autonomous way; on the other, they intervene heavily in every sphere of associated life in order to grant the omnipresence of competition among those enterprises in which individuals are supposed to be taking part. In Becker's definition, *homo eoconomicus* is the person 'who accepts reality or who responds systematically to modifications in the variables of the environment, appears precisely as someone manageable, someone who responds systematically to systematic modifications artificially introduced into the environment' (Foucault 2008, 270). The necessity to manage society meant as an organic unity that encompasses various enterprises, no matter whether they are big corporations, or are made of a single person, is thus the reason upon which neoliberalism is founded as a political project. But one would fail to understand its efficacy if one emphasized the coercive power of neoliberalism. What Foucault underscores is rather the indirect form assumed by neoliberal power. By looking at neoliberalism, what we see is:

> the image, the idea, or theme-program of a society in which there is an optimization of systems of difference, in which the field is left open to fluctuating processes, in which minority individuals and practices are tolerated, in which action is brought to bear on the rules of the game rather than on the players, and finally in which there is an environmental type of intervention instead of the internal subjugation of individuals.
>
> (Foucault 2008, 260)

There is only one trait of disciplinary power that characterizes neoliberal society, namely the inherent tendency of the latter to increase systems of securitization. According to Foucault, the exponential growth both of the demand for security and the response to this demand are a logical consequence of the regime of concurrence that neoliberalism aims at imposing on the collective. One thing is to say that the regime of concurrence is the normal and obvious feature of human intercourse when individuals are driven by profit within a market oriented context of action. A different thing is to say that human beings fight against each other in order to grant the possession of those goods, of both a material and immaterial nature, they have achieved during a life spent investing in the improvement of their own human capital. Within the classical liberal perspective, the idea that human beings compete for purchase of goods and services within the market is self-evident. Within the neoliberal one, on the contrary, it is self-evident that the regime of competition affects each aspect of associated life. The extension of competitive mechanisms explains, first, the blurring of the boundary between risk and uncertainty, and, second, the increase of those security systems the function of which is to ensure social order. Foucault is right in remembering the importance that the distinction between risk and uncertainty still had for an author like Knight, who can be considered, in this respect, as belonging to the classical liberal tradition. Nevertheless, he seems to be more interested in pinpointing the enhancement of those disciplinary measures that aim to dam the socially undesirable consequences of an extended regime of competition.

> The more you multiply enterprises, the more you multiply the centers of formation of something like an enterprise, and the more you force govern-mental action to let these enterprises operate, then of course the more you multiply the surfaces of friction between each of these enterprises, the more you multiply opportunities for disputes, and the more you multiply the need for legal arbitration. An enterprise society and a judicial society, a society orientated towards the enterprise and a society framed by a multiplicity of judicial institution, are two faces of a single phenomenon.
>
> (Foucault 2008, 149ff.)

A judicial society, within which the weight of legal arbitration is high and the necessity to enhance various forms of repression belongs to normality, can be well characterized as a disciplinary society. But Foucault highlights also the fact that neoliberalism does not simply lead to the increase of repression, as if the enforcement of law were just the expression of the necessity to maintain social order. Within a neoliberal society the management of those conflicts due to the extension of the regime of competition is just one element of the broader complex of the art of government. Those who decide to act against the legal order, in fact, are nothing but individuals who have chosen to run the risk of facing the rigours of law. The response they deserve from governmental agencies appointed to the enforcement of law is, in some way, part of the social exchange. The management of a judicial system is thus one of many possible forms of governmental intervention the scope of which is to guarantee the good functioning of the competitive mechanism that informs society.

1.2 The neo-Marxist conception of neoliberalism

The aforementioned account of Foucault's definition of liberalism had the main scope to make clear that the interpretation of the neoliberal era as that phase of modern history where the state fades and withers leaving room for the predominance of the market would be a mistake. This mistake has found a widespread acceptance within those theories that consider neoliberalism as an exacerbation of capitalism, or simply as the best definition we have in order to account for the features assumed by capitalism in recent years. It may not be necessary to add that the inclination to minimize the transformation that neoliberalism entails about the capitalist structure of society is a typical trait of a Marxist stance. In our view, the latter is problematic for several reasons. First, the authors who accept the Marxist paradigm are not prone, generally speaking, to engage in any discussion about the fact that the very term 'capitalism' should undergo profound revision. The scholarly debate about the extension that capitalism as a historical category can claim for itself is huge,[3] and it would be short-sighted – to say the least – to leave out this debate when one aims at describing contemporary society. The second point, strictly related to the first, is that Marxist theorists still embrace the classical conception of value. It might be out of place even to formulate this reproach if one just considers that the Marxist critique of capitalist society rests entirely on the idea that the process of production is nothing but a way to exploit the living force of the producer in order to extract plus value from it. Nevertheless, it would be even worse not to remember that marginalism has radically transformed the way that we look at the creation of value. It is true that the neoclassic point of view is part of those economic theories that constitute the core of neoliberalism. But, as we will show later, a valid critique of neoliberalism has not to be directed toward the soundness of the economic assumptions that inform neoliberalism itself. The unease with neoliberalism arises with regard to its political relevance as a project that aims at transforming society. And we encounter here the precise reason why the Marxist point of view seems not to provide a good account for the way in which neoliberalism has been shaping contemporary society in a way that is, to some extent, unprecedented.

The theory of value embraced by Marxism tends to subordinate the political dimension to the economic realm. What counts is how human beings satisfy their needs within civil society; the domain of the latter coincides with the object political economy examines, and actually in this discipline is to be sought the 'anatomy of civil society', as Marx states in his *Contribution to the Critique of Political Economy*. For Hegel, from whom Marx borrowed the notion, civil society was, on the contrary, part of the state organization, or, better, was the state considered as the organism that encompasses the system of needs, the administration of justice and the management of those state assets and institutions the function and scope of which the *Polizeywissenschaft* of the eighteenth century had contributed to define with precision. In Hegel's understanding, thus, it would be incorrect to consider civil society simply as the domain where social relations of an economic nature take place: civil society designates the state as far as it acts upon society through its inferior instruments of government, namely judicial and administrative powers, which remain subordinate to executive and legislative powers. Marx shifts significantly the meaning of the term and puts forward the idea that civil society should be understood as the realm within which only private interests relate individuals to each other. Therefore, civil society is set in a pre-political domain and ends up becoming indistinguishable from the base that Marx separates from the super-structure. Any relevant phenomenon that affects how individuals are governed must be evaluated in the light of what occurs at the level of production; more-over, if one wants to put in question the power structure of a given society, one has to focus primarily on the division between those who own the means of production and those whose livelihood depends on their own labour.

The weight of the separation between base and superstructure heavily affects the way in which contemporary Marxism looks at neoliberalism. It is significant how the conceptual tools that Foucault uses to describe both liberalism and neoliberalism have been reframed within the Neo-Marxist context. Biopolitics ceases to term how the governmental power affects the body and the conduct of the subject in order to manage the space of freedom that specific rules and norms grant to the subject itself. Instead of the Foucauldian use of the notion, biopo-litics becomes the ensemble of technologies of the self that capitalist organization of labour deploys to create value. In this view, the notion of *bios* sums up the creative potential of each individual, together with its motivations, desires, atti-tudes and capabilities, and should help realign Marx's theory of labour-value introduced in the first book of *Capital* in order to explain the process of valori-zation. What the capitalist puts to work is the whole of individual life, and this fact characterizes the capitalist form of exploitation since the beginning of the industrial era. The new element introduced by neoliberalism is to be seen in the extension of the mechanism of exploitation: while the set of procedures that had the function to put individuals to work was restricted, within the liberal society, to the time individuals spent within the plant or the shop floor, namely during the labour time, the form of extraction of value that occurs within a neoliberal context is new in that it targets the totality of an indivi-dual lifetime. The distinction between labour time and leisure time vanishes, as well as the boundary between the working place and the space within which one is supposed to spend time in non-productive activities. This is due to the non-productive activities that serve to improve the set of individual cap-abilities and attitudes relevant within the domain of human creativity. More-over, it is precisely creativity, together with risk taking, flexibility and readiness to change, which contributes to strengthen both the competitive advantage of the individual considered as an enterprise, and the outputs of the individual performance carried out within a firm. In this context, biopolitics coincides with all those procedures the organization of labour deploys in order to create a network suitable both to connect individuals, and to appraise their cap-abilities and skills. This network, which can be informal and not subject to strict control measures, constitutes the condition of possibility of the feature value extraction takes within neoliberalism: by cultivating the personality and by partaking in common activities outside and inside the working place; by sharing with others knowledge, information and competences, in sum by simply fostering sociability, individuals build a discursive texture that encompasses both that which enables the reproduction of the collective, and that which confers value to the goods that circulate within the market.

As Virno (2004) puts it, contemporary capitalism makes the distinction between *praxis* and *poiesis* inconsistent. The domain of labour, where one is requested to apply specific competences and skills that have been acquired during a lifelong training, is the stage on which one exerts the virtue of *poiesis*. For Aristotle the latter was inferior to the virtue of *praxis*, which is the virtue one needs to exert as a member of the collective, in other words as a free citizen. Being the ability to do something for the sake of doing it, *praxis* has in itself its end; this circumstance is the reason why *praxis* is superior to *poiesis*, which is, on the contrary, an action that has its end outside itself. Contemporary capitalism has refined its capability to extract value in the sense that it exploits what individuals do simply as human beings that communicate with each other and partake in the construction of a shared life-world. The social construction of reality, which is the result of human *praxis*, is, thus, not only the immense archive that collects those shared meanings that grant the cultural consistency of the collective, but becomes also the arena where the creation of value takes place. Therefore, if biopolitics is the notion one chooses to describe the turning of *praxis* into a variant of *poiesis*, then the analysis of biopolitical forms of extraction of value serves to shed light on how the *general intellect* Marx spoke about in the Seventh Notebook of the *Grundrisse* works within contemporary capitalism. In this collection of notes, unpublished until 1939–41, Marx shows how, within the capitalist mode of production, 'general social knowledge has become a direct force of production' (Marx 1993, 706). He refers the process along which social life has come under the control of the general intellect to the huge development of machinery within the process of production. In this sense, the general intellect is the objectification of scientific knowledge, which is the presupposition of any technological improvement ('Nature builds no machines, no locomotives, railways, electric telegraphs, self-acting mules, etc.', as Marx puts it). Nonetheless, contemporary forms of extraction of value need rather the detachment of the general intellect from its being objectified into the system of machines, in order to exist as an attribute of the living labour:

> it is necessary that a part of the general intellect not congeal as fixed capital but unfold in communicative interaction, under the guise of epistemic paradigms, dialogical performances, linguistic games. In other words, public intellect is one and the same as cooperation, the acting in concert of human labour, the communicative competence of individuals.
>
> (Virno 2004, 65)

The inclusion of the very same anthropogenesis in the existing mode of production is an event that has led those who interpret neoliberalism starting from a Marxist stance to use also the term Post-Fordism in order to define their field of analysis. First, our understanding of contemporary capitalism is supposed to gain a new momentum by using the term Post-Fordism in the sense that the latter should better account for how important has become the cognitive dimension embedded in the production process. Within a global context that forces each competing enterprise to improve the rate of innovation by implementing the incorporation of knowledge in each stage of management and production strategy, the results of the collective effort needed to cope with the pressure that competition exerts is largely dependent on the capability to embed in a network all the cognitive performances that operate in a company. Since these performances are intertwined with what one does as a social agent, in the sense that they depend on what one has learned in the course of life, the individual contribution to organizational life cannot be detached from the whole of the social relationships one maintains outside the working place. Though there is nothing wrong with this narrative, here, again, we are invited to understand the core of the way of organizing the labour process that characterizes Post-Fordism as a form of subsumption of the general intellect by capital. For this reason, the term Post-Fordism is often used in correlation with the notion of 'cognitive capitalism'.[4] Along this strain of analysis, Gorz's intuition of the immaterial nature of capital[5] meets the tradition of Italian post-operaism inaugurated by Toni Negri (Hardt and Negri 2000).

Second, while Fordism was characterized by high levels of standardization about the management of the control mechanisms within the plant or the shop floor, in order to guarantee both productivity and a low profile of the conflicts that might arise between labour forces and management, Post-Fordism is based on the capability the management has to induce the establishment of a company climate that fosters high levels of motivation, involvement, self-control, and satisfaction within the labour force. Post-Fordism, then, terms the way in which capitalist organization of labour has succeeded in convincing those who have to work in order to sustain their lives that they do not work to increase the profit of the capitalist class, but that the goal of their labour activity coincides with their self-fulfilment. Here, Foucault's analysis of entrepreneurship as the mode of existence that marks the neoliberal process of subjectivation acquires a peculiar significance. The subject turned into an enterprise, or, better, the subject that has become an enterprise, seeks its own satisfaction by working, which implies a sort of self-adaptation to the game rules that enforce the capitalist mode of production. In this way, the neoliberal rhetoric concerning the enterprise as such serves as the model where any social actor, both individual and institutional, can mirror itself, and becomes, within the discourse on Post-Fordism, nothing but the ideology of late capitalism. Like any ideological apparatus, the rhetoric of the enterprise serves to conceal the unequal power relations on which the capitalist mode of production rests.

Much more interesting for the purposes we pursue here is another strain of analysis of neoliberalism that, though still related to the tradition of Marxism, devoted its efforts to understand the role played by states and institutions within the neoliberal mode of government. This approach seems much more related to Foucault's emphasis on the fact that neoliberalism is, in the first place, a project that aims at shaping the political landscape in an unprecedented way. From a Marxist point of view, this means to embrace the way in which Gramsci has redefined the relationship between base and superstructure. Gramsci offers an interpretation of the Hegelian concept of civil society that enables understanding of how important are all those apparatuses, both private and public, which allow a hegemonic social force to exert the power it has. Far from being the sole institutional actor that operates within society, the state, according to Gramsci, shares its function as a force that guarantees for the hegemonic group to maintain its dominating position with a plethora of other governing agencies. The civil society is precisely the stage on which these governing agencies and the state provide together to ensure both the establishment of the consensus and the reproduction of the existing hegemonic structures. In this sense, Gramsci's use of the concept of civil society resembles its original Hegelian formulation: while Marx was prone to see in the civil society only the ensemble of material relation that allow for the reproduction of the system of needs, Gramsci saw in it the site where power relations are inscribed and articulated at both the cultural and the material levels (Bobbio 1998).

Starting from this Gramscian – or, better, neo-Gramscian – move, some scholars have articulated a narrative in which neoliberalism amounts to a peculiar form of managing the relationship between the state and the market. The goal of any neoliberal policy is supposed to be, more precisely, to reduce the scope of the state and to redefine its role vis-à-vis the market. This critique of neoliberalism, which finds an audience far beyond the academic milieu, has the merit to underscore – at least to a certain extent – the political nature of the neoliberal project. Further, it has provided interesting insights into the way in which the neoliberal state government works by creating an institutional network that, on one hand, has in the state its centre, but, on the other, can perform its function with a considerable degree of autonomy. This approach seems to resemble what Foucault had in mind when he introduced the notion of 'governamentalization of the state'.

If one speaks of 'neoliberal hegemonic constellations' (Plehwe, Walpen and Neunhöffer 2006), for example, it becomes clear that the neoliberal project manifests itself in a variety of forms. Within the discursive domain, neoliberalism seems to be a plural and not homogenous ensemble of theories, variously connected to each other. However, if one looks at this ensemble from the neo-Gramscian perspective, one is somehow forced to attribute a homogeneous character to neoliberalism, and this to the point that the variety of forms it can take is then interpreted as a strategic move, which is not so far from a conspiracy. In this context, it seems to be almost self-evident to confer great importance to the tradition of Austrian Economics as well as to the Chicago School. Compounding these two strains of the economic thought of the twentieth century has become almost commonsensical even within discursive domains that are not influenced by a left-wing attitude. Yet, for those who adhere – no matter how strictly – to Marxism, it sounds not only plausible, but totally obvious to affirm that both the Austrian and the Chicagoan traditions are nothing but two faces of the same coin, in so far as both envisage the market as a domain the very existence of which is supposed to justify the constraints under which the action of the state must be redefined. What is worth underscoring within the neo-Gramscian narrative about neoliberalism, however, is the effort to give room to the discursive sources that resulted in the neoliberal project, in contrast to those approaches that tend to reduce the question of neoliberalism solely to the power relations embedded in the capitalist mode of production.

Further, when one focuses, moving from the neo-Gramscian framework, on the complexity of the discursive strategies that inform the establishment of neoliberal hegemony, it becomes clear how relevant are all those institutional arenas where the neoliberal discourse is shaped, produced and reproduced in order to enforce its spread. These arenas are both important think tanks that support various forms of expertise, and transnational institutions like the World Bank or the International Monetary Fund. Not surprisingly, the Mont Pelerin Society, whose birth Hayek gave a remarkable contribution to, con-stitutes the paramount example of how the mechanism that contributes to produce and reproduce the intellectual framework of neoliberalism works (Plehwe, Walpen and Neunhöffer 2006; see also Mirowski and Plehwe 2009). As an irreplaceable neoliberal discursive community, the group of scholars who work within think tanks substantiate the neoliberal discourse not only by producing guidelines for the global economy, but above all by providing the conceptual tools that are needed to underpin the neoliberal paradigm from a scientific point of view. However various and lively it may be, the discussion that takes place at this level is far from being merely a question of producing a sustainable scientific discourse: the bulk of knowledge and expertise that stems from the global network of economic think tanks, in fact, has simply the function to legitimize the neoliberal discourse. This legitimizing role can be performed better the deeper is the impression that they act as 'independent' centres devoted solely to the production of knowledge. Thus, if one accepts the neo-Gramscian point of view, one considers the independence the various think tanks enjoy as a mask, which hides their contribution to establishing the neoliberal hegemony. Likewise – and not surprisingly – the inner differences that can be tracked within the neoliberal discourse are to be seen as a trick, which should not deceive with regard to the deep unity of the neoliberal project.

Parallel to the role of the scientific discourse that underpins neoliberalism, it is important to pay attention to the way in which the neoliberal discourse spreads and becomes part of the shared mentality of a hegemonic community. Consequently, starting from Sklair's seminal work (2001) great attention is paid to the transnational capitalist class, composed not only by transnational corporations' executives, but also by globalizing bureaucrats, politicians, pro-fessionals, merchants and media. The position that this class occupies lies between corporations and state agencies, or, better, within the network that structures different communication channels between corporations and state agencies. This matter of fact not only gives power and influence to the members of the transnational capitalist class, but also enables them to act as a hinge between different discursive domains. The result is, on one hand, the rather homogeneous character of the neoliberal discourse, which reflects, on the other, how blurring the boundaries within this class are. A career, for example, which began as a corporation executive, can end as a state bureaucrat, and vice versa. The internal mobility of this class is not fortuitous, but is the result of a conscious effort, the scope of which is to ensure the hold which hegemony has at a global level. At stake here is not only the opportunity for each member to increase the range of his personal power, but also, and above all, the collective intention to take up the greatest number of nodes of a network the dimension of which has become more and more global.[6] Especially senior members of the transnational capitalist class, who are as well part of the 'inner circle' (Useem 1984), occupy high-level positions within more than one corporation, and their interlocking role contributes substantially both to maintaining the tightness of the network and to assuring its global character. An element that facilitates the internal cohesion is the relative homogeneity of the cultural patterns that the members of this class share. Common business education on one hand, the preference accorded to similar lifestyles on the other, constitute important factors that contribute to foster this homogeneity. The fact that, at the individual level, the cultural and national roots to which one is bounded are sometimes put in evidence in order to express one's individual identity does not invalidate the 'cosmopolitan' character of the collective identity shared by all members of the group. This cosmopolitanism may confer an aristocratic scent to the individual personality of executives and top managers, but it would be better to read it as an element that facilitates the practice of good public relations. Still, the 'cultural' elements that may be taken into consideration in order to understand the common features of this group should not mislead as far as its economic role is concerned. After all, however great is the distance of the neo-Gramscian point of view towards a more traditional Marxist one, the very notion of 'class' refers to the fact that the members of this elite are those 'who own and control the major means of production, distribution, and exchange through this ownership and control of money and other forms of capital' (Sklair 2001, 17).

If one turns the attention to the state agencies that are involved in the construction of the neoliberal hegemonic project, it is hard not to focus on how contemporary capitalism works in the United States. Starting from here, some scholars seem to acknowledge that the neoliberal way of configuring the relationship between state and market is far from being a simple self-reduction of state sovereignty in favour of an expansion of markets. What neoliberalism has brought in is seen rather as a new form of state control over markets, which amounts to a twofold result. On the one hand, the nation state that is able to exert the control over global markets acquires a competitive advantage in the geopolitical arena. On the other hand, the economic actors – big corporations on the first line – that are domiciled in such a state can strengthen their global position and reduce progressively their dependence on the environment. Since the United States is the only country that succeeded in combining the support to its main economic actors with the geostrategic efforts needed to maintain its global dominant position, the analysis of neo-liberalism coincides, to a certain extent, with that of the United States as a hegemonic power on the global scene (Howard and King 2008). This power is not, according to this interpretive model, an imperial one in the classical sense of the term. Surely, the potential use of force belongs to the means thanks to which the United States created its global hegemony, and even today the maintenance of the latter is assured by American superiority in the military area. But much more important has been – and is – the capability to govern the economic sphere in such a way as to determine the constraints each country has to take into consideration in order to position itself within the broader network of global economy. This means even that decisions taken in the United States by public agencies that are responsible for the domestic balance have consequences that reach the global arena, not to mention those measures the scope of which is to limit the room of manoeuvre of other countries in the economic domain. Thus, if anybody still insists in defining the United States as an empire, it must be added that it is an empire that does not govern through the direct control of a territory, but rather through the control of the ties that bind other global actors – not only allied or friend states, but even rival countries – to the Unites States itself.

Within this perspective, the end of Bretton Woods, to be read, at the same time, as the beginning of the neoliberal era, acquires a peculiar meaning. The progressive growth of global financial markets, which took place in the after-math of the collapse of Bretton Woods's system, became the stage on which the United States performed a new strategy of dominance. The latter was based on the construction of a financial global architecture that forced other countries to open their domestic financial markets thus allowing the penetration of American firms in them. Some of these countries were – and are – good allies of the United States, but their increasing autonomy and assertiveness in the economic realm could have turned them into dangerous competitors, a possibility that the American influence exerted over the global market served to make less realistic. Here the notion of neoliberalism is used, then, to define the way a capitalist state, namely the United States, has chosen to maintain its own dominance within the global arena by assuring its corporations that operate in the financial sector that it has control over the global flow of capital.

Yet, doubt remains that even analysis based on a neo-Gramscian paradigm cannot give a convincing account of what is new in the neoliberal way of governing. It is true that the very notion of hegemony helps get rid of a deterministic way of defining the relationship between base and superstructure. Nevertheless, when the notion of neoliberalism is framed within a broader narrative supposed to explain how capitalism works, it becomes difficult to put in question the canonical view according to which economy is about production, exchange and growth of profit, whereas actions of political nature are those that define the power relations among individuals that compete for the acquirement of the goods and resources circulating in the economic realm. However sophisticated might be the way of conceiving of the relationship between the two spheres of action, the separation between them still needs to undergo a radical revision. In fact, if one keeps depicting neoliberalism as the last phase within the history of capitalism, or – which is even worse – as the last mask worn by a protean but essentially never changing capitalism, then analysing the intertwinement between economic and political sphere would ultimately mean to describe how the interests of the capitalist class meet the interests of state bureaucrats and how this match of interests favours both the economy and the self-positioning of state agencies in the global arena. Of course, if anybody adopts a comparative perspective, it becomes relevant to outline how patterns of relation between state and market differ depending on both the cultural biases affecting the actors and the constraints that characterize the past history of the nation state taken into consideration, and this move allows one to speak of historically and culturally different forms of capitalism. Yet, even in this case, a certain 'essence' of the investigated phenomenon is presupposed. The result is that the alleged essence of capitalism obscures the novelty of the neoliberal art of government, which does not simply consist in assuring the success of national based corporations through specific public interventions.

In conclusion, it is the market, more or less hypostatized, that is the part of the societal structure that is supposed to gain more within any Marxist narrative about neoliberalism. To make the point clearer, it is worth listing the main elements of this narrative, meant to account both for historical processes and for specific policies adopted in recent decades in almost all western countries. Rolling back the gains made by the working class in the advanced capitalist countries in the post-war period, these include: elimination of the Keynesian welfare state; end of any commitment to full employment; fostering of flexible labour markets; destruction of trade unions and democratic rights in order to drive down wages; privatization of state owned enterprises; introduction of user charges for public services; reduction of business taxes for corporations and the mega-rich, which contributed to the continuing fiscal crisis of the state; extension of the global reach of transnational corporations, which had as a counterpart the progressive reduction of the universal right to water, sanitation, transport, energy, health care, education and basic democratic rights. The picture is complete when one, finally, ascertains that the tendency of the rate of profit to fall could not be stopped despite all the measures adopted to favour the private sector; this ascertainment is important in so far as it serves to explain the financialization – and, parallel to it, the de-industrialization – of western economies.

It has been worth, we think, devoting so much attention to Marxist or neo-Marxist attempts to construct neoliberalism as a research object because, first, some elements of this construction are part of the mainstream criticism against neoliberalism itself, and, second, because they surely highlight some striking developments of contemporary western society. The point, however, is that insisting on focusing on the never-ending capability demonstrated by capitalism to evolve and to create the political conditions that assure its survival means, almost unavoidably, to stick to an interpretive paradigm according to which the logic that governs political behaviour is different from the one that governs economic behaviour. One may have good reasons to state that this difference exists and that it is important to maintain it as a methodological presupposition that help us read social phenomena. Nonetheless, and at the same time, one risks overlooking that precisely the attempt to make this difference not effective lies at the core of the neoliberal strategy. The latter can be better understood, in fact, not as a more sophisticated way of improving the dominance of the capitalist class, but rather as an attempt to transform the way in which institutions and organizations shape individual conduct. Furthermore, this transformation rests on the pervasiveness of a model of rationality that claims to fit any possible domain of human action.

1.3 The relationship between state action and economy

Regardless of the differences between our position, which is explicitly dependent on Foucault's analysis of neoliberalism, and the position of neo-Marxist oriented scholars, some of the aforementioned points must be taken into consideration. The theoretical frame must be different, of course, but we hold it to be important to mention them as far as they provide the historical and sociological background needed to frame the origins of neoliberalism.

First, there is the question of how national interests and economic agents relate to each other. To approach the relationship between the position of a state within the geopolitical arena and the position of its economy within the global market does not mean to address an issue related, no matter whether directly or indirectly, to the 'capitalist' feature of its economy, or to the 'neoliberal' nature of its government. It is an issue, rather, that acquires visibility and significance within the way scholars have been looking at international relations for decades.

In the aftermath of the Second World War, within the discipline that has made international relations its own object, it was almost commonsensical to regard nation states as independent entities confronting each other on a stage that was supposed to offer nothing more than a material support. Classic works like Morgenthau (1948) represents, in a typical form, this view, which mirrored a world totally organized in Westphalian terms. Still today, it seems reasonable to hold some of the basic assumptions of Morgenthau's realism – for example, that states seek to have the greatest amount of power that they possibly can, or that the legal order stemming from the existence of international treaties is not absolute, but contingent, in the sense that it depends on the value that states place upon it, and, finally, the fact that force, or the willingness to use it when necessary, is an essential part of what we understand with statehood. However, the basic assumption of realism, namely the idea according to which the nation state is to be seen as the sole actor on the stage of international relations, ends up being more nuanced. It is hard to contest that the state is the central actor on this stage, but its centrality cannot mean isolation or immunity from external influence. In other words, the substantive 'relations' points at the systemic nature of the assemblage constituted by all the international actors.

The consequences of this shift of paradigm involve a twofold acknowledgement. First, state relations are such that the role a state can play as an international actor depends heavily on the position it occupies within the geopolitical arena. This position constrains its room for manoeuvre and the frame within which any policy is carried out must be considered. Therefore, it makes sense to say – even if it might sound exaggerated – that the boundary between internal and external policies is blurred. This does not affect only states whose position is rather weak. Even states claiming to possess or effectively possessing hegemonic status depend on the interplay between all the forces operating in the global arena. Both the scholar who wants to analyse the complexity of this interplay and the decision maker who has to figure out a successful strategy must regard it as a multi-layered structure within which path dependence as well as the unpredictability of the moves made by other players affects all the subjects involved. This structure can be defined as complex not only because it encompasses so many factors, from past decisions to the habits they contribute to create and the expectations they generate in an external observer, but also because of the subject's expectations of the other's move to suppositions concerning the way the other will react to their move. It is complex, above all, because, when it becomes an object observed, the observing subject (no matter whether it is a scholar who examines international relations or a policy maker) is part of the structure itself. The results of the observation, once made public and able to produce information, contribute to modify the perception that each observer has of it.

Therefore, it would be a mistake to consider international actors as if they were isolated elements that give rise to complex systems of relations only after they begin to interact with each other: it is the systemic complexity, in fact, which engenders the unfolding of every possible interaction. The function of state sovereignty, and the way it works as a key element of the global system of international relations, can be at best explained, then, by referring to conceptual tools that stem from both institutional theory and evolutionary biology (the latter meant according to the version of Stephen Jay Gould and Niles Eldredge). Within this perspective, sovereign states act as institutions that attempt to cope, more or less successfully, with the constraints deriving from path dependence and the unpredictability of the environment, which changes after each step made by the actors involved in it (Krasner 1988).

A second fact to be taken into consideration is the agency of international actors other than sovereign states. Institutions like the WTO, the IMF or the World Bank, and organizations like multinational corporations and NGOs have contributed to make the international relations scenario much more complex. It is even possible to describe it as a global civil society, in the sense that some international institutions and transnational organizations, even if they do not exert sovereignty over a territory, do act as political forces (Rosenau 2002). This happens as far as they can negotiate their positions and defend their interests in the global arena, determine agendas that are binding even for states, manage the flux of information and then shift the focus on specific topics, create local coalitions, and, finally, contribute to generate shared behaviours and discursive patterns that influence, retroactively, the way all the actors relate to each other. Once again: this fact is not to be interpreted as the sign that the weight of states is diminishing in the global arena. Powerful states do have the capability to withstand the influence exerted by networks of non-state actors, just as they can overwhelm the will of less powerful states. The so-called 'Washington Consensus' was not just a fairy tale – though, we argue, the way in which its articulation has become part of the narrative about globalization within radical left-wing circles resembles more a conspiracy tale than the reconstruction of matters of fact. What must be underscored here, however, is the complex structure of the network within which global actors operate: the ties that bring together each element of the network are sensitive to every variation – or, better, to every noise generated within the network. Moreover, this circumstance endows all the actors with a voice, however small their negotiating capability.

In conclusion, there are two extensive processes, which are strictly inter-twined with each other, that must be taken into account if one wants to shed light on how the behaviour and actions of an economic nature become part of the broader strategy chosen by a nation state in order to define its sovereign space. On the one hand, sovereignty itself has changed as well as the perception of its function and range in the eyes of those who observe it. Sovereignty does not mean unlimited capability to create a living space and to maintain it as far as there is enough force to employ to do this. Sovereignty means rather the capability of a state to negotiate its own geopolitical position, which means, concretely, the capability to manage flows of money, resources, goods, people, and knowledge both into and out of the state boundary. The latter is porous, and it is precisely the capability of regulating the degree of its porosity which gives a concrete measure of sovereignty. On the other hand, the landscape of international relations also harbours subjects from different nation states. To equate them with the 'market forces' that are omnipresent in the discourse of left wing groups would be a mistake. These subjects may be, of course, multinational corporations, but NGOs and other actors that are able to convey specific interests are also part of the landscape. It is important to underscore as well that a nation state might seek to defend its own interests within the global arena against competitors whose domicile or headquarters is located within its own territory, but who pursue different interests.

Therefore, when specific choices in the field of political economy are made in order to exert influence upon other states and thus maintain a state's own hegemonic position, or, on the contrary, in order to eschew the burden of the external influence exerted by another state, these choices always fall within a multi-layered relationship continuum in spatial and temporal terms. The fact that the outcome cannot be foreseen in advance is constitutive as well as the possibility that unintended consequences could reverse the expected outcome.

A good example is the path that led to the establishment of a free financial market. Since the beginning, the decision to come to this result has been a political one, and this is true for all the actors who, in different moments and to diverse degrees, contributed to its attainment. Under the rule of the Bretton Woods system, it seemed obvious to all the states that were involved in it to protect the Keynesian inspired policies from the danger stemming from free speculative capitals movements. Besides that, the global trade system unfolded along a viable path underpinned by the stability of the exchange rate system foreseen by the agreements signed in 1944. It was the period characterized by those policies that, taken as a whole, are well described by the expression 'embedded liberalism' (Ruggie 1982). When the United States began to suffer from both the loss of its leading position within the field of international trade and the increasing deficit, the solution that seemed to promise the better compensation to be achieved in the easier way has been given by the opening of the financial market. To act in order to free the trade market from the constraints encumbering it would have been much more difficult because requiring that foreign states reduce or eliminate their trade barriers entails very high costs. The latter is related to the maintaining of a control system over possible free riders. In general, it is the coordination of the collective action required to maintain the openness of a free trade system that makes it costly. On the contrary, the opening of a free financial market is an action that can be carried out even unilaterally by a state in order to attract footloose capitals and financial business in its own territory. Nevertheless, creating unilaterally an open financial market proved to be a successful strategy not only because the costs for its realization were not so high, but also because it forced other states to conform to the rules imposed by the United States. Part of the design that led to the creation of the global financial market entailed the calculation that the dollar, after the end of its convertibility to gold decided in August 1971, would have become the base currency in a world of free-floating fiat currencies. The final result was that the United States, thanks to its dominant position in the open international financial system, was able to 'encourage foreigners both to finance and to bear the burden of adjustment to its growing current account and fiscal deficit' (Helleiner 1994, 202).

After losing its dominant position in the aftermath of the Second World War, the United Kingdom seized the moment offered by the American decision to create an open financial market, and animated by the desire to maintain London's position as an international financial hub. The three major British institutions involved in the financial sector, namely the Bank of England, the Treasury and the City of London, acted in a way that made it possible for London to become the centre of the Euromarkets. During the late nineteenth century, when the City occupied a hegemonic position within the financial world system, the openness of the financial market was held to be normal. Mindful of past glory, thus, since the 1960s the United Kingdom began to foster the openness of the euro-dollar market, sustained in this by the US government. In a world of extensive capital controls, in fact, both the United States and the United Kingdom took advantage of the existence of a regulation-free environment in which it was possible to trade financial assets denominated in dollars and other foreign currencies.

Japan was the third state that joined the policy of promoting openness in the financial sector. It did it later than the other two countries, starting in the 1980s, for reasons related to the enormous growth that had affected this country since the 1970s. However, Japan had a strong interest in contributing to global financial stability not only because of the huge accumulation of external financial assets that accompanied its financial rise, but also for strategic reasons. Japan took the decision to become an important global player within an open financial order envisaging the opportunity to ensure smooth bilateral relations with the United States, on which its security strongly depended.

The decision taken by some states to give birth to an open financial market, thus, can be interpreted by focusing on the strategic interests at stake. It is hardly worth bringing neoliberalism into the explanation of this phenomenon – especially if 'neoliberalism' is meant to term the preference for unleashing liberalization of global markets. The point made here suggests rather that the results of the analysis stemming from the field of international relations should invite one to be more cautious when talking about topics like 'liberalization' or 'global markets'. In addition, this caution goes hand in hand with a more circumstantial use of the notion of 'neoliberalism', which would be better used to put into question a given model of rationality and the pattern of government that it contributes to inform. Since this model of rationality seems to possess in great degree virtues like simplicity and clarity, which both surely contribute to increase its pervasiveness, it is important to devote some attention to an issue that acquired a certain relevance not only in the field of international relations, but also in that of international political economy. It is an issue strictly related to the degree of complexity reached by the world system. The hypothesis is that a governmental praxis inspired by neoliberal models probably helps reduce this complexity.

Though the effort made by some states to create an open financial market turned out well at the beginning, it became more and more difficult to cope with the effects of this openness when the amount of money circulating in the financial market reached such a level that it became impossible for any institution in the world to have an insight of it. Therefore, the positive effects that a state acting as a global player expects from its own hegemonic position risks being undermined by the autonomy the financial sector has gained in recent years. Such autonomy is, in part, an outcome of the overwhelming weight the financial market has acquired within the whole of the global economy. Nobody would think of diminishing this weight well knowing that the raison d'être of the financial market is not only to provide a separate environment for speculators who want to expand their profits at the cost of the rest of the world, but also to grant the constant availability of the liquidity needed by all economic actors. However, although it is not expensive to create an open financial market, which can attract investors and traders, it is hugely costly to even attempt to put it under control. Yet, despite the fact that almost everybody acknowledges both the necessity of the global financial market and the impossibility of restraining it, its sheer existence gives rise to great concerns regarding the possibility that a collapse could reverberate through the whole global economic system. Even in the phase in which the financial sector was taking its first steps, it would have been possible to recognize that the risk-taking attitude characterizing the financial milieu could have catastrophic consequences for the whole of the economy. The failure of Long Term Management Capital, which occurred in 1998, provided a perfect case study for that.[7] Years later, in the aftermath of the crisis of 2007–08, considerable amounts of ink have been spilled on the 'systemic risk', that is on the possibility that the failure of some big companies active in the financial sectors might engender a chain of other failures (it is the well-known 'snowball effect'), damaging not only the financial sector, but bringing the whole of the economic system to the brink of collapse. Not touched by the worrying events, nor by the criticism addressed to them, scholars within the discipline of economics – not all of them, of course, but the majority – kept on repeating the mantra of the self-regulating market, a circumstance that led to the reconstruction of the role played by economists during the crisis in terms of a tricky manoeuvre based on the tactics of agnotology (Mirowski 2013).

Still, there is something much more dreadful to be worried about within the relationship between global society and disruptive events that could occur within the financial market. Perhaps we really live on the brink of a global collapse, but nobody can foresee the date of the total breakup. What seems more likely is that democratic regimes, an international order based on sovereign states and the totally uncontrolled circulation of financial capitals around the globe are not anymore figures fitting together in the same picture of the world we live in. Therefore, it is as if the global order has to reduce its complexity to the extent that only two of the three elements can coexist. To put it in narrative form, it is as if we have to choose between one of the following scenarios. If we choose to live in a world made of sovereign and possibly democratic states, then we have to create policy measures, which are supposed to be effective on a global scale, affecting the financial market in a way that restricts its disruptive potential. If we choose to combine the existence of unrestrained financial markets with a form of global governance, which would be charged to safeguard the exercise of democratic rights, then we have to renounce living in the sovereign nation states that have constituted the architecture of international relations up to the present. In this scenario, the sacrifice of the sovereign state would be necessary because only a form of governance supposed to be stronger than an ensemble of nation states could effectively protect democratic rights at the international level in the face of a financial market with no boundaries. Finally, if we choose not to restrain in any form the financial market and, at the same time, we choose to maintain the present order based on sovereign nation states that try to cope with the capability the financial market has to interfere with every form of institution, national or international, including thus sovereign states, then we have to seriously consider the possibility that democracy can be endangered or reduced.[8] Social protests of huge proportions are easy to be imagined, in fact, if global actors belonging to the financial sector succeed in extending their global influence to the point that they can fashion the policy agenda of states. The latter, for example, in order to appease foreign investments in crucial sectors like education or health care, could undergo such a profound change that the services dispensed by public institutions cease to fulfil their main function, which is to guarantee a decent standard of living for the great majority of citizens, even for those who cannot afford the costs for their own welfare. A drastic lowering in the general quality of life, as history teaches, induces not only discontent, but also the temptation to turn one's own discontent into concrete forms of protest. There is a line (whose position is different from one society to another, and from a historical period to another) beyond which the violence caused by the expression of discontent leads to the suspension of the rule of law and democratic procedures and the imposition of a police state. As the costs for defending democracy and civil rights are very high, it is likely that most people would prefer to sit on the fence and wait until the period of upheaval is over (Hibou 2011).

Unrealistic as it may seem, even the last scenario we have just outlined must be taken into consideration if we want to understand the historical and political frame within which neoliberalism has been able to spread. The problem we are facing, it is worth repeating, is not about the relationship between state power and the economy, but it is about how a certain model of rationality has become so persuasive as to end up gaining a stronghold on the collective imaginary – to term something that is more vague as a shared mental model – both of decision makers, no matter whether they act in the private or in the public domain, and of ordinary people. As institutions, states have to manage their own self-positioning within the global arena in such a way that the starting point for each undertaking is given by the awareness of how domestic and international affairs are intertwined. Of course, the United States as a hegemonic power can keep on steering its economy by pursuing goals of both a domestic and strategic nature (Wade 2003). In other words, it can keep on behaving as an empire that has a relatively long life ahead of it. However, this does not mean that it can renounce bargaining: the use of 'soft power' is not a strategic choice; it is much more a necessity, dictated by the growing complexity that characterizes international relations.[9] Furthermore, if this is true about the United States, it is true a fortiori concerning all other countries. Therefore, it is the complexity of the global context which makes it very difficult to figure out courses of action based on a set of clear and simple assumptions. Indeed, the Bretton Woods system left room for much easier assessments both of the position one state occupied within the global arena and of the perception of where lies the boundary between domestic and international policies. The reason for that has been outlined above: markets were not 'embedded' only because capitalist countries decided to improve market efficiency by creating an international institutional framework that was supposed to combine liberalization and domestic stability; the decision to 'embed' them reflected also social expectations, norms and economic ideas that were widely shared both by the élite and a large part of public opinion. There was, then, a mutual correspondence between the world order and some of the basic assumptions about how global actors could contribute to maintaining that order.

Hence, corresponding to the increased complexity, the world system has been facing a deep change of mentality lately, affecting all the actors involved in the global arena. Neoliberalism is to be seen, we suggest, as the unifying element within the rather dispersed set of governmental practices that ensued after the collapse of the Bretton Woods system. Its unifying strength resides in the capability to provide a unique model for human action, which is supposed to work as an explanatory tool at both the macro and the micro level.

1.4 Neoliberalism and the question of systemic complexity

If we assume that the reason for the global spread of neoliberalism as a *Weltanschauung* lies in the fact that neoliberalism is a political project able to offer a set of answers to the governmental problems which decision makers have to tackle within the global arena, the discourse on the structure of neoliberalism deserves an articulated account.

Here, we introduce an issue we will pay more attention to later, namely the simple feature of the economic theory that informs neoliberalism. Based on assumptions whose relevance and pertinence are supposed to be valid only within the realm of cost-benefits analysis, it is a theory that conceals its dependence upon specific ethical and political – but one could even say metaphysical – presuppositions. As strange as it may sound, the latter ones prove to be effective precisely because they remain embedded in a theory that presents itself just as the toolbox one needs to build those policy measures that should improve the welfare of individuals. Technical measures are never merely technical and they always embody some specific conceptions of human nature whose anthropological, ethical and political character can be easily disclosed. In this case, one can lay bare to what extent the conception of welfare purported to be objective and politically neutral by the economic theory is far from being presuppositionless (Hausman and McPherson 2008). But, sticking to the Foucauldian attitude that informs our argument, it is important to avoid any confusion between the analysis of how a presupposition works within a discourse and the act of unveiling an ideology, which is supposed to be the hidden – and manipulated – 'truth' of the discourse itself.

First, welfare is meant as the satisfaction of individually-based social preferences. This is, at least, a rather narrow conception of what welfare is, but it
prevents an uninvolved observer from taking it as a moral theory. The point is
crucial: the so-called 'welfare economics' does not want to be and in fact is not
a moral theory. The narrowness of the definition of welfare it provides aims
precisely at excluding any controversy about the definition of those concepts
that, being usually related to a broader concept of welfare, belong to the field of
moral theory and, therefore, are fiercely disputed within the latter. Nevertheless,
an uninvolved observer would be right to question the neutrality with respect to
the values that marks this definition of welfare for two reasons, which are
strictly related to each other. On the one hand, economists do construct
models that are supposed to be not only well-made bricks good for building
a coherent economic theory, but also feasible guidelines for policies. An
example: the results of public choice policies, which constitute perhaps the
most striking feature of neoliberal governmentality, must be judged and
evaluated on the base of their aptness to improve individual welfare. This
simple fact challenges immediately the claim for neutrality that economists
attribute to their scientific activity.

On the other hand, the sheer fact that welfare economics focuses only on
individually-based social preferences, thus leaving aside any consideration about
social concerns, moral reasons, individual rights to certain goods or services, is
per se the result of a politically oriented choice, which can be in no way considered neutral. The 'choice' that is here at stake is not to be understood as the
fruit of a decision taken by a scientific community after a deliberation process. It
is rather the result of a discursive practice shared by those who participate in the
game of economic theory. Now, bearing in mind this important distinction, the
power of persuasion that can be attributed to the economic discourse within
the global arena depends precisely on what it excludes from the public discussion. As Bachrach and Baratz suggested in a seminal article issued several
decades ago (Bachrach and Baratz 1962), power consists in the 'mobilization
of bias', in the capability to determine both what is important – or irrelevant –
within a given agenda and what counts as a 'shared value' within a community. In
addition, perhaps the most effective way to gain power consists not in bringing to
public consideration those issues that need be decided after a deliberation that
involves the weighing of alternatives and the sifting of arguments, but rather in
simply preventing some issues from arising and receiving attention. Therefore,
if we accept the suggestions that come from Bachrach and Baratz's conception
of power, we can shed light on the connection between the lack of neutrality
that characterizes economic theory as such and its political impact. The latter
emerges precisely when economic theory conveys the idea that it is useless even
to discuss those principles according to which the members should judge the
social structure they belong to regarding both the amount of liberty and the
access to resources like education or health care.

It is perhaps worth reflecting on the fact that for a scholar that belonged to
the classical liberal tradition like Frank Knight (taken here as one of the

utmost representatives of that tradition) it would have been inconceivable to reduce economics to a theory whose main and sole scope was to define individual welfare. One can just consider, for example, an essay he issued in 1940, in which he took a stance against those scientific developments that would have made economics not only expunge from its own disciplinary field any moral or political consideration, but also remove the necessity to maintain an overt position toward the very question of what does it mean to live in a good society (Knight 1940). He recognized very clearly that the first step that would have led to these developments consisted in transforming the epistemic status of economics, turning it into a natural science. Having once taken this step, in fact, it becomes easier to look at the economic actor as a calculating machine, which has no feelings and is not interested in uttering value judgments – a position, according to Knight, that is not only untenable, but is also an expression of a lack of humour. Economic problems lie in the field where knowledge of human conduct makes sense, but the study of human conduct cannot reach those levels of certainty that characterize natural sciences. This is not to be meant as a negative judgement as regards the economic discipline. The latter can provide important insights into how human beings react to the variations of prices that mark the functioning of a sound market. Here Knight regards economics as a useful science from a social and political point of view as well: by helping determine a rigorous answer to the question of how indivi-dual behaviour changes in relation to changes of prices, economics does con-tribute to building the frame policy decision makers need to establish the 'rules of the game' according to which social actors are supposed to behave. However, when questions arise as regards how to determine the scope and limits of those rules, then economics has to recognize that other disciplines within the humanities are better geared if not to give an answer to those questions, at least to articulate their plausibility. He concludes his critical remarks towards what, precisely in that period, began to pose itself as 'positive economics' by stating that:

> [c]oncrete and positive answers to questions in the field of economic science or policy depend in the first place on judgments of value and as to procedure on a broad, general education in the cultural sense, and on 'insight' into human nature and social values, rather than on the findings of any possible positive science. From this point of view the need is for an interpretive study (*verstehende Wissenschaft*) which, however, would need to go far beyond any possible boundaries of economics and should include the humanities as well as the entire field of the social disciplines.
>
> (Knight 1940, 31)

To what extent the field of economics offers room for any form of *verstehende Wissenschaft* is well known to any student who approaches contemporary economics within their academic study. The reason why a dialogue between economics and the rest of the humanities can hardly take place lies not only in the narrow conception of welfare briefly discussed above, but also in the conception of rationality on which the entire discourse of economics rests. This conception wants to be formal, in the sense that it claims to describe the structure of individual choice. Once again, formality is related to neutrality with respect to values. According to the theory of rationality embedded in mainstream economics, individuals choose rationally if their actions are determined by their preferences, whereas their preferences, in so far as they are complete and transitive, are supposed to be rational as well. Notoriously, individuals do not always act according to the model employed by economists. Nevertheless, this has never been taken as a serious objection. If one wants to behave rationally, one must assign an ordinal number to each item ranked in a list of possible alternatives, thus expressing one's own consistent preference ranking, and then choose the preferred alternative. Any choice behaviour that would differ from this schema would be simply irrational. This procedure can be also defined as 'maximization of utilities', but it is important to notice that 'utility' is not in itself an object of preference. It is rather the element of an abstract function that allows assigning numbers to alternatives in a way that indicates preference.

Despite the formal character of this theory of rationality, which intends to remain confined to the realm of pure normativity, economists do not abstain from providing insights into the concrete content of individual preferences. They do it by assuming that most people act according to the principle of self-interest, no matter whether this principle is consciously made part of the rationale for the action or not. This assumption is indispensable if economics wants to offer generalizations on what people really prefer, as well as being an unavoidable element of the strategy that aims at strengthening the position of economics within the domain of natural sciences. The latter is supposed not only to offer generalizations of past and present events, but also to predict – with an acceptable degree of approximation – future courses of events. So, even if the principle of self-interest is taken as a useful generalization, economics is strongly committed to it, otherwise it would be very difficult to fill with content those models that are needed to explain how individuals behave as rational actors. However, here we face a circumstance that does not essentially differ from that one we met above when dealing with the burden of presuppositions that weigh on the conception of welfare. If the economic science is committed to the claim that individuals are guided by self-interest precisely when they act as rational actors, then economics is far from being simply a normative discipline, which can legitimately aspire to be taken as a useful toolbox available to anyone who wants to explain market phenomena.

There exist arguments that serve to articulate substantive objections to the theory of rationality upheld by neoclassical economics, as we will show in the two following chapters. At this point, however, it seems to be more appropriate to draw attention to the fact that neoclassical economics, despite all the objections it can receive, is far from losing its appeal. We are suggesting that the latter rests not so much on the scientific consistence one can ascribe to economic theory as such, but rather on the fact that the political project embedded in it offers an array of governmental solutions that are mainly based on procedures and not on principles of an ethical or political nature. In this sense, the neoliberal governmentality could be described as the successful marriage between economic discipline, which claims to offer an encompassing conception of human nature, and those governmental agencies that answer the question of how to manage complexity by virtue of the efficiency one generally expects from procedures.

The metaphor of marriage, we argue, seems to offer a good insight into the nature of neoliberal governmentality. This metaphor helps us, in fact, underpin the argument according to which neoliberalism is not the result of a misleading abuse of a scientific theory. Economics as a discipline and neoliberalism as a form of governmentality have crossed their paths in a way that has turned out to be fruitful for both – as happens in every marriage worthy of its name. Metaphors aside, economics was not deemed to occupy a sovereign position within the encyclopaedia of knowledge. It was, almost everywhere, a discipline that could not be easily inserted into the landscape constituted by institutionalized forms of knowledge. Nevertheless, it had something precious to offer: a set of methods and procedures that enabled the control and evaluation of the performances of public institutions and economic actors such as firms. Viewed from this point, the dominance of neoclassic economics that makes neoliberalism so peculiar is the result of a long historical and political process. Whenever public institutions have needed an expertise in order to measure the effects of a given policy, they have turned to those forms of knowledge that were supposed to assess the extent to which past interventions had been successful and future ones could be considered feasible. Economics has not simply been a science of measurement since its inception, but it has been encouraged to turn itself into a useful tool to provide guidelines for policies. This explains why the inner tendencies already present within the discipline toward a self-positioning not as a human science, but rather as a natural science, have been reinforced. We have to consider that the historical process, thus, consists in the mutual convergence of two distinct phenomena. On the one hand, public institutions need to give an account of how they govern – if not for the public opinion, as it is normally the case in democratic countries, at least for the bureaucratic apparatus that manages the flow of inputs and outputs. On the other hand, economics strives to be recognized as the discipline that can at best meet the need of public institutions to construct and improve their own image as rational actors. These two phenomena have become significant in Western countries since the age of the Enlightenment – and Foucault was not wrong in beginning his analysis of the relationship between public agencies and the economic discipline by conferring so much significance on the role played by both the *Polizeywissenschaft* and the *sciences camérales* during the eighteenth century. However, the way in which governmental technologies dovetail with the knowledge offered by the economist presents different peculiarities that can vary both geographically and historically. Although a complete account of these variations would be in the wrong place here,[10] it is worth outlining some general features of the way in which the conception of the social world provided by economics has become the 'objective' premise for governmental action. By doing so, we do not mean to suggest that Foucault's reconstruction of this issue was not complete or unsatisfying. What deserves now specific attention is the fact that the economic discipline created not only the 'truth' governmental agencies needed in order to become aware of the effects of their actions, but also those procedures that have led to a simplification of the complexity of the social world.

An insightful move in this direction, we argue, consists in considering the performativity of economics as an essential part of a strategy that aims at defining goals and limits of social engineering. In his reconstruction of the relationship between objectivity in science and social need for control and accountability Porter (1995) has persuasively shown how the scientific enterprise taken as a whole contributed not only to improve human knowledge, but also to organize both human labour and the management of resources according to data, numbers and measurements upon which not only the scientific community, but also decision makers could rely. Not by chance, many examples of his reconstruction come from the history of economics and economy. In the nineteenth century, for instance, authors like Cournot and Walras strove to be accepted by the members of those institutions whose function was to provide the solution of practical problems concerning the management of public assets. Nevertheless, they met a substantial obstacle: actuaries and engineers in post-Napoleonic France, educated in public schools like the *Ecole des Mines* or the *Ecole Polytechnique*, were keen to stand on statistics and related disciplines. That means they were not ready to embrace economics as a discipline that was supposed to bring under the same umbrella both the explanation of economic behaviour in general and the clue for answering questions raised by the administration of public goods. The mistrust of these technicians, however, can be understood by considering the fact that economics had not yet succeeded in being recognized as the 'social physics' it was striving to become. It must also be stressed that those whose effort went in the direction of strengthening the ground on which a solid science of economics could rest were not theorists interested only in the formal elegance of a pure theory: they were interested as well in giving their own contribution to the solution of problems rising from the domain of public policies. Moreover, they succeeded in this effort as soon as economics could provide numbers on which they could stand.

Another significant example comes from the practice of accounting. This practice began to be important both in the United Kingdom and the United States after the first half of the nineteenth century, but it did not take long before it spread everywhere, soon becoming coextensive with almost all social practices. At the beginning, the accounting profession offered its service in relation to the management of bankruptcy files – creditors had to be assured that they would be treated fairly. Later, as big companies in sectors such as railroad communication or production of energy grew in importance and acquired more and more economic and social weight, the accountants had to assure shareholders and other interested parties that the books were fair and honest. In both cases, independence of judgement and objectivity were required. The point Porter is interested in consists of underscoring that the scientific community had never been the sole milieu that contributed to the establishment of the ethos of objectivity. Even practitioners such as accountants made out of the pursuit of objectivity a distinguishing mark not only of their professional competence, but also of the importance of their social role. Numbers are per se mute, in other words interpreting data of no matter which sort rests on an art of interpretation, which, for its part, requires judgement – that is a mixture of good sense, attentiveness, sure instinct, tact and prudence. Those who deal professionally with the interpretation of numbers must be absolutely reliable. In addition, this reliability could be found only in a group of professionals committed to objectivity in an almost religious way. The neutrality that only objectivity can guarantee began soon to become, therefore, not only a necessary mark of those forms of knowledge that are shared within the scientific community, but also the added value of those forms of expertise that specific groups of professionals were called to provide.

Nevertheless, accounting could not remain the prerogative of a small group of professionals, albeit well established and respected. Standardized forms of accounting became soon the norm. Renouncing accurate judgments and interpretations might be a loss, but it is a peerless gain to avoid any dependence on the expertise provided by a restricted elite. In a very persuasive manner, Porter sheds light upon the process that led to the standardization of the accounting practice by showing the tie between this process and the more general process of modernization, whose main trait is precisely the fixing of some rules of common behaviour. It is true that the Weberian definition of bureaucratic administration – 'domination through knowledge' (Weber 1978, 225) – fits an ideal type that, at the beginning, found its instantiations principally in the US and Germany, but it was scarcely useful to describe the historical development of public administration in countries like the United Kingdom or France. Nevertheless, the closer one gets to the present, the feature of a global society dominated by the presence of omni-pervasive systems of accountability and monitoring stands out more and more vividly to the observer – and to an extent that Weber could not have ever imagined. The point Porter helps us to make clear is that institutions, with their need to govern conflicts, social issues, legal controversies, and distribution of resources, have triggered the process that resulted in the promotion and diffusion of objective and rigorous forms of knowledge. By no means is this to say that the contents of objective knowledge per se are a social construction.[11] However, the set of procedures used to confer normative authority on objective forms of knowledge is no doubt socially constructed. Generally speaking, it is the need to rely on authorities supposed to be impartial and unbiased that encourages the emergence of universal and incontestable forms of knowledge. Because modern science – and not, say, theology, or shamanism – is the form of knowledge that proved to be the only one that can be said to be objective, it is not surprising that the institutions of the modern nation state have increasingly put into effect methods of accountability based on science. This state of affairs exerted a great influence on those disciplines that were in need of a social and institutional recognition. The latter have been in a certain way attracted by the sphere within which the pursuit of knowledge ceases to be the object of desire of a small community of scholars and becomes a sign of distinction. Among economists, the desire of being recognized as a group of experts that can provide a socially useful form of knowledge has been always particularly strong.

The case we are discussing here is very interesting from an epistemological point of view – provided that we recognize that it is a gain, in theoretical terms, not to separate from each other the context of discovery and the context of justification.[12] The procedures that guarantee objectivity among groups of scientists that form a solid and recognized community can be brought back to 'face-to-face' communication features. They may be mediated by technological devices and take place within institutional arrangements, like symposia or research periods abroad, and of course sharing the research results through the publication in peer reviewed journals constitutes an essential tool for maintaining the internal cohesion of the community. However, the reliance on personal forms of exchange of both scientific results and opinions concerning current research programmes seems to be quite normal. This occurs, first, because it may be rather difficult to give written accounts of all the details involved in laboratory experiments, and, second, because some theoretical hypothesis that works as a blueprint for planning experimental settings, or some models that still need examining implies such a degree of complexity that informal discussions on the matter are preferred. In this case, therefore, what assures objectivity is the internal cohesiveness of the scientific community involved in the research programme. The worry about the need of an external recognition for the work carried out is irrelevant. In some ways, the social importance of the latter is not really questioned by anyone. Even if nobody outside the small community of scientists can grasp the meaning of complicated issues related, say, to particle physics, a general consensus prevails – albeit often unspoken – on the positive effects on the whole of society that derive from scientific investigation of issues supposed to reveal the deep structure of the physical world.

In the case of scientific communities involved in the definition of issues that are related to the social world the need for recognition coming from both public opinion and public institutions is felt, on the contrary, with more urgency. This explains the appeal exerted by impersonal procedures that are supposed to guarantee the production of objective knowledge. These procedures increase the reliability of a discipline that offers its services to decision makers and seeks to be recognized as a trustworthy source of guidelines for public policies. Economics is, not by chance, one of the examples chosen by Porter to illustrate the process that leads a weak discipline to strengthen itself by assuming the feature of a natural science. In this regard, the sociological perspective adopted by Porter helps expand the historical reconstruction once provided by Mirowski (1989) and seems also to reinforce McCloskey's (1985) controversial contribution on the tendency among economists to increase the degree of certainty that can be conferred to their own scientific results by using mathematical formulas.

Of course, when economists strove for a mathematization of economics that took mathematical physics as a model to be imitated, they did it because of an endogenous requirement of rigour and argumentative clarity. They pursued this goal even by stifling the voices of those who tried to put in evidence how difficult it would have been to explain in mathematical terms what individuals do when they arrange their preferences. Furthermore, they went on formalizing the grounding axioms of neoclassical theory even when they had in some way lost the awareness that they were taking the main conceptual tools supposed to entrench the scientific reliability of their discipline from the physics of the nineteenth century. Sticking so stubbornly to the research programme of neoclassical theory, thus, has come out as a way both to compensate the supposed epistemological weakness of economics and to close ranks within the discipline – concerning the last point Mirowski has shown an unequalled ability in describing the flexibility of the neoclassical model, which, in the course of time, has taken over all the possible objections that have been moved against it.

It is important, however, to show the intertwinement between the internal development of the economic discipline and the historic environment within which this development took place. Mirowski himself, concluding his work, underscores that investigating how neoclassical economics has kept on sticking to its own models of thought provides just one example among others of the institutional character of scientific work. Each scientific discipline obeys the laws that govern every institution, in the sense that the internal coherence and self-consistency of a given research programme, supposed to be the template for the activity of each scholar, is not simply a matter that concerns the unity of theory. It is, rather, a matter that concerns the unity of the discipline understood as a field, with its boundaries and the distinction the latter permits between internal and external enemies. Thus, the defence of the neoclassical model, despite the evidence collected against the claim that could explain every aspect of human behaviour in terms that resemble the way physics explains the natural world, and the willingness to offer their service to those who need a system of accountability in order to govern the social world, are two faces of the same coin.

If we now turn to the other side of the couple formed by economics – meant as a natural science that is supposed to be able to 'tell the truth' about the deep structure of society – and the neoliberal state – meant as a huge bureaucratic machine – we can realize quite well, then, that the historical process that has led to the birth of economics – and, as a consequence, to the demise of political economy – is important not only from the viewpoint of the history of economic thought. The self-affirmation of this discipline coincided with the establishment of a new way of governing people through the power of numbers (Rose 1991). It took time, of course, before economics could meet the expectations that the modern state had in this regard. It took time, too, before those bureaucratic organisms that depend on the good functioning of a routinized system of accountability for their survival, namely the modern nation state and the corporation, realized that not economics in general, but specifically the discipline of economics that had at its hard core the neoclassical model of choice and decision would suit their needs perfectly. The end point of the process is, however, clear: starting from after the First World War the situation was that public institutions and organizations obeyed the same logic, which was not the logic of profit, but rather the logic of accountability. Miller and Rose (2008) prefer to use the expression 'advanced liberal democracies' in order to describe this scenario. If it seems opportune to term this regime of governing individuals through the power of accountability as 'neoliberal', this happens not only because what is at stake here is a process that affects the whole of the planet – thus including those countries that are not ruled in a democratic way. The point that one should not miss is that mainstream economics presented itself consciously as a discipline able to support a programme of government that could not be conceived simply as the prosecution of classical liberalism.

What economists did in order to gain power from the fact that their discipline could fit perfectly the broader cultural and political environment around them is, however, only one aspect of the state of affairs we are considering here. The other aspect relates to something that, in a certain way, goes beyond the consciousness of the actors involved. It is, namely, the performative character of the economic discourse itself.

It is a great merit of Callon (1998) to have opened a new path in the investigation of this topic. The attempt made by Granovetter (1985) to draw attention to the necessity of studying economic phenomena starting from the perspective once disclosed by Polanyi's work preceded, to a certain extent, Callon's intuition that the discourse of economics is not only part of a broader social context, but it helps to create it. Callon's originality consists in having put the materiality of the economic discourse at the same level where actors meet both institutions and technological devices of various natures. It is true that Callon has largely contributed to the birth of the sociological method that made Latour's reputation grow far beyond the disciplinary boundary of the sociology of knowledge. This small aside should reduce the surprise that his way of treating economics might eventually raise. What counts here, however, is not the genealogy of the Actor-Network Theory, which has been later tied to Latour's name. The suggestion coming from Callon is crucial for a non-ideological understanding of the capability that neoliberalism has to become part of the landscape – or, better, technoscape[13] – that surrounds our everyday life.

First, Callon underlines the anthropological dimension of the calculating practice. This is tantamount to say that this practice is older than capitalism and the so-called market society. The prerogatives of *homo oeconomicus*, which are crucial for the construction of the neoliberal model of rationality, can be thus looked at from a perspective of long duration. The anthropological contextualization that Callon advances, however, is not the crucial point. Much more interesting is how Callon describes the interconnection between human actors and the set of objects that, albeit inanimate, constitute the environment that normally is said to harbour human action.[14] Callon's viewpoint is not, in other words, just one of the many versions of culturalism. He does not claim that the calculating subject is constructed, which amounts to saying that calculating depends on a broader social and political context. Calculating is, rather, the element of a network that includes specific cognitive capabilities to be attributed to human subjects, the technological devices used by human agents (various mediums, inscriptions, figures), methods of calculation, shared habits concerning how both to perform calculations and to confer value to the results of calculations. What Callon makes disappear is the conception of the calculating agent that both psychology and economics share with common sense psychology. Instead of considering the individual capability to calculate future states of the world, Callon's theory suggests a focus on calculating agencies and their performances.

If one considers that the individual calculating capacity lies at the core of rational choice theory, it is easy to imagine how broad would be the consequence that Callon's insights had for an epistemological re-framing of how economics looks at human action. However, the point that must be made here concerns the possibility offered by Callon's perspective to explain the power of economics as a part of calculating agencies. This power is not related to some specific tenets that define economics in general or some subfields of the discipline. More simply, calculative agencies without accounting tools are inconceivable. Economics, once it has developed to the extent that it has become the most powerful accounting system, provides all that is needed to put into motion the calculating machines individuals live in, be they institutions or organizations. The result of this intertwinement of economics with calculative agencies is that individuals live simultaneously in two worlds: one is the world described by economics, which studies them as calculating agents, the other is the world of economy, where they act as members of institutions or firms.

In this sense, economics, far from being the neutral science it claims to be, devoted to an objective observation of how individuals behave under market constraints, results to be a discourse that 'performs, shapes and formats the economy' (Callon 1998, 2). It is easy to imagine the rejoicing reaction to this statement that may come from those who support a postmodern attitude toward the function of knowledge in human affairs. To this reaction corresponds the opposite one coming from those who simply do not want to understand the epistemic fertility of a constructivist point of view. Callon, not differently from other scholars who endorse a constructivist approach to social science, describes something that is very concrete and has, thus, the force to trigger human action. What is at stake here is the entanglement that encompasses social actors, their beliefs, expectations, forecasts, calculations, and all the devices that make possible the flow of the latter. If we consider that scientific disciplines too are part of this entanglement, this does not amount to saying that their scientific results are flawed; the point is that, on one hand, they contribute, together with other forms of narratives, to stabilize the shared description of the world and, on the other hand, they produce outcomes whose significance fluctuates together with the dynamic of the relations among social actors.

In sum, the performativity of economics relates to its being entangled in social networks that require accountability, measurements, and forecasts. This entanglement explains not only the rapidity that characterized the spread of neoliberalism during recent decades, but above all the invisibility of the transformations in the art of government that its spread has caused. Economics, being a constitutive part of social networks and calculative agencies, its presence is taken for granted and works, thus, as an invisible element of social life.

The taken for grantedness of economics has also been explained by analysing the importance of business schools for the formation (both in the sense of creation and education) of the global elite (Thrift 2005; Ong 2006). Members of the elite are trained as students of economics and, no matter what is the position they are going to occupy, act then as supporters of the neoliberal worldview. Yet, it is perhaps more productive to look at the performativity of economics by considering how deeply economic theories are embedded in everyday practices of economic actors, thus following Callon's point of departure (MacKenzie 2006; MacKenzie, Muniesa and Siu 2007; MacKenzie 2009). It is true that these studies are mainly focused on the financial world; nevertheless they have provided a research material that has been increasingly changing the sociological way of looking at economic actors.

A further – and final – consideration regards the main effect of economics' performativity. If one asks what economics has performed during the neoliberal era, the first answer is, probably, that the whole of economic theory is there to guarantee a stable and scientific foundation of the generalized system of accountability that sustains organizations and institutions and induces both of them to act as if they were economic agents, deprived of any political finality (Power 1997). This answer, perhaps, accounts for one of the main traits of the neoliberal regime. If one looks at the issue starting from the perspective of system theory, our understanding can, however, gain in precision. The answer to our question sounds now as follows: the main performance of economics consists in providing the possibility for firms and public agencies to operate a self-reflection that does not require the recourse to contested values to be taken as benchmarks for the evaluations.

The point is clear in Luhmann (1983), which radicalizes some Weberian insights into the structure and function of neutral procedures within bureaucratic organizations. Luhmann adds to Weberian analysis the awareness that procedures are related not only to the necessity for organizations and institutions to be accountable, but above all, to the simplification they bring about in the art of government. In this sense, there is an astonishing resemblance to Luhmann's theory of procedure in Foucault's account of neoliberalism. Foucault's concern was how to explain that an economic theory – in this case the theory elaborated by the Chicago school – could ever acquire so much performative power as to become part of a governmental apparatus. In his analysis Foucault paid much attention to how the neoliberal model of rationality imposed itself in response to the increasing difficulty the liberal model had in managing a complex reality that should have brought together need for justice, liberty and security. Neoliberalism, in Foucault's account, seems to solve the problems left open by liberalism by imposing a generalized system of reduction of uncertainty, which works not because the weight of uncertainty can be really tamed, but because an economic model of rationality is called to perform a regime of control that conceals the rough reality of chance.

Luhmann's account of the spread of procedures in all realms of the associated life addresses the question of uncertainty too. Procedures, first of all, are there to reduce the psychological unsustainability of uncertainty and chance. The more the world's complexity growths, the greater becomes the need for a reduction of the latter. Procedures have revealed the simplest and most feasible way to accomplish this reduction, namely by choosing only what is pertinent to the given situation and excluding from the present horizon of experience what cannot be handled by using the available means. Procedures, in other words, are powerful devices enabling the social construction of pertinence. Not everything can be handled, not every problem can be put on the agenda for searching its appropriate solution, and a procedure that works in one context cannot find a proper application in a different one. Actions need framing; otherwise the management of the collectives would be impossible. The frame each concrete context of action needs is given by the procedure that individuals are used to recognize as proper to that context. This does not mean that procedures determine the course of human actions, it means rather that procedures provide, in each case, an answer to the question about what is required in order to follow a rule.

Considering that following a rule can mean to engage in an interpretation of it, and that interpretations are possible only if each group member is ready to discuss also the overarching principles that make it possible to judge in the concrete case at stake, we come now to the crucial point, which allows for a profitable use of Luhmann's theory for the understanding of neoliberalism. System theory as well as Foucault's genealogy is far from providing cool descriptions of what happens in the world outside there. In both cases, the central concern is about the possibility of building a critique of the present that helps, albeit in a mediated way, question the given power structure of contemporary society. Luhmann's analysis of the procedure is surely not about the emergence of the neoliberal society, but it sheds light on the main trait of it, namely the impossibility of discussing a theory of justice that makes no recourse to the neoclassical model of individual choice. Luhmann's account of how procedures serve to reduce systemic complexity can explain too how the simplifications of human action that lie at the core of the economic model of rationality have become the general frame within which institutions and organizations manage the decision making process within the neoliberal society. The totality of possible courses of action undergoes a drastic reduction without generating a totalitarian system – as Foucault used to repeat, the neoliberal policies do not amount to a new version of totalitarianism. The reduction of complexity provided by the neoliberal art of government is nevertheless remarkable. All those alternative courses of actions – and, concretely, all alternative policies – that are the result of decisions taken starting from ethical principles are excluded. Ethical principles are, in fact, controversial, and the time needed to come to the resolution of conflicts related to ethical issues is not available. The time needed for coming to a conflict resolution is not to be seen, however, as a scarce resource among others. The problem at stake here is that the complexity of the system does not allow the emergence of a superordinate agency whose function would be to decide upon the legitimacy of procedures. This agency was given in a liberal context and, to a certain extent, its realm coincided with that of politics. Precisely, the disappearance of this realm, which was supposed to be separated from procedures, made the emergence of neoliberalism possible.

Notes

1 On this, see Burchell, Gordon and Miller (1991); Barry, Osborne and Rose (1996); Dean (1999). It is worth noticing that these works had the merit of introducing Foucault's reflexion on biopolitics and governmentality before the English translation of the lectures held at Collège de France. This may explain the tendency, which can be observed in all these essays, to minimize the difference, which Foucault had underscored, between liberalism and neoliberalism.
2 On the notion of 'universal audience' we refer to, see Perelman and Olbrechts-Tytecha (1969). On the notion of justice, see Perelman (1963).
3 See Goody (2004) for a short but persuasive account of this debate.
4 On this topic, see, among others, Vercellone (2006, 2007) and Fumagalli (2007).
5 See Gorz (2010).
6 That there is a strict relationship between the capability to maintain a good network at the global level and the efficacy of one's action as an entrepreneur is a fact as old as capitalism. In this context, it is worth remembering the role that the creation of transnational networks played within the reconstruction of the beginning of capitalism provided by Braudel (1982–84).
7 For a more journalistic reconstruction of the events, see Lowenstein (2000); MacKenzie (2003) provides instead a scientific analysis of them.
8 The three scenarios here presented in a summarized form are explained at length in Rodrik (2011).
9 A question we leave aside here is the diminution which American military strength has undergone during recent decades with regard not to the quantity and quality of its military means, but to the effective capability to win a war against a counterpart with global ambitions. It is also impossible to give a detailed account of the existing literature. We restrict ourselves to mention three works that, albeit from different perspectives, help focus on the necessity to recast the great strategy that sustains the United States' ambition to maintain its hegemonic position: Posen (2014); Tangredi (2013) and Gentile (2013).

10 Fourcade (2009) gives a vivid account of how the professionalization of the economic discipline took different paths in the United States, Britain and France. The
similarities observed are equally important, however: in each of the cases studied,
there is, on one hand, the interest that state agencies had in having at their disposal
forms of expertise that could be used both to monitor and legitimize a set of policies and, on the other hand, the interest that economists have in being recognized
as a group of reliable experts.

11 We are aware of how dangerous it has become, especially in recent years, even to
use the expression 'social construction of something': the latter has ended up, in
fact, being the brand mark of all those who support a postmodern conception of
truth. Hacking (1999) provides an assessment of the question that allows speaking
of the 'social construction of something' without falling into the traps of
postmodernism.

12 The caution is due to the fact that some scholars still keep on fearing that the truth
of scientific theories must be saved from the 'contamination' that could derive from
an explanation of its genesis in historical or sociological terms. Such a fear is
groundless, since the question here is how to give account of the procedures, which
are always of a historical nature, making possible the emergence of objective
knowledge. The debate on this is, notoriously, as broad as the current discussion
within epistemology; seminal works like Knorr-Cetina (1981); Hacking (1983);
Douglas (1986); Latour (1987); Pickering (1992) and Bourdieu (2004) have paved
the way, however, toward a suitable consensus on the pivotal significance of the
matter.

13 The term comes from Appadurai (1996) and seems to be quite appropriate to the
present context.

14 This point of view will reach its complete methodological self-awareness in Latour
(2005). How fruitful it can be for economic theory to place human action into a
context that includes both human actors and the set of devices needed to make
cognition possible will be a topic discussed in the fourth chapter of this book by
taking into consideration some recent developments within the cognitive sciences.

References

Appadurai, A. (1996) *Modernity at Large. Cultural Dimensions of Globalization.*
Minneapolis, MN: University of Minnesota Press.

Bachrach, P. and Baratz, M.S. (1962) 'Two Faces of Power', *The American Political
Science Review*, Vol. 56:4, pp. 947–952.

Barry, A., Osborne, T. and Rose, N. (Eds) (1996) *Foucault and Political Reason. Liberalism, Neo-liberalism and Rationalities of Government.* Chicago: The University of
Chicago Press.

Bobbio, N. (1998) 'Gramsci and the Concept of Civil Society', in Keane, J. (Ed.) *Civil
Society and the State: New European Perspectives.* London: University of Westminster
Press, pp. 73–100.

Bourdieu, P. (2004) *Science of Science and Reflexivity.* Cambridge: Polity.

Braudel, F. (1982–84) *Civilization and Capitalism, 15th and 18th Century*, 3 vols, trans.
by Reynolds, S. New York: Harper & Row.

Burchell, G., Gordon, C. and Miller, P. (Eds) (1991) *The Foucault Effect. Studies in
Governmentality.* Chicago: The University of Chicago Press.

Callon, M. (1998) 'Introduction: The Embeddedness of Economic Markets in Economics', in Callon, M. (Ed.) *The Laws of the Markets.* Oxford, Malden, MA:
Blackwell, pp. 1–57.

Dean, M. (1999) *Governmentality. Power and Rule in Modern Society*. London: Sage.

Douglas, M. (1986) *How Institutions Think*. Syracuse, NY: Syracuse University Press.

Foucault, M. (2007) *Security, Territory, Population: Lectures at the Collège de France, 1977–1978*, edited by Senellart, M., trans. by Burchell, G. Basingstoke, England and New York: Palgrave Macmillan.

Foucault, M. (2008) *The Birth of Biopolitics: Lectures at the Collège de France, 1978–1979*, edited by Senellart, M., trans. by Burchell, G. Basingstoke, England and New York: Palgrave Macmillan.

Fourcade, M. (2009) *Economists and Societies. Discipline and Profession in the United States, Britain and France, 1890s to 1990s*. Princeton, NJ: Princeton University Press.

Fumagalli, A. (2007) *Bioeconomia e capitalismo cognitivo. Verso un nuovo paradigma di accumulazione*. Rome: Carocci.

Gentile, G.P. (2013) *Wrong Turn. America's Deadly Embrace of Counterinsurgency*. New York: The New Press.

Goody, J. (2004) *Capitalism and Modernity: The Great Debate*. Cambridge: Polity.

Gorz, A. (2010) *The Immaterial. Knowledge, Value and Capital*. London: Seagull Books.

Granovetter, M. (1985) 'Economic Action and Social Structure: The Problem of Embeddedness', *American Journal of Sociology*, Vol. 91:3, pp. 481–510.

Hacking, I. (1983) *Representing and Intervening: Introductory Topics in the Philosophy of Science*. Cambridge: Cambridge University Press.

Hacking, I. (1999) *The Social Construction of What?* Cambridge, MA: Harvard University Press.

Hardt, M. and Negri, A. (2000) *Empire*. Cambridge, MA: Harvard University Press.

Hausman, D.M. and McPherson, M.S. (2008) 'The Philosophical Foundations of Mainstream Normative Economics', in Hausman, D.M. (Ed.) *The Philosophy of Economics. An Anthology*. Cambridge, New York: Cambridge University Press, pp. 226–250.

Helleiner, E. (1994) *States and the Reemergence of Global Finance. From Bretton Woods to the 1990s*. Ithaca, NY, London: Cornell University Press.

Hibou, B. (2011) *Anatomie politique de la domination*. Paris: La Découverte.

Howard, M.C. and King, J.E. (2008) *The Rise of Neoliberalism in Advanced Capitalist Economies. A Materialist Analysis*. Basingstoke, England and New York: Palgrave Macmillan.

Knight, F. (1940) 'What is Truth in Economics?', *The Journal of Political Economy*, Vol. 48:1, pp. 1–32.

Knorr-Cetina, K.D. (1981) *The Manufacture of Knowledge. An Essay on the Constructivist and Contextual Nature of Science*. Oxford, New York: Pergamon Press.

Krasner, S.D. (1988) 'Sovereignty. An Institutional Approach', *Comparative Political Studies*, Vol. 21:1, pp. 66–94.

Latour, B. (1987) *Science in Action*. Cambridge, MA: Harvard University Press.

Latour, B. (2005) *Reassembling the Social. An Introduction to Actor-Network Theory*. Oxford, New York: Oxford University Press.

Lowenstein, R. (2000) *When Genius Failed. The Rise and Fall of Long Term Capital Management*. New York: Random House.

Luhmann, N. (1983) *Legitimation durch Verfahren*. Frankfurt am Main: Suhrkamp.

MacKenzie, D.A. (2003) 'Long-Term Capital Management and the Sociology of Arbitrage', *Economy and Society*, Vol. 32:3, pp. 349–380.

MacKenzie, D.A. (2006) *An Engine, Not a Camera. How Financial Models Shape Markets.* Cambridge, MA: The MIT Press.

MacKenzie, D.A., Muniesa, F. and Siu, L. (Eds) (2007) *Do Economists Make Markets? On the Performativity of Economics.* Princeton, NJ: Princeton University Press.

MacKenzie, D.A. (2009) *Material Markets. How Economic Agents Are Constructed.* Oxford, New York: Oxford University Press.

Marx, K. (1976) *Capital. A Critique of Political Economy.* Volume One, trans. by B. Fowkes. Harmondsworth: Penguin.

Marx, K. (1993) *Grundrisse. Foundation of the Critique of Political Economy (Rough Draft),* trans. with a foreword by Nicolaus, M. London: Penguin Books in association with *New Left Review.*

McCloskey, D. (1985) *The Rhetoric of Economics.* Madison, WI: University of Wisconsin Press.

Miller, P. and Rose, N. (2008) *Governing the Present.* Cambridge, Malden, MA: Polity.

Mirowski, P. (1989) *More Heat Than Light. Economics as Social Physics: Physics as Nature's Economics.* Cambridge, New York: Cambridge University Press.

Mirowski, P. (2013) *Never Let a Serious Crisis Go to Waste: How Neoliberalism Survived the Financial Meltdown.* London: Verso.

Mirowski, P. and Plehwe, D. (Eds) (2009) *The Road from Mount Pèlerin: the Making of the Neoliberal Thought Collective.* Cambridge, MA: Harvard University Press.

Morgenthau, H. (1948) *Politics Among Nations. The Struggle for Power and Peace.* New York: Knopf.

Ong, A. (2006) *Neoliberalism as Exception. Mutations in Citizenship and Sovereignty.* Durham and London: Duke University Press.

Perelman, C. (1963) *The Idea of Justice and the Problem of Argument,* trans. by Petrie, J. London: Routledge & Kegan Paul.

Perelman, C. and Olbrechts-Tytecha, L. (1969) *The New Rhetoric: a Treatise on Argumentation,* trans. by Wilkinson, J. and Weaver, P. Notre-Dame, IN: University of Notre-Dame Press.

Pickering, A. (Ed.) (1992) *Science as Practice and Culture.* Chicago, London: The University of Chicago Press.

Plehwe, D., Walpen, B. and Neunhöffer, G. (2006) 'Introduction: Reconsidering Neo-liberal Hegemony', in Plehwe, D., Walpen, B. and Neunhöffer, G. (Eds) *Neoliberal Hegemony. A Global Critique.* New York: Routledge, pp. 1–24.

Porter, T.M. (1995) *Trust in Numbers. The Pursuit of Objectivity in Science and Public Life.* Princeton, NJ: Princeton University Press.

Posen, B.R. (2014) *Restraint. A New Foundation for U.S. Grand Strategy.* Ithaca, NY: Cornell University Press.

Power, M. (1997) *The Audit Society. Rituals of Verification.* Oxford, New York: Oxford University Press.

Robbins, L. (1932) *An Essay on the Nature and Significance of Economic Science.* London: MacMillian.

Rodrik, D. (2011) *The Globalization Paradox: Democracy and the Future of the World.* New York, London: W.W. Norton & Company.

Rose, N. (1991) 'Governing by Numbers: Figuring Out Democracy', *Accounting, Organizations and Society,* Vol. 16:7, pp. 673–692.

Rosenau, J.N. (2002) 'Governance in a New Global Order', in Held, D. and McGrew, A. (Eds) *Governing Globalization. Power, Authority and Global Governance.* Cambridge: Polity, pp. 70–86.

Ruggie, J.G. (1982) 'International Regimes, Transactions, and Change: Embedded Liberalism in the Postwar Economic Order', *International Organizations*, Vol. 36:2, pp. 379–415.

Sklair, L. (2001) *The Transnational Capitalist Class*. Oxford: Blackwell.

Smith, A. (1976a) *The Theory of Moral Sentiments*, edited by D.D. Raphael and A.L. Macfie. Oxford: Clarendon Press.

Smith, A. (1976b) *An Inquiry into the Nature and Causes of the Wealth of Nations*, Edited by W.B. Todd. Oxford: Clarendon Press.

Tangredi, S.J. (2013) *Anti-Access Warfare. Countering A2/AD Strategies*. Annapolis, MD: Naval Institute Press.

Thrift, N. (2005) *Knowing Capitalism*. Los Angeles, London: Sage.

Useem, M. (1984) *The Inner Circle*. Oxford: Oxford University Press.

Vercellone, C. (Ed.) (2006) *Capitalismo cognitivo. Conoscenza e finanza nell'epoca postfordista*. Rome: manifestolibri.

Vercellone, C. (2007) 'From Formal Subsumption to General Intellect: Elements for a Marxist Reading of the Thesis of Cognitive Capitalism', *Historical Materialism*, Vol. 15:1, pp. 13–36.

Virno, P. (2004) *A Grammar of the Multitude: For an Analysis of Contemporary Forms of Life*. Cambridge, MA: Semiotext(e).

Wade, R.H. (2003) 'The Invisible Hand of the American Empire', *Ethics & International Affairs*, Vol. 17:2, pp. 77–88.

Weber, M. (1978) *Economy and Society. An Outline of Interpretive Sociology*, 2 vols, edited by Roth, G. and Wittich, C. Berkeley, CA and Los Angeles: University of California Press.

2 The building of economics as a science

This chapter will be dealing with the shift from the classical notion of political economy to the notion of neoclassical economics.[1] As previously stated (see Introduction), the notion of political economy was a direct derivation of the influence of classical liberalism during the modern age; neoclassical economics, raised at the end of the nineteenth century and developed during the twentieth, has been the root of the so-called neoliberalism which emerged during the post-modern age.

There are as many substantial differences between political economy and economics, as well as between classical liberalism and neoliberalism. The popularization of the notion of neoclassical economics is deeply rooted in Lord Robbins' definition of economy as 'the science which studies human behaviour as a relationship between ends and scarce means which have alternative uses' (Robbins 1932, 16). Gary Becker gave the ultimate definition of neoclassical economics, when he defined its key characteristics: maximizing behaviour, market equilibrium, and stable preferences (Becker 1976).

The road from Robbins to Becker in considering economics 'predominantly as a science of choice' (Williamson 2002) has been long, though. After an intense period of methodological transformations, and a geographical transition from European academia to the most prominent universities in the United States, neoclassical economics reached its status of mainstream within the discipline in Samuelson's comparative statics (Samuelson 1947) as well as in Friedman's definition of economics as a positive science (Friedman 1953). Both Samuelson's and Friedman's methodological positions are grounded in the rational choice theory as the best framework to understand the formalization of individual and social economic behaviour.

In order to explain this process of transformation, it is important to describe the rise of marginalism as the first step for transforming a political science dealing with the wealth of a nation to a formal science focused on describing individual and social rational behaviour.[2] It is also essential to define the building and the reinforcement of neoclassical economics in Europe during the 1930s (Düppe and Weintraub 2013). Finally, it is fundamental to clarify that the transition from institutionalism to neoclassic economics in the

United States (Morgan and Rutherford 1998) had been influenced by the migration of European economists in the late 1930s (Weintraub 2002).

The historical framework of the interwar period in Europe, where totalitarian regimes spread, allows understanding of the development of economics as a formal science, as a value-free discipline. The formalization of the discipline within general economic equilibrium theory as well as the introduction of econometrics, during those two decades, were not only instruments to reorganize the scientific nature of the economic theory; they were also formidable tools used by European economists to avoid any political and even personal relations with totalitarian regimes (Leonard 1998, 2010).

During the cold war, American economists, mainly at the University of Chicago, definitely shaped the discipline into what today is neoclassical economics and endorsed the Western political model, based on that model, presenting it as the most rational and efficient system, able to increase social progress and individual freedom (Christ 1994; Emmett 2009a; Schliesser 2010).

As previously stated, although both neoclassical economics and neoliberalism have been presented as renewed forms of classical economy and classical liberalism, there are some crucial differences between them: the nature of the market as well as the meaning of individual freedom are the main examples of their idiosyncratic relationship.

Classical doctrines looked at the market as an institution that enabled a higher division of labour, as a necessary condition to increase the wealth of a nation. Neoclassical economics and neoliberalism consider the market as the only natural institution that enables relations amongst rational agents. The theoretical *strength* of rational choice theory has gradually converted this vision into an anthropological dimension that found its outcome in the rise and the development of neoliberalism (see Chapter 3).

2.1 The revolution of marginalism: how political economy became economics

Adam Smith's definition of political economy was an 'inquiry' about the causes of the 'wealth of a nation' (Smith, 1776). In 1844, John Stuart Mill claimed that 'political economy was a *political* science which studies the production and distribution of wealth' (Mill 1844). In 1890, Alfred Marshall defined economy as the 'study of mankind in the ordinary business of life; it examines that part of individual and social actions which is closely connected with the attainment and with the use of material requisites of well-being' (Marshall 1890, 1).

In 1900, Pareto defined pure economics as a science for determining a state of equilibrium:

> [pure economics] arrives at identifying the choices that are available to individuals, by taking into account the obstacles the latter encounter and

by hypothesizing that not only can such choice be completely ordered, but they are also identical if they only differ because of the order of consumption, since the faculty to enjoy the goods is more important than the way they are enjoyed.

(Pareto [1900] 1982, 388)

In 1932, as previously already reported, Robbins defined economics as 'the science which studies human behaviour as a relationship between given ends and scarce means which have alternative uses' (Robbins 1932, 16).

The path from marginalism to Robbins has been the track for the rise of neoclassical economic theory as mainstream economics; and the old classical liberalism has been gradually transformed into a new liberalism.

Neoclassical economics can be dated back to the work of the founding fathers of marginalism (Menger 1871; Jevons 1871; Walras 1874), and their immediate followers (Edgeworth 1881; Marshall 1890; Pareto 1906).[3]

In 1871, Jevons' *Political Economy* and Menger's *Grundsätze* appeared without any reciprocal influence (Jevons 1871; Menger 1871). Three years later, Walras published his *Éléments* (Walras 1874). Historians of economic thought consider these three books as the pillars of the so-called marginalistic revolution, or marginalism. Marginalism has been rightly considered the starting point of the transformation of political economy from a branch of moral philosophy (as it was regarded from Adam Smith to Marx and John Stuart Mill) to economics as a science (Milonakis and Fine 2009).

Both positivism and neopositivism deeply influenced the transformation of the discipline (Caldwell 1980; Weintraub 1985; Mirowski 2002).[4] Later in the twentieth century, during the interwar period, the specific scientific feature of economics as a science became much more related to physics. Along with the development of this process, ethics was discarded from economics, as it was supposed to be alienated from any other social science (Sen 1987; Putnam 2002).

The main differences between classic political economy and marginalism can be listed as follows:

1 Methodological individualism: in marginalism, economic agents are individuals (either consumers or firms) and no longer social classes (rentiers, workers, capitalists) like in Smith's, Ricardo's and Marx's theory.
2 Strict subjectivism: the marginalistic theory of value is based on individual utility, and no more on the cost of production (Smith) or on the sole labour (Ricardo-Marx).[5]
3 In marginalism, the final aim of economic theory is general economic equilibrium, and no longer an inquiry of the wealth of a nation (mainly based on the introduction of the division of labour, or alternatively, in a Marxian perspective, on the alienation of workers' labour and on the following collapse of the rate of profit in the latest phase of capitalism).
4 The principle of maximization of economic agents' expected utility function: in marginalism, general economic equilibrium is made possible when

economic agents are featured as rational agents able to rank their preferences and to make an optimal choice under a condition of scarcity of
available means.

5   In marginalism, market price is seen as the only possible mechanism able
to get a final general economic equilibrium;[6] in the classical school,
market is still regarded as a historical institution where if exchange and
trade are free, the national wealth is bound to increase.

In the 1890s a second phase of marginalism occurred. Alfred Marshall in
Cambridge and Vilfredo Pareto, the successor of Walras in Lausanne, were
the main representatives and most influential economists of that period.

Around 1900, the father of American institutionalism, Thorstein Veblen,
coined the term *neoclassical* in order to define Marshall's economy theory as 'the
best work that is being done under the guidance of the classical antecedents'
(Veblen 1919, 171.)

In fact in his *Principles* Marshall was able to bridge the gap between the
classical school of political economy and the recent development (marginalism) within the discipline. Marshall made possible the shift of subjectivism
from the demand side (the theory of consumer, upon which marginalism was
grounded) to the supply side (upon which classical economic theory was
rooted). In fact, Marshall introduced the concept of representative firm as an
individual agent able to minimize inputs' costs in order to maximize profits.
Furthermore, Marshall introduced the notion of price as the equilibrium
point between demand (as in marginalism's theory of utility) and supply
(classical theory of cost of production).

Pareto made a step forward to the notion of economics as a science. The
Italian and Lausanne-based economist introduced the notion of pure economics, centered on the description of logical actions of individuals, who are
able to rank their preferences, and to follow a rational way of behaving in a
contest that will be heading to general economic equilibrium. The substitution
of the subjective approach with classical objectivism made it possible to ana-
lyze economics and the market through an individualistic approach, based on
the idea that individuals' behaviour is *reasonably* oriented to satisfy their
needs.[7]

Marginalistic economic theory had been strongly influenced by British
utilitarianism: this is evident not only in Jevons' notion of utility, who directly
quoted from Bentham,[8] but also later in Edgeworth's ideas, that Pareto would
redefine as the set of efficient allocation occurring during an economic
exchange.

If Marshall was able to build a strong continuity between classic political
economy and marginalistic economics, the notion of economics as a science
that starts from individuals' preferences had been grounded in Pareto's
toolbox.

Charles Gide was the first scholar who became aware of the fact that along
with the transformation of political economy into a scientific discipline, a new

doctrine of liberalism was occurring, that was much more suitable for the emergent definition of economy. The French philosopher specifically used the term 'new liberal school' to address Maffeo Pantaleoni.

According to Gide, Pantaleoni was one of those 'mathematical economists':

> adepts of 'Neo-liberalism' (along with Warlas and Pareto) who apply economic theory to an 'hedonistic world' (...) in which each contracting party will weigh in a subjective balance, infallibly exact, the final utility of the object to be disposed of and of the object to be acquired (...), a world where the law of supply and demand will bring about the maximum of utility for both individual and society, and will always send back the barometric needle, at once and without friction, to 'set fair' – I mean to the fair price.
>
> (Gide 1898, 494–495)[9]

The role of Pareto in the building of economics as a science has been crucial. In Pareto's *Cours* (1896) and *Manuale* (1906), 'pure economy' is the only scientific form of classical political economy, and it has to be described in mathematical terms even though in a different way than Walras had done. The French economist had used a deductive approach, based on the internal coherence of the logical procedure without any concern about the realism of the initial hypotheses. Following a different path, Pareto applied the method of natural sciences (experimentalism) to economic theory: by trial and error, he found that it is possible to build an economic theory free from any metaphysical residuals. The experimental approach is also be concerned about the realism of the initial hypotheses. In his *Cours*, economic theory is like any other natural science: the application of mechanical physics allows for a gradual entrance into the formulation of general economic equilibrium. The use of mathematics is possible, and somehow necessary, because human actions follow some regular patterns 'qui constituent des *lois naturelles*' (Pareto 1896, 397).

In the *incipit* of his *Cours*, Pareto firmly claimed that, in his book, no solution for any concrete problem will be found, and his definition of economics as a science will involve the notion of *ophélimité* as the measure of pure economic satisfaction.[10]

After the publication of his first book, Pareto's urgency to find the objective side within economic theory led him to introduce a 'pure experimental method' as well as to discard the use of non-empirical categories like utility, *ophélimité*, value, hedonism.[11] In his later *Manuale* (Pareto 1906), the principle of maximization of the utility function is no longer used to describe general economic equilibrium, rather that is reached starting from the application of a neutral tool: the indifference curves' set and – as a consequence – the application of the ordinal ranking of preferences.

On March 1900, in a paper published in *Giornale degli Economisti*, Pareto claimed that indifference curves represent human choice when this is directly affected by experience. Hence, it is necessary to start from preferences to get general economic equilibrium. Unlike *ophélimité*, whose measurement presents many difficulties, indifference curves represent ordinal preferences and they allow a perfect combination of deductive and inductive methods, which is the only scientific way to formulate general laws beginning from concrete facts (Pareto 1900, 81). In that article, Pareto defined pure economy as an experimental science (Pareto 1900, 91), which uses induction to cope with concrete phenomena as well as deduction to deal with the logical relation between premises and consequences. The use of mathematics is a part of the deductive process. A third momentum is required, according to Pareto, in fact deductions have to be compared with real facts either to reveal eventual discrepancies or to confirm them.

In his *Manuale*, Pareto complained about the fact that a definitive and firm distinction between science and practice in economics had not happened yet. Pareto's aim was to consider economics like a natural science: both are based on abstraction of regularities from concrete phenomena; upon those regularities, general laws can be formulated. Even though concrete phenomena (either natural or social) cannot be wholly known, general knowledge can be reached using approximation (Pareto 1906).

The well-known Pareto's distinction between logical and not-logical actions represents the starting point of the introduction of general economic equilibrium: individuals' logical actions, massively and regularly repeated, to get material satisfactions can be expressed in mathematical terms. They allow the building of pure economics, which has no practical aim.[12]

While writing his *Manuale*, Pareto was involved in a debate on the nature of economics along with the Italian philosopher Benedetto Croce (Croce 1900, 1901; Pareto 1901, 1902). Their well-known *querelle*, which was hosted in *Giornale degli Economisti* between 1900 and 1902, allows a description of the transformation of economics into a formal science in a broader cultural sense.

As Kirzner pointed out:

> Croce was aware of a new general element in his experience of human affairs. This element was not moral, it was not technical, nor did it coincide with any other already-named abstractions. In his formulations, Croce made a vigorous attempt to present this abstraction to the attention of the world by ascribing to it the word 'economic' (....) If in the effort to provide an adequate definition of economics, an attempt is made to analyse the concept of economy, for example, one necessarily becomes involved in a problem of economic *science* itself [emphasis added].
>
> (Kirzner 1976, 11)

Croce had started the debate. The Italian philosopher, influenced by historical Hegelism, and supporter of a conception of economics as a 'practical form of the Spirit' that deals with 'useful things', was well aware of the revolutionary feature of the advent of marginalism within economics. He considered Pareto as one of the most important economists of this new doctrine, able to show that 'economics has nothing to do with history and with practical issues: it is a science following its own principle, the *economic principle*' (Croce 1900, 16). In his first paper, Croce rhetorically asked Pareto what was the nature of this economic principle: Croce's main objection was that the mechanical definition (provided by Pareto) of the economic principle (able to make measurability possible) is problematic and obscure. Croce insisted on the fact that economic choice is a practical activity and it depends on human will. According to the philosopher, economics cannot follow mechanical laws. Furthermore, Pareto did not clearly explained what logical actions really are. Following Hegel, Croce claimed that logics belongs to a theoretical realm, while economic phenomena are practical activities, and they may be related to ethics (Croce 1900).

Pareto's reply to Croce was centred on the idea that there is a sort of *uniformity* within economic phenomena. This uniformity allows a definition of economic laws, which can be expressed in mathematical terms. The same process happens within natural sciences: the use of mathematics allows an objective description of relations amongst quantities, and it has nothing to do with relations amongst mental concepts. Pareto admitted that something else can be present in economic phenomena (Pareto 1901), but this does not change the scientific nature of economics (and other sciences). In fact, any science deals with functional relations, not causal relations, which occur amongst phenomena.

In his following reply, Croce pointed out that Pareto was still confusing the nature of a *science* with the *way to explain scientific results*: the formal representation of economic phenomena is not science, because it does not explain the nature of economic relations and phenomena (Croce 1901). Croce's critique went even beyond this point. Almost in a paradoxical way, the philosopher accused the economist of being metaphysical in his reduction of human facts (as economic phenomena are) to physical facts, and he added that, even in physics, facts can only be described, but never wholly understood (Croce 1901).

In Pareto's following and last reply, which concluded their debate, the economist rejected Croce's accusation that he was metaphysical in his definition of economics as a science. 'I am the most nominalist amongst nominalists' Pareto claimed (Pareto 1902, 131); and he added that there were no differences between the regularities amongst physical facts and human phenomena: scientists' aim was to find them out and to describe how they work. Mathematical description was the most suitable and simple way to do it.[13]

Pareto purged economics from any metaphysical residual as well as he purged economic agents from any psychological influence, by coping with preferences in an axiomatic way. Later during the interwar period, mathematical economists developed this approach (see below). Many other non-mathematical economists expounded upon it in a non-formalistic way: Robbins shared Pareto's opposition to a psychological subjective theory of value, as well as Pareto's attitude of considering economics as the science of rational behaviour under certain circumstances (Bruni and Sudgen 2007).

Lionel Robbins' contribution between the late 1920s and early 1930s is important in order to describe the transformation of the discipline which today we recognize as neoclassical economics.

Robbins' main concern was that infinite disputes amongst economists have deprived economics of a proper definition about its nature and its significance. In 1929, Robbins wrote in his diary that a proper definition of economics was still unsettled, and he pointed out the wide variety of available definitions of economics. According to him, there was a 'too vague' sociological definition, based on exchange and money measurement (Pigou, Mises, and Schumpeter); also, there was a 'too narrow' definition of economics, as the study of material welfare (Cannan); finally, there was a 'misleading and confusing' definition of economics, focused on the notion of scarcity and the operation of economizing (Cassel and Schumpeter). Robbins also added that the use of some words, such as 'welfare', is dangerous because of its ethical implications (Howson 2011, 144).

In his *Essay*, Robbins' aim was twofold: 'to arrive at a precise notion concerning the subject-matter of Economic Science and the nature of the generalizations of which Economic Science consists. Second, it attempts to explain the limitations and the significance of these generalizations' (Robbins 1932, vii). As it is well known, Robbins' formula in defining economics was exposed in the first chapter of his book: 'economics is the science which studies human behaviour as a relationship between ends and scarce means which have alternative uses' (Robbins, 1932, 16).

In this definition, Robbins embedded Menger's and Mises' individualism along with Pareto's technicalities. In his general definition of economics, Robbins was able to merge the formal aspect of the discipline with its implicit subjectivism. Furthermore, he defined economics unequivocally as a science able to describe and to forecast a special behaviour, the behaviour imposed by a situation of scarcity of means to achieve given ends.

The scientific character of economics has been especially underlined by Robbins' definition of economics' neutrality about ends. In his words: 'economics is entirely neutral between ends' (Robbins 1932, 24).[14]

The use of purely formal conceptions within economics was fundamental when Robbins defined the nature of an economic good: 'Whether a particular thing or a particular service is an economic good depends entirely on its relation to valuations. Thus wealth is not wealth because of its substantial qualities. Wealth is wealth because it is scarce' (Robbins 1932, 47).

Given the formal nature of the relationship between ends and means, Robbins described the economic laws upon which economic science rests: price theory as well as the law of diminishing marginal utility directly derive from the definition of economics as the disposal of scarce goods with alternative uses.

The pure theory of equilibrium is the final achievement of economics:

> [it] enables us to understand how, given the valuations of the various economic subjects and the facts of the legal and technical environment, a

system of relationships may be regarded as tending. It enables us to describe that distribution of resources which, given the valuations of the individual concerned, satisfies demand most fully. *But it does not by itself provide any ethical sanctions* (...) There is no penumbra of approbation round the Theory of Equilibrium, equilibrium is just equilibrium [emphasis added].

(Robbins, 1932, 127)

At the end of his book, Robbins went back on the necessity to free economics from any ethical issue. Likely pushed by what has recently been called emotivism amongst economists (De Martino and McCloskey 2016), Robbins almost obsessively stressed the urgency to fix the boundaries of economics within the assumption of human rationality, and to let ethics remain strictly outside them. Robbins wrote:

There is nothing in Economics which relieves *us* of the obligation to choose. There is nothing in any kind of science, which can decide the ultimate problem of preference. But to be rational, we must know what it is we prefer. We must be aware of the objective implications of the alternatives of choice. For rationality in choice is nothing more and nothing less than choice with complete awareness of the alternatives rejected.

(Robbins 1932, 136)

Deeply influenced by Mises, Robbins was able to give a precise definition of positive economics, which was based on the subjectivism of individuals' choice in a context of objective scarcity, without any ethical implication. Robbins' postulates were the existence of an order of preferences, the existence of more than one factor of production, and the uncertainty about future conditions of scarcity. Even though in his postulates Robbins did not feature '*the* fundamental assumption of economics, namely, the postulate of rational behaviour' (Giocoli 2003, 86), and his book is much more complex than a simple manifesto of mainstream economics (Masini 2009), Robbins built up the most persuasive compromise for a scientific definition of economics.

Robbins' book was one of the most influential methodological works in twentieth century economics, and its influence needs to be understood within the context of the 1930s development of marginalism (Wade Hands 2009). This was especially true after the enthusiastic acceptance and endorsement Robbins' work got from Stigler (Stigler 1942) and Samuelson (Samuelson 1948). In addition, Koopmans (Koopmans 1957) explicitly linked the axiomatic method with the Robbins definition of economics (Backhouse and Medema 2009b). Furthermore, in 1962, Friedman implicitly invoked Robbins when he claimed that: 'an economic problem exists whenever *scarce* means are used to satisfy *alternative* ends' (Friedman 1962a, 6). Robbins got a similar endorsement from Becker, whose definition of economics was 'the study of the allocation of scarce means to satisfy competing ends' (Becker 1971, 1).

From Becker onward, the use of Robbins' definition of economics (Backhouse and Medema 2009b, 2009c) had a huge influence even outside the discipline: it narrowed economics to the theory of constrained maximization or rational choice, and justified the imperialism of economics among the other social sciences (Boulding 1969; Tullock 1972; Cartwright 1999; Lazear 2000; Backhouse and Medema 2009a).

2.2 General economic equilibrium and econometrics in the 1930s: from Vienna to Chicago

Before focusing on the Department of Economics at the University of Chicago, it is necessary to take a step back in order to describe how neoclassical economics had been gradually rooted on its two pillars: general economic equilibrium and econometrics.

In interwar Vienna, Abraham Wald, Karl Schlesinger and John von Neumann had accomplished the final systematization of general economic equilibrium. They were members or they were somehow related to the *Mathematical Colloquium* (founded by Karl Menger in 1928). As Kenneth Arrow pointed out, von Neumann's article on an expanding economy and Wald's paper on the existence of equilibrium were very close, despite being of no reciprocal reference (Arrow 1989). Both Wald and von Neumann tried to solve analytical problems still unresolved in the Walrasian model. Wald developed the static Cassel's system with inequalities (Cassel 1918; Wald 1934; 1936),[15] and von Neumann provided a proof of the existence of general economic equilibrium, using a generalization of Brower's fixed-point theorem[16] (von Neumann 1937; Menger 1952; Koopmans 1964; Weintraub 1983; 1985).[17]

Along with the systematization of general economic equilibrium, in the 1930s, econometrics arose and developed. The term, 'econometrics', was coined by Ragnar Frisch in 1926 to merge in one word the terms 'economics' and 'statistics'. In 1930, in Cleveland, Ohio, Ragnar Frisch and fifteen other scholars founded The Econometric Society. Among them were Joseph Schumpeter, Karl Menger, Harold Hotelling, Henry Schultz, and Norbert Wiener (Bjerkholt 1995). The Econometric Society started to organize general meetings in Europe and in 1933 *Econometrica*, its official journal, was founded, which is well known outside the discipline and is still amongst the most prestigious economic journals today.

According to the founder, Ragnar Frisch, econometrics was intended as the tentative effort to apply mathematical economics to statistical data, in order to find out an eventual general uniformity within economic phenomena, in a realistic realm. The aim of econometrics has been intended as a 'unification of the theoretical-quantitative and the empirical-quantitative approach to economic problems that are penetrated by constructive and rigorous thinking similar to that which has come to dominate in the natural sciences' (Frisch 1933, 1).

The foundation of the Econometric Society was the first tentative attempt to create a joint scientific project (the building of a formal economics to be intended as a science) amongst European and American economists within an institutionalized context, such as the academic community.

The result of this project was twofold: the systematization of the discipline converged into mathematical economics and econometrics (that were direct derivations of the neoclassical approach to economics); both mathematical economics and econometrics gradually became the mainstream approach within economics.

The migration to the United States of many European economists, right before and after the Second World War, implemented the success of this project. After the Second World War, the Department of Economics at the University of Chicago became the stronghold of neoclassical economics.[18]

The urgency to define the scientific nature of economics was an aim of the *International Encyclopaedia of Unified Science,* promoted, above all, by the Viennese philosopher and economist Otto Neurath, one of the most active members of the Vienna Circle,[19] and the Chicagoan philosopher Charles Morris, between 1938 and 1969 (Becchio 2013). Between 1934 and 1941, Neurath, Carnap and Morris jointly organized many international congresses to present the project for the *International Encyclopaedia of Unified Science* that had been officially launched in 1934 in Prague, where many Viennese, German and American philosophers had gathered for a philosophical congress (Stadler 2001).[20] The intent of this philosophical movement was focused on the explanation of what they defined 'the scientific conception of the world: i.e. 'a basic attitude [whose] goal [was] *unified science*', *Einheitswissenshaft*,[21] (Neurath 1973, 306).[22] American philosophers like Charles W. Morris,[23] mainly influenced by Carnap, emphasized the link between the Viennese new empiricism and American pragmatism.[24]

From 1938 to 1969, 20 books (divided into two volumes) of the *Encyclopaedia* appeared, published by The University of Chicago Press.[25] The volume on economics was published by Gerhart Tintner in 1968; it dealt with mathematical economics and econometrics. The genesis of this volume is an emblematic example of the transformation of neoclassical economics into mainstream economics.

The volume on economics appeared late though, 30 years after the launching of the project, and 20 years after the definitive transfer of the entire project to the USA. The reason was quite simple: it was necessary to wait for economists to finally agree on a commonly shared scientific definition of economics. The original idea of economics pursued by Neurath (who suddenly died in 1945) was too far away from what Morris and Carnap had in mind when talking about the integration of economics into the notion of unified science. Even though Neurath had been included economics among the disciplines to be freed from any of 'metaphysical admixtures', his notion of economics was still a combination 'history' and 'political economy' to be merged into the project of unifying science (Neurath 1973; 2004). Morris and

Carnap were much more interested in the new developments of economic theory, i.e. mathematical economics as well as econometrics (Gibrat 1936).

There was a general agreement amongst the members of the project about the still unclear definition of economics. In a letter of 23 April 1941, M. K. Hubbert discouraged Morris from including economics in the project of unifying science, comparing it to astrology and alchemy. In the same year, Zilsel openly claimed that the stage of economics at that present moment was not scientific enough to be part of the unified science (De Santillana and Zilsel 1941).[26] According to him, economics was still in fact a sort of hybrid: from a theoretical point of view it was initially a branch of moral philosophy (political economy) but, from a historical point of view, it spread from the practical needs of the economy as capitalism developed. According to Zilsel, political economy could not be considered 'scientific' yet, because its aims from the outset had been to control and predict economic processes in order to find causal explanations of economic phenomena useful for formulating economic laws. Moreover, in the nineteenth century, statistical methods had been added and had proved to be highly successful. Zilsel also claimed that when 'rational deduction and mathematics [that] do play a large part in certain economic theories' become the 'language' of economics, it could be considered 'scientific' and included in the unified science project. According to Zilsel, the situation is even worse if we think that political economy is too often exposed to 'selfish interests, political pressure, and wishful thinking than is the case in any other science'. Zilsel stressed that:

> in political economy scientific agreements could be reached only on comparatively unimportant questions; in fact, there are separate schools which do not even recognize each other. Some of them cling to experience; the results of their inquiries are collections of material rather than theories in which facts are causally explained. Others deal with nothing but laws of economy; they investigate them by means of rational analysis of a few basic concepts and construct large deductive systems based upon scanty observations.
>
> (De Santillana and Zilsel 1941, 832–833)

More than 20 years later, in a letter dated 21 June 1960, Morris wrote to Carnap that it was time to find someone able to write the volume of the *Encyclopaedia* dealing with economics. He was thinking of involving Tinbergen (at that time teaching at The Hague), asking him for a book entitled 'Mathematical Tools in Economics'. Three year later, on Carnap's suggestion, Morris proposed the volume on economics to Gerhart Tintner, who had been a student of Carnap's. The genesis of Tintner's volume was rather difficult: there were three versions, but finally, in 1968, *Methodology of Mathematical Economics and Econometrics* appeared.

Following the overall aim of the Unity of Science Movement, Tintner addressed his text 'to a public which does not necessarily consist of economists' (Tintner 1968, vii). He maintained in his volume that economics can adopt two different methods: mathematical economics and econometrics, both of which are valid tools for raising the scientific level of economics and for including it in the ideal of unified science.[27]

The core of Tintner's book was its introduction. He explicitly borrowed the definition of economics from Robbins and Lange: 'the science which studies human behaviour as a relationship between given ends and scarce means which have alternative uses' (Robbins 1945, 16) or, on the other hand, as 'the science of administration of scarce resources in human society' (Lange, 1942). Tintner considered 'deplorable' the influence of ideology on economists 'on the left and on the right' who 'have sometimes illegitimately presented value judgments as scientific truth' (Tintner 1968, 6). According to Tintner, even though economics is like any other social science that deals with human action, it is fundamental to keep separate the ideological motivations of a scientist from any possible scientific result. In his view, this goal was far from being achieved in economics because of the ideological bias of most economists; hence he suggested that the only method for transforming economics into an objective science was the introduction of mathematical tools and statistics.

Tintner specified that the use of mathematics in economic theory had grown increasingly common in previous decades and had become the tool best suited to 'theoretical economics', even if 'the bulk of the results of theoretical economics has been achieved without mathematical means' (he recalled the struggle of theoretical economics against the German historical school and the American institutionalism), and he stated that 'mathematical economics and econometrics are the *only* methods for the study of problems in economics'. The aim of economics, according to Tintner, is 'to construct fundamental models to apply to concrete economic problems'; he stressed the need to bridge the gap between theoretical concepts and empirical observations. Quoting Carnap and Popper, Tintner recalled the neo-positivist philosophical approach that emphasized the unity of scientific method in the natural and social sciences, and he maintained that economics could be included in this project only when it used mathematics and/or applied it to empirical cases in an econometric sense, because only mathematical economics and econometrics could be regarded as theoretical economics at this stage of the discipline's development.

The story of the place of economics within the project of Unified Science symbolized the transformation of political economy to economics, as well as the final definition of mainstream economics as the union of mathematical economics and econometrics, based, from a methodological point of view, on neoclassical assumptions. Neurath considered economics as 'political economy' connected with the technical aspects of production and distribution of a society's wealth. In Tintner's volume, economics was formalized and described as 'theoretical', and mathematics and statistics were recognized as its only possible tools to handle the economic phenomena. In this work economics reached a 'positive' stage, becoming finally a 'neutral' science *à la* Robbins-Pareto. On considering the historical development of the meaning of economics from Neurath to Tintner (from the mid-1930s to mid-1960s), it does not seem coincidental that one of the main causes for its transformation was the Americanization of the project itself.

2.3 The Americanization of the discipline: building mainstream economics

During the interwar period, economics in the United States had adopted a pluralistic approach. This changed during the 1950s in Chicago, where two stories converged: the building of mainstream economics around the systematization of the general economic equilibrium theory and the development of econometrics, and the popularization of neoclassical economics. Popularization was intended as the general consensus amongst scholars within and outside a discipline about the definition of the nature of the discipline itself. The popularization of economics as a science within a neoclassical framework started with the collaboration between Robbins and Hayek at the LSE during the 1930s and ended up in Chicago in the 1950s when Knight and Hayek began their collaboration.

In Schumpeter's terms (Schumpeter 1954), general economic equilibrium and econometrics became the toolbox of mainstream economics, and a neoclassical approach to economics became the vision shared by mainstream economists. Both toolbox and visions had been moving from Europe to the United States where the old institutionalism was still predominant. Although the relationship between old institutionalism and neoclassical economics is much more complex than a simple antithetical position (Rutherford 2010, 2011), during this process of the transformation of the discipline between the 1940s and 1950s, the old American institutionalism lost its primacy within American universities (Hodgson 2000; 2001), as well as in interwar Europe, where political economy had been transformed into neoclassical economics.[28]

After Robbins' *Essay,* the most prominent and influential contributions on the methodology of economics were Paul Samuelson's *Foundations* (Samuelson 1947) and Milton Friedman's *Essays* on positive economics (Friedman 1953). Robbins clarified the vision within economics as a science forged from marginalism to general economic equilibrium and econometrics; Samuelson and Friedman's methodological and theoretical assumptions are the analytical pillars of neoclassical economics. The combination between Robbins' systematization as well as Samuelson's *Foundations* and Friedman's *Essays* became the mainstream in economics.

Samuelson clearly described the process of the foundation of economic analysis starting from physics. Quoting E.H. Moore, Samuelson wrote: '*the existence of analogies between central features of various theories implies the existence of a general theory which underlies the particular theories and unifies them with respect to those central features*' (Samuelson 1947, 3). Samuelson admitted the uniformity of economic phenomena and the existence of *operationally meaningful* theorems in economics.[29] According to him, economic theorems proceed from the general hypothesis that the conditions of equilibrium are equivalent to the maximization of some magnitude.

Samuelson's methodology has been defined as a comparative statics without any normative connotation around the concept of equilibrium.[30] It was a special application of the more general practice of scientific deduction in which the behaviour of a system is intended in terms of a given set of functional equations and initial conditions (*ceteris paribus*) and tastes, technology, institutional framework and governmental data.[31]

Samuelson recognized the foundation of his approach to describe economics as science – 'as a purely deductive science based upon certain postulates' (Samuelson 1947, 21) – in the theory of maximizing behaviour that can be described in terms of thermodynamics.

As Samuelson wrote:

> The general method involved may be very simply stated. *In cases where the equilibrium values of our variables can be regarded as the solutions of an extremum (maximum or minimum) problem, it is often possible regardless of the number of variables involved to determine unambiguously the qualitative behavior of our solution values in respect to changes of parameters.*
>
> (Samuelson 1947, 21)

Entrepreneurial behaviour as well as consumers' behaviour can be described as acts of maximization able to reach a stable equilibrium in the system, even though they cannot be intentional. The process of maximization combines dynamic individual acts of behaviour with the static stability of the final equilibrium. The same process happens in physics:

> in some cases, it is possible to formulate our condition of equilibrium as those of an extremum problem, even though it is admittedly not a case of any individual's behaving in a maximizing manner, just as it is often possible in classical dynamics to express the path of a particle as one which maximizes (minimizes) some quantity despite the fact that the particle is obviously not acting consciously or purposively.
>
> (Samuelson 1947, 23)

In Friedman's work, economics is *positive:* it is in principle independent of any particular ethical position or normative judgment (Friedman 1953, 4), and it has to be regarded as an objective science in the same sense as any of the physical sciences (Mäki *et al.* 2009). Friedman is not totally rejecting normative economics, rather he was clearly claiming that normative economics cannot be independent from positive economics: 'a theory has to be judged by its predictive power for phenomena which it is intended to explain'.[32] According to Friedman, economics must be more than a set of tautologies; and it is important to accept the substantive hypotheses that shape the categories into which empirical phenomena are organized.[33] The interest for realism in economics was, according to Friedman himself, the main difference between Chicago and Harvard (Hammond 1992).

Describing the role of assumptions, Friedman maintained that they have to be presented '*as if* they occurred in a hypothetical and highly simplified world containing only the forces that the hypotheses assert to be important' (Friedman 1953, 40), and that complete realism is clearly unattainable.[34]

Friedman thought that progress in positive economics requires not only testing of existing hypotheses, but also the construction of new ones, in a context of dispersed knowledge and costly information.[35] This has nothing to do with formalism, because the act of building up new hypotheses is:

> a creative act of inspiration, intuition, invention; its essence is the vision of something new in familiar material. The process must be discussed in psychological, not logical, categories; studied in autobiographies and biographies, not treatises on scientific method; and promoted by maxim and example, not syllogism or theorem.
>
> (Friedman 1953, 43)[36]

Summing up, Samuelson, on one side, and Friedman, on the other, represented not only the foundation of economics, but also the popularization of the discipline as a science during the late 1940s and early 1950s. In this perspective, there is continuity between their and Robbins's work in the building of neoclassical economics. The Chicago school of economics as a label to describe economic theory represented the outcome of this long process of transformation of political economy to economics. As Stigler clearly remarked, Robbins's definition made economics 'the study of all purposive human behavior' (Stigler 1984, 302), and it could be applied – as a general method based on efficiency – to law (Coase and Posner), to history (Fogel), to sociology (Becker's research on social structure and behaviour) and finally to politics (Buchanan and Tullock).

Economics had been reaching toward that predominant position, also known as 'imperialistic' (Stigler 1984). Stigler wrote:

> The statement of economics began to be abstract and general, and increasingly to use mathematical language, in the 1890s with Marshall, Pareto, Fisher, Edgeworth and others. By 1907 Pareto was saying that an economic problem contained only two ingredients: goals and obstacles to their achievement. Goals (or tastes) and obstacles can be found everywhere. It took two generations for this transformation to be completed: by 1940 the new Ph.Ds at good universities began to be proficient in the viewing and handling of economics as a general analytical machine, the machine of maximizing behavior. The abstraction increased the distance between economic theory and empirical economic phenomena – not without some cost to economics – and made the extensions to other bodies of phenomena easy and natural. If that explanation is correct, there will be no reversal of the imperialism.
>
> (Stigler 1984, 312)

The role of Frank Knight at the department of economics of the University of Chicago is emblematic of the transformation of economics as described above (Emmett 2009b, 2013; Stapleford 2011). Knight's contributions were focused on a strong defence of the neoclassical economics in an anti-positivistic perspective. Like Friedman, he considered economics a positive science, having a deductive and abstract structure. Knight wrote:

> Economics and other social sciences deal with knowledge and truth of a different category from that of the natural sciences, truth which is related to sense observation – and ultimately even to logic – in a very different way from that arrived at by the methodology of natural science. But it is still knowledge about reality.
>
> (Knight 1940, 5–6).

Knight was also deeply engaged in an accurate strategy for the popularization of the nature of economics in those terms. Not by chance, his well-known article on the nature of economic science (Knight 1934) is an explicit endorsement of Lionel Robbins's book (Robbins 1932).

The role of Knight in the story of the transformation of economics in Chicago is emblematic in explaining the definitive transition from political economy to economic science that took place in Chicago. As Emmett perfectly explained, without Knight's introduction of the toolbox of price theory, the neoclassical Chicago tradition would not exist; yet the methodology of the Chicago school of economics (Friedman's positive economics and Stigler-Becker's approach) have nothing in common with Knight's vision (Emmett 2009c).

Furthermore, later in 1950, Knight was involved, along with Hayek, in the introduction of Carl Menger's work to the English speaking academic community (Knight 1950). In order to explain the reasons why this story can be regarded as an important episode of the process of popularization of the idea of economics as a science, it is necessary to recall the genesis of Robbins's book on the nature of economics.

In early 1930s, Hayek went to the LSE under Mises' suggestion, and joined the newly appointed professor, Robbins. Besides becoming close friends, they were deeply engaged in a challenging new project: the development of an economic theory based on a strict methodological individualism by following and merging with the pure essence of Austrian tradition as well as the traditional British moral philosophical outlook. The most important results of this project were the renaissance of Menger's work, whose *opera omnia* was reprinted and introduced by a long article by Hayek (Hayek 1934),[37] as well as the publication of Robbins' book (Robbins 1932).[38] Robbins and Hayek's intent was to define economics as a science of subjective choice under some conditions of scarcity (means, time, and knowledge). They found in Menger a formidable forerunner of this approach: in Menger's *Principles* the subjective theory of value, exchange, price, and money was grounded on the idea of scarcity; and in Menger's methodology (Menger 1883, 1884) there was a strictly individualistic method of analysis.

In a paper published in 1937, George Stigler praised the project of the LSE to rediscover classics in order to reinforce this approach, and he underlined the importance of Menger as the most important theorist of subjective value. Stigler also regretted 'Menger's failure to develop generally the method by which the individual maximizes his want-satisfaction' (Stigler 1937, 239).

In 1950, Hayek moved to Chicago, where Frank Knight was leading the Department of Economics. Even though Hayek was never admitted as a faculty member to the Department of Economics, Knight regularly attended Hayek's seminars on liberalism and the liberal tradition (Emmett 2011b, 60).

Although Knight was not particularly enthusiastic about Menger's analytical results,[39] he decided to edit the first translation of his *Principles* into English (Menger 1950). Knight's interest in translating Menger's work was much more related to Menger's vision, able to embed marginalism within the framework of free market competition in a liberal political system. Knight's purpose was to shape the nature of economics around a subjectivist approach, based on economic rationality within a system of free competition as the only possible political framework.

As Knight wrote one year later:

> economic principles are simply the more general implications of the single principle of freedom, individual and social, i.e. free association, in a certain sphere of activity. The sphere is that of economizing, i.e. conduct in which quantitative means are used to achieve quantitative ends.
>
> (Knight 1951, 7)

The primacy of subjectivism has as an immediate consequence the primacy of the market:

> the perfect market (miscalled perfectly competitive) is unreal but conceptually necessary. It is the embodiment of complete freedom (...) The freedom in question centers in the right of each to be the judge of his own values and of the use of his own means to achieve them.
>
> (Knight 1951, 8)

It was the perfect time for economists, like Knight and Hayek, to be involved in a cultural project for the development of new liberalism, based on a 'neoliberal evolutionary economics' (Mirowski 2011). In fact, in 1947, Knight and Hayek, along with many other economists in Chicago, jointly organized the foundation of the Mont Pélerin Society.

2.4 The rise of neoliberalism in Chicago: the hegemonic role of both neoliberalism and neoclassical economics

Scholars of several disciplines have lately described the story of the rising of neoliberalism in detail. In particular, economists and historians of economics have been engaged in pointing out the relationship between neoliberalism and economics (Hartwell 1995; Harvey 2005; Mirowski and Van Horn 2009; Stedman Jones 2012).[40]

Neoliberalism is usually regarded as the *de facto* doctrine of the Chicago school of economics in a double perspective: supporters of neoliberal policy during the last three decades have presented themselves as close to the Chicago school's economic theory. Furthermore, economists of the Chicago school either explicitly (Simons 1934, Friedman 1951) or implicitly (Stigler, Becker) have been supporters of neoliberalism (Van Horn 2011).

The foundation of the Mont Pèlerin Society is usually seen as one of the most important initiatives for the development of neoliberalism made by economists outside academia. In fact, amongst the 36 founders of the Mont Pèlerin Society, most were economists. There were, to name but a few, Friedrich von Hayek, George Stigler, Milton Freedman, Aaron Director, Frank Knight, who were faculty members at the University of Chicago: also Lionel Robbins, Ludwig von Mises, Michael Polanyi, and the German ordoliberals Wilhelm Röpke and Walter Eucken.[41]

Although the term neoliberalism was used for the first time by Charles Gide to label marginal economists, such as Maffeo Pantaleoni at the end of the twentieth century (see the first paragraph), the Mont Pèlerin Society was the symbol of neoliberalism as the most prominent result of mainstream economics outside its theoretical boundaries. Even though the influence of 'heterodox' economics such as German ordoliberalism (Oliver 1960; Biebricher 2013) as well as the Austrian school of economics (Plehwe 2009)[42] had a massive influence on the rise of neoliberalism, neoclassical economics, as shaped in Chicago, were the authentic matrix of neoliberalism as conceived in the United States during the Cold War.

Hayek had indeed a pivotal role in this story. In the first meeting of the Mont Pèlerin Society, he insisted on the urgency for a new liberalism able to cope with real problems no longer avoidable (Hartwell 1995; Turner 2008). As Hayek wrote:

> This task involves both purging traditional liberal theory of certain accidental accretions which have become attached to it in the course of time, and also facing up to some real problems which an over-simplified liberalism has shirked or which have become apparent only since it has turned into a somewhat stationary and rigid creed.
>
> (Hayek [1947] 1967, 149)

In his opening address to the Mont Pèlerin Society, Hayek listed the agenda of this new project for the reinforcement of liberalism on a global scale in order to avoid the raise of totalitarian regimes as happened in interwar Europe. To get this aim, old liberalism is no longer enough: 'what we need are people who have faced the arguments from the other side, who have struggled with them and fought themselves through to a position from which they both critically meet the objection against it and justify their views' (Hayek [1947] 1967, 151). For the first meeting of the Mont Pèlerin Society, Hayek suggested a programme based on these following points: a serious discussion on the relationship between free enterprise and a really competitive order; the inflationary high-pressure in many countries; the fight against the development of a collectivistic vision (mainly due to the way history had been taught lately); the future of Germany; and finally, the actual possibility of a European federation.

Hayek was mainly influenced by Popper's notion of piecemeal social engineering (Popper [1936] 1957, 1945) and by Röpke's critique of classical liberalism (Röpke [1942] 1950), as well as by Mises' more recent critique of socialism and by Michael Polanyi's vision of practicing scientists (Polanyi 1946). Although there is no doubt about the fact that Hayek 'provided both the intellectual impetus and the organizational spade-work for both the Chicago school and the Mont Pèlerin Society' (Mirowski and Van Horn 2009, 159; Mirowski 2011),[43] it was Friedman who clearly explained the different nature of neoliberalism in respect to old classical liberalism.[44]

If Hayek insisted on the urgent revival of 'true liberalism', based on individual freedom, against 'the aggressive rationalism which would recognize no values except those whose utility (for an ultimate purpose never disclosed) could be demonstrated by individual reason' (Hayek [1947] 1967, 155); Friedman rooted the idea of a new liberalism as a direct consequence of the rationality of economic theory. In this passage we attest to the initial distance between Hayek and Friedman, or in broader terms, between Austrians and Chicagoans. Hayek's 'false rationalism' leads to 'an intellectual hubris' that is the opposite of 'the essence of true liberalism that regards with reverence those spontaneous social forces through which the individual creates things greater than he knows' (Hayek [1947] 1967, 155). The role of economic rationality as intended by Friedman was indeed different and led him to consider the superiority of economics over politics, and consequently, he promoted the urgency of handling politics by using economics as a benchmark to measure either the efficiency or the failure of a political system, such as a democracy. In Friedman, the shift from old classical liberalism to neoliberalism had been accomplished.[45]

In a paper Friedman wrote in 1951, he introduced neoliberalism as a political programme to be organized in order to attain its goals, because the traditional and classical belief of a self-regulated market was no longer acceptable. After having praised Dicey's thesis on the distinction between legislation and public opinion (Dicey 1905), Friedman stressed the fact that the opinion according to which legislation is always in opposition to freedom is obsolete. It was a fault of old nineteenth century liberalism to consider the state as a harmful institution. According to Friedman, a new philosophical outlook was necessary, a philosophy enabling the estimation of the danger of monopoly and 'the danger that private individuals could through agreement and combination usurp power and effectively limit the freedom of other individuals' (Friedman 1951, 90). This new faith, in Friedman's words, is called 'neo-liberalism' (Friedman's terminology).

He wrote:

> Neo-liberalism would accept the nineteenth century liberal emphasis on the fundamental importance of the individual, but it would substitute for the

nineteenth century goal of laissez-faire as a means to this end, the goal of the competitive order. It would seek to use competition among producers to protect consumers from exploitation, competition among employers to protect workers and owners of property, and competition among consumers to protect the enterprises themselves. The state would police the system, establish conditions favorable to competition and prevent monopoly, provide a stable monetary framework, and relieve acute misery and distress. The citizens would be protected against the state by the existence of a free private market; and against one other by the preservation of competition.

(Friedman 1951, 91)

The different nature of classical liberalism and neoliberalism is clear in this passage. Given that the present world is a very complex system, the competitive order within the market is the most suitable principle to create efficiency for both individuals and society, and the state should assume an active role to determine the conditions for the development of such a system.[46] Friedman merged Hayek's spontaneous order (Hayek 1948) and Simons' programme for liberty (Simons 1948) into a new form of liberal theory, only inspired by classical liberalism, but not completely adherent to it, and mainly shaped by the new way of thinking that had been emerging within neoclassical economics. Furthermore, according to Friedman, monetary stability was one of the two conditions, along with a strong deregulation of the market, that made the spread of neoliberalism possible (Friedman 1951).

A few years later, Friedman explained the differences between old and new liberalism in a lecture he gave at Wabash College in 1956 (Friedman 1962b) about the relationship between economic and political freedom. In his paper, published in the latter part of his book *Capitalism and Democracy*, Friedman claimed the intimate connection between economics and politics, both based on individual freedom. A capitalistic society where a free market is guaranteed is the only possible framework for the coordination of different individuals' plans. In a complex society the role of politics, led by the state, cannot be anything else but central. In Friedman's words:

government is essential both as a forum for determining the 'rules of the game' and as an umpire to interpret and enforce the rules decided on. What the market does is to reduce greatly the range of issues that must be decided through political means, and thereby to minimize the extent to which government need participate directly in the game. The characteristic feature of action through political channels is that it tends to require or enforce substantial conformity. The great advantage of the market, on the other hand, is that it permits wide diversity.

(Friedman 1962b, 21)

According to Friedman, the only alternative system is a totalitarian regime. In fact, a pure free world, where anarchy would lead the system, is impossible, due to the anthropological condition of individuals, who are far from being perfect.[47] Friedman's focus on individuals in order to describe the neoliberal feature of the market and the state was central in a later writing, *Free to Choose* (Friedman 1980). In this book, Friedman dealt with political and economic systems as 'markets in which the outcome is determined by the interaction among persons pursing their own self-interests (broadly interpreted) rather than by the social goals the participants find it advantageous to enunciate' (Friedman and Friedman 1980, x).

Friedman's shift towards the description of individual nature within a discourse on neoliberalism, a general political philosophy, was possible mainly because his analysis was deeply rooted in neoclassical economics, which had reached its strong dominant position also because of its ability to construct a strong economic agent, a rational economic agent able to maximize (see Chapter 3).

How about an eventual neoliberal economics? Does it exist? And what are its main features? In a recent publication, Mirowski listed 'the Thirteen Commandments' of the neoliberalist economic doctrine (Mirowski 2013, 53) as follows:

1. A good society is not natural; its conditions must be constructed.
2. Even though the notion of market remains vague within neoliberal economic theory, the state and the civil society are subordinated to the market.
3. The neoliberal narrative is based on the idea of the market as a natural institution that is able to dynamically reach more complex degree of organization, and on the rejection of market failures as they are described in neoclassical economic theory.
4. The neoliberal project is aimed at a redefinition of the practices of the state.
5. Neoliberal economics deals with politics as if it were a market in order to avoid the conflict between democracy and neoliberal programmes.
6. Individuals are forced to behave in a fixed way following the 'theory of everything', that implies the golden rule of maximization.
7. The concept of freedom has been shaped around the neoliberal programme.
8. Neoliberal globalized finance combines the freedom of international trade with the freedom of capital flows.
9. Inequalities of the system are a power tool to improve progress, and the concept of 'social justice' is a dangerous misunderstanding of the neoliberal mechanism of the market.
10. Corporations and monopolies are tools for better development of society.
11. The neoliberal market has a solution for any problem, not only an economic problem.
12. From a neoliberal perspective, while criminal law is designed for non-affluent people, tort law is designed for rich people.
13. Neoliberalism has its own moral code, based on individual freedom, even though the concept of freedom without a corpus of moral values makes things complicated.

We might ask at this juncture, how many of these 'Commandments' are direct derivations from neoclassical economics? *Strictu sensu*, only Commandment 6: the golden rule of maximization. The other Commandments are a direct development of neoclassical economics' vision and they should not be conceived without the dominance achieved by mainstream economics in Western democratic societies. Even though neoliberalism was developed in a broader context than economic theory,[48] the origin of the version of neoliberalism, as it emerged in the late 1940s and spread the message during the second half of the twentieth century, has a special connection with neoclassical economics as it was built up in Chicago during the same period.

Both neoclassical economics and neoliberalism reached a position of hegemony, and, especially after the financial and economic crisis that began in 2007–2008, they became the object of serious critique for a vast audience (Plehwe and Walpen 2006; Delazay and Garth 2006). In order to better understand the evolution of the strict interconnection between neoclassical economics and neoliberalism, it is central to consider the development of economic rationality within neoclassical economics. Without the idea that economic agents are rational agents in the context of scarcity, the power of neoliberalism as it has developed on a global scale would not be fully understood.

Notes

1 For a recent discussion about the complex notion of neoclassical economics, see Lawson (2013).
2 It will be useful to consider the use, and in some cases abuse, of the founding fathers' work in order to make the new definition of economics much stronger. An example can be found in the story of how Menger's work was presented to the English speaking academic world (Hayek 1934; Knight 1950), first by Robbins and Hayek in the 1930s, and later by Knight and Stigler during the 1950s in Chicago (Becchio 2014). Another example has been the use of Adam Smith's notion of an invisible hand as the most suitable representation of the market (Houseman 2003; Kaushik 2011; Samuels and Johnson and Perry 2011).
3 For a study on the relationship between marginalism and neoclassic economics, see Aspromorgous (1986).
4 A massive literature deals with the debate around the link between positivism and economics from Hutchinson onwards (Hutchinson 1938; Lipsey 1963; Blaug 1980; Boland 1989; Lawson 1997; Mäki 2009).
5 For a study on the role of subjectivism within economic theory from Smith to the Austrians, see Davis (2011) and Scott (2012).
6 In 1912, the Italian economist Enrico Barone showed that general economic equilibrium could also be reached in a system of planned economy: hypothetically a Minister of Production can perfectly allocate resources in order to get the best possible social performance (Barone [1912] 1935). As reminded by Hayek, this does not mean that 'Pareto and Barone have *solved* the problem of socialist calculation. What they, and many others, did was merely to state the conditions by which a rational allocation of resources would have to satisfy and to point out that these were essentially the same as the conditions of *equilibrium* of a competitive market [emphasis added]' (Hayek 1948, 90). Later during the interwar period, and after

the Bolshevik revolution, a massive debate on the feasibility of a planned economy was carried on by supporters like Dobb and Lange (Dobb 1933; Lange 1935), and detractors, like Mises and Hayek (Mises 1935; Hayek 1935), to name but a few. For a complete list of contributions to that debate, see Boettke (2000). Intermediate positions, based on alternative social models, were also part of the debate, especially in interwar Vienna (Neurath 2004; Polanyi 1922, 1924).

7 The concept of 'economic rationality' had gradually become central within economic theory along with the centrality of individuals intended as economic agents who are supposed to make economic choices in a rational way (see Chapter 3).

8 'By utility is meant that property in any object, whereby it tends to produce benefit, advantage, pleasure, good, or happiness (all this, in the present case, comes to the same thing), or (what comes again to the same thing) to prevent the happening of mischief, pain, evil, or unhappiness to the party whose interest is considered.' (Bentham [1789], 1832, 82).

9 Pantaleoni was one of the masters of marginalism in the Italian Academia during the late nineteenth century and early twentieth century.

10 In Pareto's words: 'parmi les sciences sociales, la science de l'ophelimité est la seule dont les résultats aient atteint un degré de précisione et de certitude comparable à celui des propositions des autres sciences naturelles, telles que la chiemie, la physique, etc.' (Pareto 1896, 6). Most likely, before the publication of his *Cours*, Pareto was a supporter of late nineteenth century positivism, based on the idea that the deductive method, founded on hedonistic hypotheses, would have made objective truth possible in social science as well as in natural sciences (Bruni 2002).

11 Pareto's search for realism was constantly linked to his theoretical assumptions: even his concept of ophelimity is related to empirical data (Montesano 2006).

12 In *Manuale*'s 'Appendix', Pareto reformulated Edgeworth's indifference curves (Pareto 1906, 367).

13 Although Pareto's approach to economics represented one of the most powerful and well-grounded pillars of formal economics and economics as a science, his following work on sociology revealed a different development (Pareto [1916] 1963). He introduced his so-called theory of residues and derivations in order to describe and possibly to explain the complexity of social phenomena.

14 Some years before the writing of his *Essay*, in a review article about Hawtrey's book (Hawtrey, 1926), Robbins had already clearly stated that economics has nothing to do with ethical issues. As Robbins wrote: 'It is not because we believe that our science is exact that we wish to exclude ethics from our analysis, but because we wish to confine our investigations to a subject about which positive statement of any kind is conceivable' (Robbins 1927, 176). Robbins mentioned Hawtrey's position on ethics in his *Essay* too (Robbins 1932, 132).

15 As Wald wrote: 'in mathematical economics, certain processes are described by systems of equations in which certain economic magnitudes are used as data and others as unknowns. As a rule, economists have contented themselves with equating the number of equations and unknowns and have assumed, without further investigation, that the system of equations had a meaningful solution from an economic viewpoint, and that this solution was unique. But the equality of the number of equations and un-knows does not prove that a solution exists, much less the uniqueness of a solution' (Wald 1951, pp. 369–370). Wald's model of equilibrium was developed later by Arrow and Debreu (Arrow and Debreu 1954), as well as by McKenzie (McKenzie 1954, 1981), as Weintraub clearly described (Weintraub 2011).

16 Using convex sets, von Neumann introduced a minimax solution as a mathematical instrument with which to prove the verifiability of the general economic equilibrium model.

17 In von Neumann's model, the realism of hypotheses and the correspondence between reality and the mathematical model were abandoned (Champernowne 1945). This represents a turning point in the history of neoclassical economics: the adherence between model and reality were no longer a priority as long as the model gave a scientific status to the discipline that, still, in the 1930s, had a nebulous aspect.

18 The foundation of the Cowles Commission in 1932 is part of this story. In 1939 the Cowles Commission, the main financial supporter of *Econometrica*, was relocated to Chicago. Friedman and Savage occasionally attended Cowles' seminars and meetings, and members of the Commission joined their classes. The contribution of the Cowles Commission to Econometrics was twofold: 'the exposition and advocacy of probability models, and the development of simultaneous equation models to a useable stage' (Hildreth 1985, 128). In 1943 Jacob Marshak was appointed professor in the Department of Economics in Chicago and he was named director of the Cowles Commission. After his arrival, the synergy between the Commission and the department became increasingly stronger (Emmett 2011a).

19 The Vienna Circle was founded in Vienna by Moritz Schlick in 1922. During the 1920s, many scholars joined the group. Amongst them were the philosopher Rudoph Carnap, one of the fiercest adversaries of Heiddeger, the mathematicians Hans Hahn and Kurt Reidmeister, the economist Otto Neurath, the historian Victor Kraft, and the lawyer Felix Kaufmann. In 1929, the group published their *Manifesto* (Hahn, Neurath and Carnap 1929). In the *Preface* they explained that all knowledge in every discipline had to be verified in order to achieve the status of science. The project of the *International Encyclopaedia of Unified Science* was part of the scientific programme that involved social scientists of the Vienna Circle and American pragmatists. Followers of Moritz Schlick's theory of knowledge (Schlick 1918), they converged towards a new scientific model that was able to reject any kind of metaphysics (including idealism and neo-Kantism) in order to find a proper logical description and an exact definition for any empirical observation (neo-empiricism).

20 After the *Anschluss* (1938), many Austrian scholars moved to the United States (Craver 1986; Vaughn 1994; Timms and Hughes 2003; Rutherford 2004), and Morris and Carnap, both at the University of Chicago (Feigl 1969; Stadler 2001; Richardson and Uebel 2007), led the project of the *International Encyclopaedia*.

21 *Einheitswissenshaft* was not a sort of 'super-science' able to legislate to a specific science; it had to be regarded as a tool able to unify scientific language, in order to avoid the many so-called metaphysical questions.

22 The ideal of a unified science pursed by members of the Vienna Circle during the 1930s involved many scholars outside Vienna. Their aim was to 'unmask [philosophical problems] as pseudo-problems and to transform them into empirical problems [to be] subjected to the judgement of experimental science' (Neurath 1973, p. 306). Any form of metaphysical residual, such as intuition and apriorism, was discarded as a possible source of knowledge.

23 Morris' pragmatism was mainly focused on the foundation of a unified theory of language and signs to be applied to all areas of knowledge without any metaphysical residual (Morris 1938).

24 The first official contact between Viennese philosophers of Schlick's circle and American philosophers came about in 1931, when Herbert Feigl and Albert Blumberg introduced Viennese logical positivism, as 'a unified theory of knowledge in which neither logical nor empirical factors are neglected', to the American audience (Feigl and Blumberg 1931, 282). Herbert Feigl was one of the most prominent students of Schlick's and later one of the most active members of the

Vienna Circle. In 1930, he obtained a fellowship for a visiting position in Harvard College, Cambridge, MA, where he started to work with Albert Blumberg, an American philosopher, who had received his PhD in Vienna under the supervision of Schlick and was teaching at The Johns Hopkins University.

25 Morris arranged to find the financial support for organizing the entire *Encyclopaedia* project. In a letter of 28 January 1935, he requested W. Weaver (Rockefeller Foundation) to furnish financial support for the unified science movement (Morris 1946; 1960).

26 Zilsel was a Viennese scholar, member of the Gomperz Circle (which included Popper).

27 The book consisted of three chapters: Mathematical Economics, Econometrics, and Welfare Economics and Economic Policy. Mathematical Economics was described in Hilbertian terms: economic theory that 'uses the logical-deductive method and derives conclusions from certain fundamental assumptions or axioms, such as rationality and profit maximization' (Tintner 1968, 14). Econometrics was described as 'an important special method for the evaluation of mathematical economic models in numerical terms and for the verification of economic theories; it uses the methods of modern statistics for this purpose ... based upon applied probability' (Tintner 1968, 56). The final chapter on welfare economics and economic policy was shorter than the previous two (its length is about ten pages): it dealt mostly with the distinction between positive and normative economics and with explanation of the welfare utility function from Bergson to Arrow.

28 The remarkable success of the Chicago school of economics in the postwar period has been recognized even by outside economists. According to historians of economics, the pillars of the Chicago's excellence were manifold. According to Van Overtveld there was a formidable work ethic, a strong belief in economics as a science, a strict criterion of excellence as the only measurement for career advancement, the central role of internal seminars and discussions, and the geographical and academic isolation of the University (Van Overtveldt 2007). Other scholars consider as central both the long-lasting defence of liberalism against socialism as well as the introduction of neoliberalism (Amadae 2003; Van Horn 2007). Emmett underlined the formidable synergy between theoretical and empirical research shared in a lively academic environment that was aimed to produce a policy oriented toward liberal (or neoliberal) principles (Emmett 2011a).

29 According to Samuelson, a hypothesis about empirical data could be refuted only under ideal conditions; there are no deductions from any a priori propositions.

30 This implies the investigation of changes in a system from one position of equilibrium to another without regard to the transitional process involved in the adjustment.

31 Samuelson considered it sterile and misleading to speak of one variable as causing another because the only sense in which the use of the term causation is admissible is in respect to changes in external data.

32 As an example, Friedman mentioned the evidence that from an increase in money supply inflation is derived in the short run.

33 Friedman explained that in building hypotheses and in testing their validity, two caveats occur: (1) any particular fact is incidental of the collection of data and the knowledge of the researcher; (2) the initial stage is always a fictitious starting point.

34 As an example, Friedman claimed that relative price theory from Marshall onward is true in a static monetary theory that explains absolute prices, aggregate output, quantitative monetary theory and everything in a static form.

35 Hayek's role of dispersed knowledge deeply influenced Stigler (Stigler 1961) as well as Friedman in describing the market process and the nature of economics (Hammond 2011).

36 Friedman's monetarism is the obvious consequences of his methodology: he identifies the natural state of economy as the general economic equilibrium in the

long run, where a natural unemployment rate occurs and individuals' expectations are fully realized (Friedman 1968). In the short run, a discrepancy exists between expected and actual economic values. This discrepancy makes fluctuations possible.

37 Menger's latest work, i.e. the second edition of his *Principles* (Menger 1923), was not reprinted though. Hayek's article is a long and exhaustive presentation of Menger's economic theory and methodology for an English-speaking audience.

38 As Robbins' main biographer admits, Robbins was much influenced by Mises and Hayek while he was working on his book (Howson 2011).

39 In his long *Introduction*, Knight criticized Menger from a theoretical and methodological point of view, by accusing him of being less rigorous than Walras and Jevons, and adopting an obsolete Aristotelian framework to explain the scientific nature of economics (Knight, 1950).

40 According to Stedman Jones, neoliberalism went through three phases (Stedman Jones 2012). The first occurred in interwar Europe: the term indicated a new market-based society that was able to avoid the failure of old classical liberalism based on Lippman's book (Lippman 1937) and German ordoliberalism. The second phase occurred between 1950 and 1980, i.e. from the emergence of the Chicago school of economics as a neoliberal leader in economics as well as in economic policy up to the advent of Thatcher and Reagan. The final phase occurred after 1980 and was centered on the spread of neoliberal agenda outside Western society.

41 The 35 attendees were: 'Maurice Allais (Paris), Carlo Antoni (Rome), Hans Barth (Zurich), Karl Brandt (Stanford), John Davenport (New York), Stanley Dennison (Cambridge, England), Aaron Director (Chicago), Walter Eucken (Freiburg), Erich Eyck (Oxford), Milton Friedman (Chicago), Harry Gideonse (Brooklyn), Frank Graham (Princeton), F.A. Harper (Irvington-on-Hudson), Henry Hazlitt (New York), T.J.B. Hoff (Oslo), Albert Hunold (Zurich), Carl Iversen (Copenhagen), John Jewkes (Manchester), Bertrand de Jouvenel (Chexbres), Frank Knight (Chicago), Fritz Machlup (Buffalo), L.B. Miller (Detroit), Ludwig von Mises (New York), Felix Morley (Washington, DC), Michael Polanyi (Manchester), Karl Popper (London), William Rappard (Geneva), Leonard Read (Irvington-on-Hudson), Lionel Robbins (London), Wilhelm Röpke (Geneva), George Stigler (Providence, Rhode Island), Herbert Tingsten (Stockholm), Francois Trevoux (Lyon), V.O. Watts (Irvington-on-Hudson), and C.V. Wedgwood (London)' (Hayek [1947] 1967, 148).

42 About the differences between Austrians and Chicagoans, see Chapter 3 of this volume.

43 Along with the thesis pursued by Mirowski and Van Horn, there is an opposite position that considers neither Hayek nor the Chicagoans as the founders of neoliberalism (Caldwell 2011).

44 On the differences between Hayek and Friedman on neoliberalism, see Chapter 3 of this volume.

45 A few years later, Buchanan (Buchanan 1954) and Coase (Coase 1960) will represent a development of the differences between Hayek and Friedman about the role of social rationality in an analysis of the place of freedom within institutions (Coleman 2013).

46 Friedman's main reference in this passage is Henry Simons (Simons 1948).

47 The influence of Hayek's work (Hayek 1944, 1948) in Friedman's thought is evident. In *Road to Serfdom* (1944), Hayek had described liberalism in the twentieth century as a spontaneous order without strict rules, and able to gradually increase either individual freedom or social well-being.

48 This is in agreement with Mirowski's position against 'the fallacy of identifying neoliberalism exclusively with economic theory' (Mirowski 2009, 427).

References

Amadae, S. (2003) *Rationalizing Capitalistic Democracy: The Cold War Origins of Rational Choice Liberalism*. Chicago: University of Chicago Press.

Arrow, K. (1989) 'Economic Theory and the Hypothesis of Rationality', in Eatwell, J., Milgate, M. and Newman, P. (Eds) *The New Palgrave Utility and Probability*. New York: Norton, pp. 25–37.

Arrow, K. and Debreu, G. (1954) 'Existence of an Equilibrium for a Competitive Economy', *Econometrica*, Vol. 22:3, pp. 265–290.

Aspromorgous, T. (1986) 'On the Origin of the Term "Neoclassical"', *Cambridge Journal of Economics*, Vol. 10:3, pp. 265–270.

Backhouse, R. and Medema, S. (2009a) 'Retrospectives: On the Definition of Economics', *Journal of Economic Perspectives*, Vol. 23:1, pp. 221–233.

Backhouse, R. and Medema, S. (2009b) 'Robbins' Essay and the Axiomatization of Economics', *Journal of the History of Economic Thought*, Vol. 31:4, pp. 485–499.

Backhouse, R. and Medema, S. (2009c) 'Defining Economics: The Long Road to Acceptance of the Robbins Definition', *Economica*, Vol. 76:s1, pp. 805–820.

Barone, E. [1912] (1935) 'The Ministry of Production in the Collectivistic State', in Hayek, F. (Ed.) *Collectivistic Economic Planning: Critical Studies of the Possibilities of Socialism*. London: Routledge and Kegan Paul, pp. 245–290.

Becchio, G. (2013) 'Economics in the International Encyclopaedia of Unified Science', *History of Economic Thought and Policy*, Vol. 9:2, pp. 145–156.

Becchio, G. (2014) 'From Social Needs to Social Goods in Carl Menger's Final Work', *History of Political Economy*, Vol. 46:2, pp. 247–264.

Becker, G. (1971) *Economic Theory*. New York: Knopf.

Becker, G. (1976) *The Economic Approach to Human Behavior*. Chicago: University of Chicago Press.

Bentham, J. [1789] (1832) *An Introduction to the Principles of Morals and Legislation*, Oxford Clarendon Press, reprinted *The Schoolmasters, and Edinburgh Weekly Magazine*. Glasgow: John Anderson and John McLeod and Atkinson and Co.

Biebricher, T. (2013) 'Europe and the Political Philosophy of Neoliberalism', *Contemporary Political Theory*, Vol. 12:4, pp. 338–375.

Bjerkholt, O. (1995) 'Introduction', in Bjerkholt, O. (Ed.) *Foundations of Econometrics: The Selected Essays of Ragnar Frisch*. London: Edward Elgar, pp. 1–49.

Blaug, M. (1980) *The Methodology of Economics*. Cambridge: Cambridge University Press.

Boettke, P. (Ed.) (2000) *Socialism and the Market. The Socialist Calculation Debate Revised. Marginalist Economics and the Socialist Economy*. London: Routledge.

Boland, L. (1989) *Methodology of Economic Model Building: Methodology after Samuelson*. London: Routledge.

Boulding, K. (1969) 'Economics as a Moral Science', *American Economic Review*, Vol. 59:1, pp. 1–12.

Bruni, L. (2002) *Vilfredo Pareto and the Birth of Modern Microeconomics*. Cheltenham, UK: Edward Elgar.

Bruni, L. and Sudgen, R. (2007) 'The Road Not Taken: How Psychology Was Removed from Economics, and How It May Be Brought Back', *Economic Journal*, Vol. 117:516, pp. 146–173.

Buchanan, J. (1954) 'Social Choice, Democracy and Free Markets', *Journal of Political Economy*, Vol. 62:2, pp. 114–123.

Caldwell, B. (1980) 'Positivist Philosophy of Science', *Journal of Economic Issues*, Vol. XIV:1, pp. 53–76.

Caldwell, B. (2011) 'The Chicago School, Hayek, and Neoliberalism', in Van Horn, R., Mirowski, P. and Stapleford, T. (Eds) *Building Chicago Economics*. Cambridge: Cambridge University Press, pp. 301–334.

Cartwright, N. (1999) *The Dappled World. A Study on the Boundaries of Science*. Cambridge: Cambridge University Press.

Cassel, G. (1918) 'Abnormal Deviations in International Exchange', *The Economic Journal*, Vol. 28:112, pp. 413–415.

Champernowne, D. (1945) 'A Note on J. v. Neumann's Article on "A model of Economic Equilibrium"', *The Review of Economic Studies*, Vol. 13:1, pp. 10–18.

Christ, C. (1994). 'The Cowles Commission Contributions to Econometrics at Chicago: 1939–1955', *Journal of Economic Literature*, Vol. 32:1, pp. 30–59.

Coase, R. (1960) 'The Problem of Social Costs', *Journal of Law and Economics*, Vol. 3:1, pp. 1–44.

Coleman, W. (2013) 'What Was "New" About Neoliberalism?', *Economic Affairs*, Vol. 33:1, pp. 78–92.

Craver, E. (1986) 'The Emigration of the Austrian Economists', *History of Political Economy*, Vol. 18:1, pp. 1–32.

Croce, B. (1900) 'Sul principio economico, lettera al professore Vilfredo Pareto', *Giornale degli Economisti*, Vol. 21:7, pp. 15–26, English translation in Wood, J. and McLure, M. (1999) *Vilfredo Pareto: Critical Assessments of Leading Economists*, Vol. 1. London: Routledge, pp. 237–244.

Croce, B. (1901) 'Sul principio economico, replica all'articolo del prof. Pareto', *Giornale degli Economisti*, Vol. 22:2, pp. 121–130, English translation in Wood, J. and McLure, M. (1999) *Vilfredo Pareto: Critical Assessments of Leading Economists*, Vol. 1. London: Routledge, pp. 262–268.

Davis, A. (2011) *Individuals and Identity in Economics*. Cambridge: Cambridge University Press.

Delazay, Y. and Garth, B. (2006) 'The National Usages of a Global Science: the International Diffusion of New Economic Paradigms as Both Hegemonic Strategy and Professional Stakes within the National Fields of Reproduction of State Elites', *Sociologie du Travail*, Vol. 48:3, pp. 308–329.

De Martino, G. and McCloskey, D. (2016) 'Introduction', in De Martino, G. and McCloskey, D. (Eds) *The Oxford Handbook of Professional Economic Ethics*. New York: Oxford University Press, pp. 3–10.

De Santillana, G. and Zilsel, E. (1941) 'The Development of Rationalism and Empiricism', in Neurath, O., Carnap, R. and Morris, C. (Eds) *International Encyclopaedia of Unified Science*, Volume 2. Chicago: University of Chicago Press.

Dicey, A. (1905) *Lectures on the Relation between Law & Public Opinion in England during the Nineteenth Century*. London: Macmillan and Company.

Dobb, M. (1933) 'Problems of a Socialist Economy', *The Economic Journal*, Vol. 43:172, pp. 114–123.

Düppe, T. and Weintraub, R. (2013) *Finding Equilibrium*. Princeton, NJ: Princeton University Press.

Edgeworth, F. (1881) *Mathematical Physics: an Essay on the Application of Mathematics to the Moral Sciences*. London: Kegan Paul.

Emmett, R. (2009a) 'Realism and Relevance of a Free Society', *Journal of Economic Methodology*, Vol. 16:6, pp. 341–350.

Emmett, R. (2009b), 'Frank Knight, Max Weber, Chicago Economics, and Institutionalism', in Emmett, R. (Ed.) *Frank Knight and the Chicago School in American Economics*. London and New York: Routledge, pp. 111–123.

Emmett, R. (2009c) 'Did the Chicago School Reject Frank Knight? Assessing Frank Knight's Place in the Chicago Economics Tradition', in Emmett, R. (Ed.) *Frank Knight and the Chicago School in American Economics*. London and New York: Routledge, pp. 145–155.

Emmett, R. (2011a) 'Sharpening Tools in the Workshop. The Workshop System and the Chicago School's Success', in Van Horn, R., Mirowski, P. and Stapleford, T. (Eds) *Building Chicago Economics*. Cambridge: Cambridge University Press, pp. 93–115.

Emmett, R. (2011b) 'Discussion and the Evolution of Institutions in a Liberal Democracy: Frank Knight Joins the Debate', in Farrant, A. (Ed.) *Hayek, Mill, and the Liberal Tradition*. London: Routledge, pp. 57–77.

Emmett, R. (2013) 'Frank Knight on Institutionalism and Economics', *Research in the History of Economic Thought and Methodology*, Vol. 31:B, pp. 117–124.

Feigl, H. (1969), 'The Wiener Kreis in America', in Fleming, D. and Baylin, B. (Eds) *The Intellectual Migration*. Cambridge, MA: Harvard University Press, pp. 630–673.

Feigl, H. and Blumberg, A. (1931) 'Logical Positivism', *Journal of Philosophy*, Vol. 28:11, pp. 281–296.

Friedman, M. (1951) 'Neo-liberalism and Its Prospect', *Farmand*, Vol. LX:7, pp. 89–93.

Friedman, M. (1953) *Essays in Positive Economics*. Chicago: Chicago University Press.

Friedman, M. (1962a) *Price Theory: A Provisional Text*. Chicago: Aldine.

Friedman, M. (1962b) *Capitalism and Freedom*. Chicago: University of Chicago Press.

Friedman, M. (1968) 'The Role of Monetary Policy', *American Economic Review*, Vol. 58:1, pp. 1–17.

Friedman, M. and Friedman, R. (1980) *Free to Choose*. New York and London: Harcourt Brace Jovanovich.

Frisch, R. (1933) 'Editor's Note', *Econometrica*, Vol. 1:1, pp. 1–4.

Gibrat, R. (1936), 'La Science Economique. Methodes et Philosophie?', in *Actes du congrès international de philosophie scientifique*. Paris: Hermann & Cle Editeurs, pp. 22–31.

Gide, C. (1898) 'Has Co-operation Introduced a New Principle into Economics?', *The Economic Journal*, Vol. 8:32, pp. 410–511.

Giocoli, N. (2003) *Modelling Rational Agents. From Interwar Economics to Early Modern Game Theory*. Cheltenham, UK: Edward Elgar.

Hahn, H., Neurath, O., and Carnap, R. (1929) *Wissenschaftliche Weltauffassung. Der Wiener Kreis*. Vienna: Arthur Wolf Verlag.

Hammond, D. (1992) 'An Interview with Milton Friedman on Methodology', *Research in the History of Economic Thought and Methodology*, Vol. 10, pp. 91–118.

Hammond, D. (2011) 'Markets, Politics, and Democracy at Chicago', in Van Horn, R., Mirowski, P. and Stapleford, T. (Eds) *Building Chicago Economics*. Cambridge: Cambridge University Press, pp. 36–63.

Hartwell, R. (1995) *A History of the Mont Pélerin Society*. Indianapolis, IN: Liberty Fund.

Harvey, D. (2005) *A Brief History of Neoliberalism.* Oxford: Oxford University Press.

Hawtrey, R. (1926) *The Economic Problem.* London: Longmans.

Hayek, F. (1934) 'Carl Menger', in Hayek, F. (Ed.) *The Collected Works of Carl Menger,* reprinted as *Series of Reprints of Scarce Tracts in Economics and Political Science,* Vol. 17. London: London School of Economics and Political Science.

Hayek, F. (Ed.) (1935) *Collectivistic Economic Planning: Critical Studies of the Possibilities of Socialism.* London: Routledge and Kegan Paul.

Hayek, F. (1944) *Road to Serfdom.* London: Routledge.

Hayek, F. [1947] (1967) 'Opening Address to a Conference at Mont Pèlerin', in Hayek, F. *Studies in Philosophy, Politics and Economics.* Chicago: University of Chicago Press, pp. 148–159.

Hayek, F. (1948) *Individualism and Economic Order.* Chicago: University of Chicago Press.

Hildreth, C. (1985) 'The Cowles Commission in Chicago', *Discussion Paper 225,* Minneapolis, MN, Center for Economic Research, Department of Economics: University of Minnesota.

Hodgson, G. (2000) 'What is the Essence of Institutional Economics?', *Journal of Economic Issues,* Vol. 34:2, pp. 317–329.

Hodgson, G. (2001) *How Economics Forgot History: The Problem of Historical Specificity in Social Science.* London: Routledge.

Houseman, G. (2003) 'The Use and Abuse of Adam Smith', *Challenge,* Vol. 46:3, pp. 108–111.

Howson, S. (2011) *Lionel Robbins.* Cambridge: Cambridge University Press.

Hutchinson, T. (1938) *The Significance and Basic Postulates of Economic Theory.* London: Macmillan.

Jevons, W. (1871) *The Theory of Political Economy.* London: Macmillan.

Kaushik, B. (2011) *Beyond the Invisible Hand: Groundwork for a New Economics.* Princeton, NJ: Princeton University Press.

Kirzner, I. (1976) *The Economic Point of View.* Menlo Park, California: The Institute for Human Studies.

Knight, F. (1934) 'The Nature of Economic Science in Some Recent Discussion', *The American Economic Review,* Vol. 24:2, pp. 225–238.

Knight, F. (1940) 'What Is Truth in Economics?', *Journal of Political Economy,* Vol. 48:1, p. 1–32.

Knight, F. (1950) 'Introduction', in Menger, C. *Principles of Economics.* Glencoe, IL: Free Press, pp. 9–35.

Knight, F. (1951) 'The Role of Principles in Economics and Politics', *American Economic Review,* Vol. 41:1, pp. 1–29.

Koopmans, T. (1957) *Three Essays on the State of Economic Science.* New York: McGraw-Hill.

Koopmans, T. (1964) 'Economic Growth at a Maximal Rate', *Quarterly Journal of Economics,* Vol. 78:3, pp. 355–394.

Lange, O. (1935) 'Marxian Economics and Modern Theory', *Review of Economic Studies,* Vol. 2:3, pp. 189–201.

Lange, O. (1942) 'The Foundation of Welfare Economics', *Econometrica,* Vol. 10:3, pp. 215–228.

Lange, O. (1945) 'The Scope and Method of Economics', *Review of Economic Studies,* Vol. 13:1, pp. 19–32.

Lawson, T. (1997) *Economics and Reality.* London: Routledge.

Lawson, T. (2013) 'What Is This "School" Called Neoclassical Economics?', *Cambridge Journal of Economics*, Vol. 37:5, p. 947–983.

Lazear, E. (2000) 'Economic Imperialism', *Quarterly Journal of Economics*, Vol. 115:1, pp. 99–146.

Leonard, R. (1998) 'Ethics and the Excluded Middle. Karl Menger and the Social Science in Interwar Vienna', *Isis*, Vol. 89:1, pp. 1–26.

Leonard, R. (2010) *Von Neumann, Morgenstern and the Creation of Game Theory*. Cambridge: Cambridge University Press.

Lippman, W. (1937) *The Good Society*. Boston: Little, Brown & Co.

Lipsey, R. (1963) *An Introduction to Positive Economics*. London: Weidenfeld and Nicolson.

Mäki, U. (Ed.) (2009) *The Methodology of Positive Economics: Reflections on the Milton Friedman Legacy*. Cambridge: Cambridge University Press.

Marshall, A. (1890) *Principles of Economics*. London: Macmillan.

Masini, F. (2009) 'Economics and Political Economy in Lionel Robbins' Writings', *Journal of the History of Economic Thought*, Vol. 31:4, pp. 421–436.

McKenzie, L. (1954) 'On Equilibrium in Graham's Model of World Trade and Other Competitive Systems', *Econometrica*, Vol. 22:2, pp. 147–161.

McKenzie, L. (1981) 'The Classical Theorem on the Existence of Competitive Equilibrium', *Econometrica*, Vol. 49:3, pp. 819–841.

Menger, C. [1871] (1981) *Principles of Economics*. New York: New York University Press.

Menger, C. [1883] (1965) *Investigations into the Method of the Social Sciences with Special Reference to Economics*. New York: New York University Press.

Menger, C. (1884) *Die Irrthümer des Historismus in der Deutschen Nationalökonomie*. Vienna: Alfred Hölder.

Menger, C. (1923) *Grundsätze der Volkswirtschaftslehre. Zweite Auflage*. Vienna and Leipzig: Hölder-Pichler-Tempsky A.G.

Menger, C. (1950) *Principles of Economics*. New York: New York University Press.

Menger, K. (1952) 'The Formative Years of Abraham Wald and His Work in Geometry', *Annals of Mathematical Statistics*, Vol. 23:1, pp. 14–20.

Mill, J. S. (1844) *Essays on Some Unsettled Questions of Political Economy*. London: Longmans, Green, Reader, and Dyer.

Milonakis, D. and Fine, B. (2009) *From Political Economy to Economics: Method, the Social and the Historical in the Evolution of Economic Theory*. London: Routledge.

Mirowski, P. (2002) *Machine Dreams: Economics Becomes a Cyborg Science*. Cambridge: Cambridge University Press.

Mirowski, P. (2009) 'Postface', in Mirowski, P. and Plehwe, D. (Eds) *The Road from Mont Pèlerin: the Making of the Neoliberal Thought Collective*. Cambridge, MA: Harvard University Press, pp. 417–455.

Mirowski, P. (2011) 'On the Origins (at Chicago) of Some Species of Neoliberal Evolutionary Economics', in Van Horn, R., Mirowski, P. and Stapleford, T. (Eds) *Building Chicago Economics*. Cambridge: Cambridge University Press, pp. 237–275.

Mirowski, P. (2013) *Never Let a Serious Crisis Go to Waste. How Neoliberalism Survived the Financial Meltdown*. London and New York: Verso.

Mirowski, P. and Van Horn, R. (2009) 'The Rise of the Chicago School of Economics and the Birth of Neoliberalism', in Mirowski, P. and Plehwe, D. (Eds) *The Road from Mont Pèlerin: the Making of the Neoliberal Thought Collective*. Cambridge, MA: Harvard University Press, pp. 139–180.

Mises, L. (1935) 'Economic Calculation in the Socialist Commonwealth', in Hayek, F. (Ed.) *Collectivistic Economic Planning: Critical Studies of the Possibilities of Socialism*. London: Routledge & Kegan Paul, pp. 87–130.

Montesano, A. (2006) 'The Pareto Theory of Ophelimity in Close and Open Cycles', *History of Economic Ideas*, Vol. 14:3, pp. 77–100.

Morgan, M. and Rutherford, M. (1998) 'American Economics: The Character of the Transformation', *History of Political Economy*, Vol. 30: supplement, pp. 1–26.

Morris, C. (1938) 'Foundations of the Theory of Signs', in *International Encyclopedia of Unified Science*. Chicago: University of Chicago Press.

Morris, C. (1946) 'The Significance of Unity of Science Movement', in *International Phenomenological Society*, Vol. 6:4, pp. 508–515.

Morris, C. (1960) 'On the History of the International Encyclopaedia of Unified Science', *Synthese*, Vol. 12:4, pp. 517–521.

von Neumann, J. (1937) 'Uber ein okonomische Gleichungssystem und eine Verall-gemeinerung des Brouwerschen Fixpunktsatzes', in Menger, K. (Ed.) *Ergebnisse eines Mathematischen Kolloquiums*. Leipzig and Vienna: Franz Deuticke, pp. 73–83.

Neurath, O. [1944] (1969) 'Foundations of the Social Sciences', in *International Encyclopedia of Unified Science*, Vol. 2:1. Chicago: University of Chicago Press.

Neurath, O. (1973) *Empiricism and Sociology*. Dordrecht, The Netherlands: Reidel.

Neurath, O. (2004) *Economic Writings. Selection 1904–1945*. Dordrecht, The Netherlands: Kluver Academic Publishers.

Oliver, H. (1960) 'German Neoliberalism', *Quarterly Journal of Economics*, Vol. 74:1, pp. 117–149.

Pareto, V. (1896) *Cours d'Economie Politique*. Geneve: Droz.

Pareto, V. (1900) 'Sunto di alcuni capitoli di un nuovo trattato di economia pura del prof. Pareto', *Giornale degli Economisti*, Vol. 20:3, pp. 216–235; and Vol. 20:6, pp. 511–549, reprinted in Marchionatti, R. (Ed.) *Early Mathematical Economics 1871–1915*. London: Routledge, pp. 79–129.

Pareto, V. [1900] (1982) *Escrits d'Economie Politique Pure*, in Busino, G. (Ed.) *Oeuvre Completes*, Vol. XXVI. Geneve: Droz.

Pareto, V. (1901) 'Sul fenomeno economico, lettera a Benedetto Croce', *Giornale degli Economisti* Vol. 21:8, pp. 139–162, English translation in Wood, J. and McLure, M. (1999) *Vilfredo Pareto: Critical Assessments of Leading Economists*, Vol. 1. London: Routledge, pp. 245–261.

Pareto, V. (1902) 'Sul principio economico', *Giornale degli Economisti* Vol. 22:2, pp. 131–138, English translation in Wood, J. and McLure, M. (1999) *Vilfredo Pareto: Critical Assessments of Leading Economists*, Vol. 1. London: Routledge, pp. 269–274.

Pareto, V. (1906) *Manuale di economia politica con una introduzione alla scienza sociale*. Milano: Società editrice libraria.

Pareto, V. [1916] (1963) *The Mind and Society. A Treatise on General Sociology*. New York: Dover Publications.

Plehwe, D. (2009) 'Introduction', in Mirowski, P. and Plehwe, D. (Eds) *The Road from Mont Pèlerin: the Making of the Neoliberal Thought Collective*. Cambridge MA: Harvard University Press, pp. 1–45.

Plehwe, D. and Walpen, B. (2006) 'Between Network and Complex Organization: The Making of Neoliberal Knowledge and Hegemony', in Walpen, B., Plehwe, D. and

Neunhoffer, G. (Eds) *Neoliberal Hegemony: A Global Critique*. London: Routledge, pp. 27–50.

Polanyi, K. (1922) 'Sozialistische Rechnunslegung', *Archiv für Sozialwissenschaft und Sozialpolitik*, Vol. 49:2, pp. 377–418.

Polanyi, K. (1924) 'Die funktionelle Theorie der Gesellschaft und das Problem der sozialistischen Rechnungslegung (Eine Erwiderung an Prof. Mises und Dr. Felix Weil)', *Archiv für Sozialwissenschaft und Sozialpolitik*, Vol. 52:1, pp. 196–217.

Polanyi, M. (1946) *Science, Faith and Society*. Chicago: University of Chicago Press.

Popper, K. [1936] (1957) *The Poverty of Historicism*. London: Routledge.

Popper, K. (1945) *The Open Society and Its Enemies*. London: Routledge.

Putnam, H. (2002) *The Collapse of the Fact/Value Dichotomy and Other Essays*. Cambridge, MA: Harvard University Press.

Richardson, A. and Uebel, T. (2007) *The Cambridge Companion to Logical Empiricism*. Cambridge: Cambridge University Press.

Robbins, L. (1927) 'Mr. Hawtrey on the Scope of Economics', *Economica*, Vol. 7:20, pp. 172–178.

Robbins, L. [1932] (1945) *An Essay on the Nature and Significance of Economic Science*. London: Macmillan.

Röpke, W. [1942] (1950) *The Social Crisis of Our Time*. London: W. Hodge.

Rutherford, M. (2004) 'Institutional Economics at Columbia University', *History of Political Economy*, Vol. 36:1, pp. 31–75.

Rutherford, M. (2010) 'Chicago Economics and Institutionalism', in Emmett, R. (Ed.) *The Elgar Companion to the Chicago School of Economics*. Cheltenham, UK: Edward Elgar, pp. 25–39.

Rutherford, M. (2011) *The Institutional Movement in American Economics 1918–1947: Science and Social Control*. Cambridge: Cambridge University Press.

Samuels, W., Johnson, M. and Perry, W. (2011) *Erasing the Invisible Hand: Essays on an Elusive and Misused Concept in Economics*. Cambridge, MA: Harvard University Press.

Samuelson, P. (1947) *Foundations of Economic Analysis*. Cambridge, MA: Harvard University Press.

Samuelson, P. (1948) *Economics*. New York: McGraw-Hill.

Schlick, M. (1918) *Allgemeine Erkenntnislehre*. Berlin: Julius Springer.

Schliesser, E. (2010) 'Friedman, Positive Economics, and the Chicago Boys', in Emmett, R. (Ed.) *The Elgar Companion to the Chicago School of Economics*. Cheltenham, UK: Edward Elgar, pp. 175–195.

Schumpeter, J. (1954) *History of Economic Analysis*. Oxford: Oxford University Press.

Scott, S. (2012) *Architectures of Economic Subjectivity. The Philosophical Foundations of the Subject in the History of Economic Thought*. London: Routledge.

Sen, A. (1987) *On Ethics and Economics*. Oxford: Basic Blackwell.

Simons, H. (1934) *A Positive Program for Laissez Faire: Some Proposals for a Liberal Economic Policy*. Chicago: Chicago University Press.

Simons, H. (1948) *Economic Policy for a Free Society*. Chicago: Chicago University Press.

Smith, A. (1776) *An Inquiry into the Nature and the Causes of the Wealth of Nations*. London: Edwin Cannan.

Stadler, F. (2001) *The Vienna Circle. Studies in the Origins, Development, and Influence of Logical Empiricism*. Vienna and New York: Springer.

Stapleford, T. (2011) 'Positive Economics for Democratic Policy', in Van Horn, R., Mirowski, P. and Stapleford, T. (Eds) *Building Chicago Economics.* Cambridge: Cambridge University Press, pp. 3–35.

Stedman Jones, D. (2012) *Masters of the Universe.* Princeton, NJ: Princeton University Press.

Stigler, J. (1937) 'The Economics of Carl Menger', *Journal of Political Economy*, Vol. 45:2, pp. 229–250.

Stigler, J. (1942) *The Theory of Competitive Price.* New York: Macmillan.

Stigler, J. (1961) 'The Economics of Information', *Journal of Political Economy*, Vol. 69:3, pp. 213–225.

Stigler, J. (1984) 'Economics: The Imperial Science?', *The Scandinavian Journal of Economics*, Vol. 86:3, pp. 301–313.

Timms, E. and Hughes, J. (Eds) (2003) *Intellectual Migration and Cultural Transformation. Refugees from National Socialism in the English-Speaking World.* Vienna and New York: Springer.

Tintner, G. (1968) *Methodology of Mathematical Economics and Econometrics.* Chicago: University of Chicago Press.

Tullock, G. (1972) 'Economic Imperialism', in Buchanan, J. and Tollison, R. (Eds) *Theory of Public Choice.* Ann Arbor, MI: Michigan University Press, pp. 317–329.

Turner, R. (2008) *Neo-Liberal Ideology. History, Concepts and Policies.* Edinburgh: Edinburgh University Press.

Van Horn, R. (2007) *The Origins of the Chicago School of Law and Economics.* South Bend, IN: Notre Dame University.

Van Horn, R. (2011) 'Jacob Viner's Critique of Chicago Neoliberalism', in Mirowski, P. and Van Horn, R. (Eds) *Building Chicago Economics.* Cambridge: Cambridge University Press, pp. 279–300.

Van Overtveldt, J. (2007) *The Chicago School: How the University of Chicago Assembled the Thinkers Who Revolutionized Economics and Business.* Chicago: Agate.

Vaughn, K. (1994) *Austrian Economics in America: The Migration of a Tradition.* Cambridge: Cambridge University Press.

Veblen, T. (1919) *The Place of Science in Modern Civilization and Other Essays.* New York: Huebsch.

Wade Hands, D. (2009) 'Effective Tension in Robbins' Economic Methodology', *Economica*, Vol. 76:s1, pp. 831–844.

Wald, A. (1934) 'Uber die eindeutige positive Lösbarkeit der neuen Produktionsgleichungen', in Menger, K. (Ed.) *Ergebenisse eines mathematischen Kolloquiums*, Vol. 6. Leipzig and Vienna: Franz Deutiche, pp. 33–34.

Wald, A. (1936) 'Uber die Produktionsgleichungen der okonomischen Wertlehre', in Menger, K. (Ed.) *Ergebnisse eines mathematischen Kolloquiums*, Vol. 7. Leipzig and Vienna: Franz Deutiche, pp. 1–6.

Wald, A. (1951) 'On Some Systems of Equations in Mathematical Economics', *Econometrica*, Vol. 19:4, pp. 368–403.

Walras, L. (1874) *Éléments d'Economie Politique Pure ou Théorie de la Richesse Sociale.* Lausanne: Imprimerie L. Corbaz & Cie.

Weintraub, R. (1983) 'The Existence of a Competitive Equilibrium: 1930–1954', *Journal of Economic Literature*, Vol. 21:1, pp. 1–39.

Weintraub, R. (1985) *General Equilibrium Analysis: Studies in Appraisal.* Cambridge: Cambridge University Press.

Weintraub, R. (2002) *How Economics Became a Mathematical Science.* Durham, NC: Duke University Press.

Weintraub, R. (2011) 'Retrospectives: Lionel McKenzie and the Proof of the Existence of a Competitive Equilibrium', *Journal of Economic Perspectives*, Vol. 25:2, pp. 199–215.

Williamson, O. (2002) 'The Theory of the Firm as Governance Structure: From Choice to Contract', *Journal of Economic Perspectives*, Vol. 16:3, pp. 171–195.

3 The building of individuals as rational agents

As described in the previous chapter, the genesis of neoclassical economics was a transformation of classical political economy into a scientific discipline, starting from marginalism up to the present mainstream economics, and based on Samuelson's and Friedman's models. While classical political economy was grounded in the old classical liberalism of the nineteenth century, neoclassical economics has been much more related to neoliberalism as it developed in the twentieth century. A similar story happened to the notion of the individual within economic theory: classical political economy was mainly focused on social classes, and individuals were considered free when they operated in a free market and society. In neoclassical economics, individuals have been transformed into rational maximizer agents, especially within the Chicago school of economics (Van Overtveldt 2007; Emmett 2008). Paradoxically, in neoliberalism, individuals gradually lost their freedom: in a neoliberal society, we can attest to a kind of inverse relation between individual rationality and individual liberty. Without the transformation of individuals into rational agents, which occurred in neoclassical economics, the pervasive role of neoliberalism as well as its powerful rhetoric could not be fully understood.

Hence, this chapter will deal with the building of a rational choice theory within the perspective of the relationship between neoclassic economics and neoliberalism. Rational choice theory is the methodological and anthropological pillar of neoclassical economics and is focused on the methodological assumption that individuals are rational economic agents able to rank their preferences, and, given budget constraints, they can choose the optimal solution. Although the formal nature of preferences as well as the concept of rationality have been deeply problematized and criticized within and outside the neoclassical economic theory, these critiques did not reduce the power of that paradigm.

The two theorems of welfare economics are the translation of rational choice theory from an individual level to a social level.[1] They are based on the assumption that a society will develop and increase its welfare by maximizing its social utility function in the same way individuals maximize their expected utility function.[2]

The story of rational choice theory began with Pareto's concept of revealed preferences (Pareto 1896), later developed by Samuelson, who enunciated and revealed preference axioms (Samuelson 1937, 1948, 1950).[3] Rational choice theory finally ended up with the Chicago school of economics, especially with Becker's concepts on the economic approach to human behaviour as the combination of 'maximizing behavior, market equilibrium, and stable preferences' (Becker 1976, 7).[4]

The theoretical *strength* of rational choice theory has been gradually converted into an anthropological dimension through the rise and the development of neoliberalism. On this specific issue, it is important to understand the role of the Austrian School of Economics, and to show the differences between the Austrian School and the Chicago School on the nature of economics as a science, on the meaning of individual freedom, and on the nature of the market. The place of economists, like Mises and Hayek, in this story is not as clear as it appears in most of the secondary literature (see section 2).

As prophetically anticipated by Polanyi's notions of 'disembedded economy' and 'economic fallacy' (Polanyi 1944, 1947a, 1977), the displacement of the neoclassical economic rationality within the realm of government led to its application to the performance of non-economic phenomena, including phenomena related to moral values and justice (see section 3). In Polanyi's vision, what he called the 'great transformation', the role of rational choice theory has become crucial to cope with the complexity of Western neoliberal society (Nell and Errouaki 2013).

Although the definition of neoliberalism is something more sophisticated than the usual – even though complex – set of definitions (see Introduction), it is a very simple practice. Neoliberalism is a specific way to think about the mechanism of rational human choice in an individualistic as well as at an aggregate level. Although the meaning of economic rationality is much more complex than this definition (Herfeld 2013), neoliberalism has simplified and reduced the concept of the individual's rationality into a pure logic of choice: neoliberalism is the use of maximization as the general rule to get any rational outcome in any framework. Choice involves means; ends are given, and they are not questionable. Individuals, social groups, institutions which are able to follow this way of choosing are bound to get the most rational possible result (benefit) and, simultaneously, to get it by the minimization of effort (cost). Any idiosyncratic result from this way of behaving is regarded as a deviation from the standard model.

3.1 Economic rationality and *homo oeconomicus*: from Vienna and Lausanne to Chicago

The act of choosing within a framework of economic rationality, as displaced in neoclassical economics, is a behaviour that allows getting the means in order to satisfy a need in a contest of scarcity. Given the general economic principle according to which there is a trade-off between costs and benefits, individuals are supposed to act in order to get more benefits than costs. This way of behaving implies a commitment to utilitarianism, which gave emphasis to the quantification of pain (cost) and pleasure (benefit) as detailed in Bentham's work (Bentham 1789).

In John Stuart Mill's version of utilitarianism there is room for a qualitative approach (Mill 1871),[5] even though it still based on a vague sense of moral obligation that leads individuals to classify pleasure of a higher and lower degree. In Adam Smith's works on ethics and economics, individual behaviour has been described as a composition of sympathy and self-interest (Smith 1759, 1776). Along with the tradition of classical political economy, in Mill's and Smith's philosophical outlook, ethics still had a fundamental role in describing individual behaviour and social phenomena (Witzum 1997).

Furthermore, it is fundamental to clarify that utilitarianism, that deeply influenced the classical school of political economy, is much more related to hedonism than neoclassical economics, that is based on the assumption of the measurability of revealed preferences.[6] The shift from a hedonistic concept of utility (based on a cardinal measurement) to a method of measurement based on a scale of preferences (ranked in an ordinal way) clarifies the passage from a selfish, but also emphatic, individual within the classical school of economics to an indifferent rational maximizer economic agent within neoclassical economics.

Once again, as happened in the transformation of political economy into economics, the building of individuals as rational agents occurred in marginalism, where rational choice theory is grounded.

Even though still deeply embedded into an Aristotelian principle of causation, Menger's subjectivism opened the gate for rational choice theory. According to Menger, an economic good is determined by four prerequisites, which must be simultaneously present: a human need; a causal connection between the thing and the satisfaction of a human need; human knowledge of this causal connection; and the ability to get the thing which is able to satisfy the need (Menger 1871). The first prerequisite is an impulse, a natural propulsion to feel something missing. Hence, it has nothing to do with the ability of humans to get anything to satisfy it. The other three prerequisites implicitly or explicitly cope with human rationality: individuals understand the nexus between causes (needs/ends) and effects (the search for means to satisfy needs), and they are able to choose how to get a proper mean to satisfy the initial impulse (need).[7]

Menger's model is dynamic and takes account of time and ignorance, thus follows Austrian tradition (Aimar 2014; Rizzo 2015; O'Driscoll and Rizzo 2015). Walras' *homo oeconomicus* is the anti-Menger individual: in fact in Walras, *homo oeconomicus* operates in a free market, where knowledge and information are complete and tastes are data. Focusing on the nature of the Walrasian economic agent, it becomes evident how much the idea that Walras' system can be regarded as a formalization of Adam Smith's invisible hand has been misleading:

> Adam Smith exemplified the liberal tradition in his lively concern with the self-interest pursuit of goals and its ramifications in economic theory. By contrast, Walras had defined the pure science to which he aspired as

the study of relationship between *things*, not *people* and sought, with notable success, to eliminate human relationships from his purview.

(Bowles and Gintis 1993, 84)

Furthermore, in Adam Smith there is no trace of individual rationality as it has been conceived in neoclassic economics.

> Smith had a firm grasp of the way in which the market mechanism is capable of coordinating the independent decisions of buyers and sellers, but anything so fundamental as the functional relationship of demand and price escaped him. It never occurred to him that it was possible to demonstrate precisely in what sense a decentralized economy produces optimum results and when Walras and Pareto worked out the logic of Smith's convictions a hundred years later, their demonstration of the optimal properties of a competitive regime bore no resemblance to Adam Smith's view about the workings of 'the invisible hand'.
>
> (Blaug [1961] 1997, 3)

Edgeworth's curves of contracts merged the marginalistic subjectivism with Jevons' utilitarianism (Jevons 1871), into a formal framework that will be later developed by Pareto (Edgeworth 1881; Pareto 1896, 1906), even though Edgeworth's model of human behaviour is much more hedonistic than Pareto's. Edgeworth started the so-called dehumanization of political economy (Heilbroner 1953): in Edgeworth's words, *homo oeconomicus* is a 'pleasure machine', and mathematical physics is able to rationalize human behaviour (Edgeworth 1889).

Although supporters of a different measurement of utility, both Edgeworth and Pareto shared the use of individual preferences as the only possible starting point to describe the dynamics of consumers' demand.[8] Pareto's curves of indifferences made the model of the individual's representation of utility very persuasive and much less naïve than in Edgeworth's hedonism. In fact, Pareto assumed that economic choice could be described by pure economics without any concern about pleasure and pain (Pareto 1900). In Pareto's *Manuale*, the Italian economist clearly defined the principle of maximization under constraint as the sole paradigm to describe economic rationality (Ingrao and Israel 1990; Zouboulakis 2014). He introduced a definition of economic rationality able to discard any link to psychology. Pareto's anti-psychological perspective paved the way for Robbins' definition of economics (Blaug 1961; Maas 2009), to Hicks' consumer theory and axioms of general equilibrium theory, and to Samuelson's theory of revealed preferences (Zouboulakis 2014). In this passage, discarding ethics has been completed: according to Robbins, it is not possible to compare individual utilities, because this operation implies the introduction of value judgments, and value judgments are outside the realm of economics as a science.

The process proceeds along the following steps: given a trade-off between two alternatives, given preferences, and the presence of a budget constraint, the rationality of economic choice will get a Pareto optimal solution. Emotions, irrational behaviour, bias and mistakes are regarded as deviations from standard economic rationality mainly because of their psychological nature.

Once having properly ranked his indifference curves, *homo economicus'* behaviour leads the market to general economic equilibrium. The microfoundation of economic theory has been completed in the building of the paradigm of economic rationality as described above, and as it is described in Econ 101: microeconomics manuals started from individual rationality to proceed towards a scientific explanation of economic phenomena and the functioning of the market system.

A further step towards a notion of an 'imperialistic economic rationality' was taken in Chicago in the late 1960s, when Becker got home from Columbia University,[9] and in the 1970s, where Chicagoan economists extended economic rationality, intended as the process of maximization under certain constraint, outside economic choice (Becker 1976; Stigler and Becker 1977). Economic rationality gradually became the only possible tool for explaining human choice in any contest:

> the ambitiousness of our agenda deserves emphasis; we are proposing the hypothesis that widespread and/or persistent human behaviour can be explained by a generalized calculus of utility-maximizing behaviour, without introducing the qualification 'tastes remaining the same'. It is a thesis that does not permit of direct proof because it is an assertion about the world, not a proposition in logic.
>
> (Stigler and Becker 1977, 76)

It is worthy to remember that Gary Becker was awarded the Nobel Prize in Economics in 1992 'for having extended the domain of microeconomic analysis to a wide range of human behavior and interaction, including nonmarket behavior' (Becker 2014). As Becker stated: 'now everyone more or less agrees that rational behavior simply implies consistent maximization of a well-ordered function, such as a utility or profit function' (Becker 1962, 1) and, given some incentives, even irrational agents often react in a rational way.

Becker's efforts to define 'economic approach [as a way] to understand *all human behavior* in a variety of contexts and situations' [emphasis added] (Becker 1976, 1) started with his studies on human capital (Becker 1964) and his reformulation of the theory of consumer behaviour (Becker 1965; Michael and Becker 1973).

Becker's definition of human capital is focused on the study of how an individual's education can be regarded as an investment incentive similar to a firm's investments in input and machinery; human capital corresponds to any stock of knowledge and skills individuals have in their life; human capital massively influences an individual's productivity.[10]

Becker's new theory of consumer behaviour is rooted in his theory of allocation of time between different activities and its empirical applications: when earnings, income, prices and the productivity of working and consuming change, time is reallocated and this involves a reallocation of demanded goods and supplied commodities (Becker 1965). In the traditional consumer theory of choice, consumer behaviour maximizes a utility function, given income, tastes and prices. The weakness of this model is its scarce range of applicability; hence, Becker proposed an alternative theory, i.e. the household production function approach that would open the gate of economic approach to non-economic fields. The household production function:

> systematically and symmetrically incorporates numerous constraints on the household's behavior, strengthens the reliance on changes in income and prices as explanations of observed behavior, and correspondingly reduces the reliance on differences in tastes and preferences (...) the new approach *expands the applicability of the economist's theory of choice into the non-market sector* and hence makes the theory more useful in analyzing household behavior in its many dimensions [emphasis added].
>
> (Michael and Becker 1973, 394)

After having discarded as useless and vague the definition of economics in terms of the allocation of material good and welfare, Becker recognized in Robbins' definition of economics (Robbins 1932), the most general of all concepts, even though it is too broad and often it excludes nonmarket behaviour. In spelling out the main attributes of the economic approach, Becker firmly wanted to present its 'uniquely' power to 'integrate a wide range of human behavior' (Becker 1976, 5).

As previously recalled, Becker considered 'the combined assumptions of maximizing behavior, market equilibrium, and stable preferences' as 'the heart of economic approach' (Becker 1976, 5). It can be applied to any human decision and any human behaviour, such as health,[11] marriage,[12] education,[13] not to mention discrimination,[14] democracy,[15] legislation,[16] and fertility.[17] In Becker's words, the economic approach provided a 'unified' and 'comprehensive framework' to the understanding of human behaviour (Becker 1976, 14), even though some noneconomic variables can affect human behaviour under duress (as was stressed by Friedman and Samuelson when they compared individuals to physical particles) (see Chapter 2). This is like the renewal of the paradigm of 'unified science', based on the special *hybris* that is a typical feature of any philosophical reductionism or determinism, and that is common to other social sciences, like sociology (Becker himself pointed out some similarities between his approach and Robert Merton's) and psychoanalysis.

Economists in Chicago, from Stigler and Knight to Friedman and Becker, have been the pillars of mainstream economics, and consequently of neoliberalism (Emmett 2010; Mirowski 2013). Neoliberalism is the practical application of Becker's reductionism to any aspect of human society, based neither on the idea of market equilibrium (De Martino 2000), nor on the notion of capitalistic imperialism (Petras and Veltmeyer 2013; McGuian 2016), but mostly on the concept of economic rationality as it has been developed in neoclassical economics. This specific point is fundamental to understand the distance between the Chicago and Austrian schools of economics in developing neoliberalism.

3.2 The theoretical and methodological distance between Vienna and Chicago

The Austrian and the Chicago schools of economics have been regarded as similar in their conception of marketplace and both were involved in neoliberalism (Harvey 2005; Stedman Jones 2012; Schmidt and Thatcher 2013), especially outside economists (Barnett 2010).[18] Yet, from a theoretical point of view as well as from a methodological perspective, there are many differences between Austrians (mainly Menger, Mises, and Hayek) and Chicagoans (mainly Stigler, Friedman, and Becker).[19] Moreover, the distance between Vienna and Chicago increases when we are reminded that there are substantial dissimilarities between the old classical liberalism and neoliberalism.

The main source of the distance between the Austrian school of economics and the Chicago school of economics is in their origins. Austrians are the off-spring of Menger, Schumpeter, Mises and Hayek;[20] Chicagoans are the heirs of the Walras-Pareto-Hicks-Samuelson tradition. As Streissler wrote:

> [H]ardly an author can be found, not even Keynes himself, who is so much the exact antipode of Milton Friedman in every part of that economist's theoretical vision as Carl Menger; and this in spite of the fact that Menger and Friedman were of the same political persuasion, which goes to show that *Weltanschauung* and scientific vision need hardly be related at all.
>
> (Streissler, 1973, 164)

The Austrian school of economics is embedded in the tradition of classical political economy, which was part of the tradition of classical liberalism; the Chicago school of economics is the most persuasive result of the transformation of the discipline into a formalized discipline, namely neoclassic economics.

The foremost differences between the Austrian school of economics and the Chicago school of economics are the status of the discipline; the nature of individuals as rational agents; the nature of social performance and the market; finally, the role of individual freedom in a liberal and neoliberal society.[21]

The status of the discipline

In defining economics as a theoretical science whose aim is 'investigating and describing general economic phenomena' (Menger [1883] 1985, 39), Menger claimed that this particular meaning of economics, the 'scientific' aspect of the discipline, is only a part of the general meaning of the discipline itself. In fact, besides theoretical economy, there are historical sciences (history and statistics) as well as practical sciences of national economy (economic policy and science of finance). Those three different aspects (general, historical and practical) constitute the status of the discipline. In his methodological work, Menger stressed the fact that it was urgent to develop the scientific aspect of political economy (Menger [1883] 1985).[22] He defined economic 'exact' laws, which enable us to establish social knowledge, and empirical regularities that enable us to explain social order. From Menger's spontaneous order was derived the idea of catallaxy within a process of market-coordination, in opposition to the idea of economics within a framework of general economic equilibrium (Barry 1982; Oakeshott 2006). The meaning of the word catallaxy, which derives from ancient Greek, is a way to relate individuals within a community where interpersonal relationships spontaneously evolve toward a mutual order (Mises 1949; Hayek 1978).

This is very different from the neoclassic idea of formal economics as it was developed in Chicago, and that Hayek had defined as the pure logic of choice. Hayek defined it as 'a set of self-evident propositions which, like mathematics or geometry, are subject to no other test but internal consistency' (Hayek 1937, 34); and it reduces 'the economic problem of a society [to] merely a problem of how to allocate "given resources"' (Hayek 1948, 77).

The logic of pure choice reached its apogee in the Chicago school of economics, where the Walras-Pareto tradition,[23] Weber's notion of science,[24] Robbins' definition of economics, Samuelson's axiomatization, and Friedman's definition of economic science, converged.

The notion of economics as a positive science, supported by the Chicagoans, should have freed economics from any political involvement; however, the interconnection between neoclassic economics and the neoliberalism doctrine reversed this situation. The Chicagoans were much more politically oriented than the Austrians.[25] The historically well-known aversion for Marxism in Mises and Hayek was a consequence of the nature of political economy, not the result of a formalized demonstration based on an unrealistic assumption made possible by the 'scientific' nature of economics.[26] Furthermore, Hayek was suspicious of economics as a positive science. As he said, '[what] I most regret [has been] not having returned to a criticism of Keynes' treatise, but it is as much true of not having criticized Milton [Friedman]'s *Positive Economics,* which in a way is quite as dangerous a book' (Hayek 1994, 145).

On the individual's rationality

Menger first introduced the role of an individual's will in order to explain the relation between human needs and economic goods. The four prerequisites for the definition of an economic good are strictly individualistic: an economic good *per se* does not exist; it depends on whether it is useful to satisfy an individual need. The role of scarcity, which can be regarded as an objective trait of an economic good, has actually a second order value. Given the huge number of individuals in a market place, and assuming they have more or less the same needs to satisfy, in a homogeneous context, scarcity will determine prices. Menger's definition of economic choice is strictly based on the relationship between individual needs and the effective amount of economic goods that nature and the market can actually provide. In Menger, at the very first level, individuals are driven by their biological impulses (Menger 1923). The dynamic of an individual's behaviour, as well as the evolution of human associations and institutions, in Menger's work, is very complex.

The dynamics of individuals is central in Schumpeter's work, too (Schumpeter [1908] 1980). Schumpeter's entrepreneur and his creativity are the primary factors for social development and economic growth. Entrepreneurs are risk-prone; they are driven by instincts and intuition; they like to challenge the market by introducing innovations. In Mises' thought, praxeology concerns individual dynamics as well (Mises 1949, 1960).

Hayek's methodological individualism sums up the previous contributions of his predecessors. Individuals make decisions because they have plans; although their knowledge is limited and information available is restricted and incomplete, they follow their expectations and are able to achieve their goals by choosing amongst available means (Hayek 1937, 1948, 1967).

According to Hayek, the market enable us to understand:

> how the spontaneous interaction of a number of people, each possessing only bits of knowledge, brings about a state of affairs in which prices correspond to costs, etc., and which could be brought about by deliberate direction only by somebody who possessed the combined knowledge of all those individuals.
>
> (Hayek 1937, 39)

As shown in the previous chapter, from the Chicagoans' (neoclassical) perspective, individuals are rational economic agents who are able to maximize an expected utility function; in a framework of perfect competition, they are able to optimize their behaviour. Given a model of full knowledge and complete information, their rationality is a tool that allows them to calculate benefits and costs in order to make the optimal choice. The prerequisite to achieve an optimal choice is the fact that individual preferences can be ranked in a special way. As Stigler claimed, quoting Pareto: 'the utility theory allowed a unified explanation of behaviour: everyone was a utility-maximizer, and all economic problems became simply problems of tastes and obstacles (so, Pareto)' (Stigler 1972, 578).

The Chicagoan economic agent and the Austrian individual are not described starting from the same kind of rationality. The neoclassical model of individuals as homogeneous agents is a holistic procedure to describe the realm of economic choice. The neoclassical economic agent is a computational agent: no matter whether human rationality is full or bounded, agents are able to 'construct' the best way to make rational choices. This is reminiscent of what Hayek named 'false individualism', a form of individualism based on the Cartesian rationalism: a form of *hybris* according to which humans have the ability to plan their achievements in the private sphere as well as in public life (Hayek 1948). Hayek's definition of true individualism is based on

> the contention that, by tracing the combined effects of individual actions, we discover that many institutions on which human achievements rest

have arisen and are functioning without a designing and directed mind,
[they] are result[s] of human action but not the result[s] of human design.
(Hayek 1948, 6–7)

True individualism can also be recognized in Mises' praxeology (the science
of 'human action as purposeful behaviour'), who clarified that 'action is not
simply given preference', because 'action always involves both taking and
renunciation', and it is a 'real thing always rational' (Mises 1949, 12).

Social performance and role of the market

The Chicagoans' economics enables what Hayek called 'Cartesian rationalism'
to be shifted from an individual perspective to a social dimension. The theoretical meaning in the concept of a social utility function as well as the two
theorems of welfare economics represent that translation into social terms of
the neoclassical model of an individual's behaviour. The result in terms of
society is the ability to reach a general economic equilibrium: this model is
static, and does not allow a real description of how societies work.

With the Austrian school, the social performance is not determined by the
rationality of individuals as neoclassicals intend it; on the contrary, social
performance is regarded as a spontaneous order, determined by free individuals whose rationality is much closer to a reasonable common sense than to
a computational planning tool. Society results as a complex system where
order can be only described, not fully explained, and, especially in Hayek's
society, the dynamics of society is very similar to a complex theory founded
either on the concept of emergence (Lavoie 1989; Rosser 2012) or on an evolutionary approach (Hodgson and Knudsen 2010; Lewis 2012). This perspective
allows the inclusion of a historical framework, sociological determinants, and
path dependence within the economic model of market society.

As Lavoie wrote, subjectivism and spontaneous order were the two related
principles that defined the Austrian way of describing how the process of
communication makes social performance ordered (Lavoie 1990); nothing is
spontaneous in the neoclassical model of describing social performance, and
subjectivism is reduced to a mere ability to maximize a utility function.

As Kirzner pointed out, it is necessary to distinguish the principle of maximization (the objective allocation of scarce means among competing ends)[27] from
the principle of economizing (a subjective choice based on the scarcity of means
that will be later defined by Robbins).[28] They are both neoclassical and formalized; while the Austrian principle of economy is 'acting in the praxeological
sense: [it] consists in selecting a pattern of behaviour designed to further the actor's
purposes' (Kirzner 1960, 161). They also allow society to avoid violence in order
to achieve the individual's aims, as Schumpeter claimed (Schumpeter 1942). The
market is able to coordinate individual choice in a framework where there is
uncertainty and heterogeneity of intents. Society as a whole benefits from the role
of the market as an institution. Development is guaranteed by innovations and

growth is an effect of developments. It is also one of the most ancient social institutions able to make connections amongst individuals possible. From a cultural point of view, social, economic and civil emancipation of people is a consequence of this dynamic. The more freedom there is in the market, the more proficient is the outcome of these connections.

This approach is a typically Austrian description of market dynamics in the context of uncertainty (Borch 1973). The central role of uncertainty to describe social performance in a realistic framework was introduced first by Menger in his *Principles* (Menger 1871). It is also present in Böhm-Bawerk's idea of uncertain income expected in future and the role of entrepreneurship (Böhm-Bawerk [1881] 1962; McCaffrey and Salerno 2014), as well in Schumpeter's process of innovation (Schumpeter 1934), in Mises' sense of contingency in human action (Mises 1957), and above all in Hayek's theory of knowledge (Hayek [1945] 1948).

In neoclassical economics, the market is similar to a Cartesian plan that makes exchange possible in order to achieve an individual's goals. In the neoclassical approach, there is no room for uncertainty. Market[s] work[s] in an efficient way because of the rationality of economic agents; because of perfect knowledge and complete information available; and because of perfect competition. The possibility to calculate benefits and costs at margin allows economic agents to choose by following the principle of efficiency. Society is formed by this principle: Becker's 'rationality at the market level', which includes irrational behaviour, properly describes the market's performance under the theory of individual rational choice (Becker 1962).

In this passage, from the nature of human rationality to the nature of market, the role of neoliberalism emerges. Society as a whole, which includes every sphere of public and private life, not only economic exchange, is shaped by efficiency: policy, culture and organizations are ruled according to this principle.

Classical liberalism versus neoliberalism

Given the differences listed above between the Austrian and Chicago schools of economics, is it possible to maintain that Austrians could be regarded as classical liberals and Chicagoans could be considered as neoliberals? To answer this question it is fundamental not just to think about laissez-faire policy, but also to consider that Austrians and Chicagoans are supporters of a different idea of freedom. Furthermore, it is fundamental to consider that classical liberalism and neoliberalism present some similarities (they both originated from liberalism in the age of the Enlightenment, a broad cultural movement challenging the power of tradition and emphasizing individualism), as well as many differences.

Classical liberalism was grounded on the principle that freedom was the most important value for individuals, and consequently, for a society as a whole. Following the Scottish moral sense of tradition (Shaftesbury 1737–38; Hume [1739–1740] 1896; Hutcheson 1755), freedom in classical liberalism was based on moral assumptions: i.e. it was grounded on ethics. Neoliberalism is much more focused on the opposite tradition of moral rationalism, in conjunction with the development about economic rationality, or instrumental rationality (as in Weber's thought) within neoclassic economics, based on efficiency (Wright 2003). Efficiency has gradually become the benchmark for liberty. Efficiency enables individuals to behave in a rational way, and, consequently, allows shaping social performance in a rational way.

Hayek defined this approach as 'constructivist rationalism, a conception which leads to the treatment of all cultural phenomena as the product of deliberate design, and on the belief that it is both possible and desirable to reconstruct all grown institutions in accordance with a preconceived plan', and against this approach, Hayek defined true liberalism as 'based on an evolutionary interpretation of all phenomena of culture and mind and on an insight into the limits of the powers of the human reason' (Hayek [1966] 1967, 161).

In the Austrians' work, especially Hayek's and Mises', the market makes individuals free in order to enable them to mutually and spontaneously coordinate their plans: a society shaped like this is a free society in a classical liberal way. As Mises wrote: 'human society is an association of persons for cooperative action. As against the isolated actions of individuals, cooperative actions on the basis of the principle of the division of labor, as the advantage of a greater productivity' (Mises [1927] 1985, 19).

Knight's position in the mid-1930s was still closer to an Austrian approach than to a neoclassical model. He wrote:

> the substance of society, in so far as it is free or moral, is the body of such rules made by human beings for their own association, with a view either to making their activity itself as interesting and satisfying as possible, or else to fulfilling what they conceive to be their 'task' as human beings. Economic efficiency and economic liberty are beyond doubt vitally important in this connection; but their relations to the project and to each other are not of the sort pictured in a mathematical function to be maximized.
>
> (Knight 1934, 237)

The later development within the Chicago school went beyond Knight's position, though.

An efficient society, based on the principle of maximization, as developed by Chicagoans from Stigler-Friedman to Becker, is much closer to a designed model of society rather than a model of spontaneous order. Neoliberalism, oriented towards the Chicagoans' approach, promotes efficiency in a neutral framework rather than freedom in a moral structure.[29] Also on this specific point, the Austrians, especially Mises and Hayek, and the Chicagoans diverged.

According to Mises, 'the observance of the moral law is in the ultimate interest of every individual, because everyone benefits from the preservation of social cooperation. (...) Liberalism is not anarchism, nor has it anything whatsoever to do with anarchism' (Mises [1927] 1985, 36–37). In Mises' definition, liberalism is seen as:

> a political doctrine, not a theory, developed by praxeology and especially economics to define problems of human action within society (...). As a political doctrine, liberalism *is not neutral with regard to values and the ultimate ends sought by action*. It assumes that all men or at least the majority of people are intent upon attaining certain goals. It gives them information about the means suitable to the realization of their plans [emphasis added].
>
> (Mises 1949, 154)

In Hayek's words: 'the order of the market rests not on common purposes but on reciprocity, that is on the reconciliation of different purposes for the mutual benefit of the participants (...) we may call such a free society a *nomocratic* (law-governed) as distinguished from an unfree *teleocratic* (purposed-governed) social order' (Hayek 1967, 163).[30]

The Chicagoans went beyond the respectful separation between science and freedom: Stigler identified the ultimate meaning of freedom with 'a wider domain of choice' due to the human ability to maximize their utility against Hayek's definition of liberty (Hayek 1960) as 'freedom from coercion by other men' (Stigler 1978, 214).[31]

Hayek's expression 'teleocratic' (a purposed-governed) social order perfectly fits Friedman's definition of neoliberalism, as described in the previous chapter, 'a new faith, (...) supposed to act in order to create conditions for making laissez faire effective' (Friedman 1951, 90).[32]

Neoliberalism in Friedman's purpose was a specific political programme, and his agenda for a neoliberal policy looks more like what Hayek would be later referring to as a form of legislation (the deliberate making of law) rather than the rule of law (an asset of enforced rules of conduct), on which spontaneous order is rooted (Hayek 1973, 1976, 1979).

Table 3.1 Classical liberalism *versus* neoliberalism

	Classical liberalism	*Neoliberalism*
Individuals	Citizens and laymen whose freedom is their maximum value, both in private and public life.	Economic agents with an expected utility function to maximize in a framework of scarcity of means and given preferences.
Institutions	Systems able to integrate individual choice. Subjected to historical and cultural changes.	Systems able to integrate individual choice, in a static performance of efficiency.

Table 3.2 Austrian *versus* Chicago school of economics

	Austrians	*Chicagoans*
Economics	Human discipline/social science with general regularities (laws).	Formalized science into a model of physics: mathematical economics and econometrics.
Market	Social institution for the coordination of individual plans through a spontaneous order.	Social institution where general economic equilibrium is reached through an optimal allocation of resources.
Individuals	Free and socially connected; they have limited information and dispersed knowledge.	Maximizer economic agents able to act as if they would have complete information and perfect knowledge in any sphere of their life.
Society	A combination of individuals whose actions are coordinated in a spontaneous way under the rule of law.	A model of coexistence based on the principle of efficiency as the best performance.
Freedom	Includes moral values.	Intended as the application of efficiency.

3.3 Karl Polanyi's critique of neoliberalism

In the 'Foreword' of a recent reprint of Karl Polanyi's masterpiece, *The Great Transformation*, Stiglitz claimed that Polanyi had been a forerunner of the opposition to the Washington consensus, 'the modern-day version of the liberal 'orthodoxy'' (Stiglitz 2001, xii). In fact, between the mid-1940s and 1960s, Polanyi had anticipated some features of the neoliberal society,[33] such as the transformation of the classical political economy into a formal economics (Polanyi 1944, 1957, 1977), the *hybris* of economic rationality in neoclassic economics (Polanyi 1947a, 1977), and the annihilation of individual freedom in a future efficient-shaped society (Polanyi 1944).

What Polanyi defined a 'complex society' is to be intended as the present neoliberal society, and his concern about the features of that society sounds like a kind of prophecy.

In his writings, Polanyi has introduced some social and historical categories to describe the complex situation as well as the radical changes that were occurring in the interwar Western society. Polanyi's idea of the 'great transformation' (the collapse of liberal Western society after the First World War) is a consequence of the emergence of what he defined as a disembedded economy (the idea that economy has no relation with politics and ethics).[34] The notion of a disembedded economy is rooted in what Polanyi called an economistic fallacy (the logical and fallacious identification of economic phenomena with market phenomena). This cultural transformation was made possible by the emergence of economic determinism, of which two components were economic rationalism (the logical and mental procedures of the human beings that lived and worked in a market society, i.e. the equivalent of instrumental rationality) and economic solipsism, i.e. the distance between the economic field and the political one (Polanyi 1977).

According to Polanyi, the combination and the following development of these features would lead to a new complex society that might seem to be much more efficient, but also much less free (Polanyi 1944, 1957 unpublished, 1977).

On the formalist meaning of economics. Polanyi versus Robbins

Polanyi claimed that the transformation of classical political economy into economics originated a form of disembedded economy, i.e. the combination of a situation in which the economic sphere is regarded as completely autonomous, and the belief is of a market overtly capable of self-regulation. Polanyi called *economic determinism* the acceptance of the idea that the market is a self-regulated institution led by perfect rational agents (Polanyi 1947a). Economic determinism is based on an *economic fallacy*,[35] the mistaken identification between human economy and market economy, and between economic phenomena and market phenomena (Polanyi 1977). According to Polanyi, the notion of economic determinism emerged in Robbin's *Essay*. In Polanyi's words: 'from Hume and Spencer to Frank H. Knight and Northrop, social thought suffered from this limitation wherever it touched on the economy. Lionel Robbins' E*ssay* (1932), though useful to economists, fatefully distorted the problem' (Polanyi 1953, 4).[36] This mystification changed the nature of the market itself: no longer seen as a historical phenomenon, it became a *natural* phenomenon, a self-regulated system, or a 'distortion in thought' (Block and Somers 2014, 59). This is the meaning of what Polanyi has defined the *economistic transformation* of isolated markets into a self-regulating *system* of market. Furthermore, this transformation was the 'crucial step' for the alteration of labour and land as money into fictitious commodities (Polanyi 1977).[37]

According to Polanyi, the economistic transformation happened because neoclassical economists like Robbins defined the discipline around the sole formal meaning of 'economic', and they set completely apart the substantive meaning of the word 'economic' (Polanyi 1957).[38]

The formal meaning derives from the logical character of the means-end relationship *á la* Robbins. It implies a situation in which there are scales of given preferences and a scarce amount of goods of definite utility. In such a system, *equilibrium* could be reached either in a liberal system (in which the scales of preference may be given by the needs and wants of an individual) or in a collectivist society (in which those scales of preference are determined by the Supreme Economic Council). Polanyi claimed that during the process of transformation of economics into a science, 'economists felt so safe within the confines of such a purely theoretical market system that they only grudgingly conceded to nations more than a nuisance value' (Polanyi 1953, 15). According to Polanyi, this process created a false identification between (scientific) economics and capitalism, but this identification was a mystification. In fact, political economy is a broader concept than neoclassical economics; as with capitalistic economy, which is not a general form of economy, it has been historically determined by the special organization of man's livelihood that took shape in Western society over the past two centuries. Both capitalism and neoclassical economics 'consisted in a system of price-making markets [in which] the rules of choice happened to be singularly applicable' (Polanyi 1953, 18).

On the other side, according to Polanyi, the substantive meaning of economic derives from 'man's dependence for his livelihood upon nature and his fellows. It refers to the interchange with his natural and social environment' (Polanyi 1957, 243). It does not involve the necessity of a choice induced by the limiting effect of the scarcity of means. It enables the building of a model of the economy 'as an instituted process of interaction serving the satisfaction of material wants' (Polanyi 1953, 31), i.e. a process that 'provide[s] material means in society' (Polanyi 1953, 34). This two-tier process consists of the interaction between man and his surroundings and the institutionalization of that process (Polanyi 1977).[39]

Polanyi explicitly asserted the supremacy of the substantive meaning over the formal one from a theoretical point of view: 'only the substantive meaning of economic can yield the basic concepts that are required by the social sciences for an investigation of the empirical economies of the past and the present' (Polanyi 1953, 2). Furthermore, the supremacy of the substantive meaning over the formal one is claimed also from a moral point of view: only the substantive economy enables individuals to act in a cooperative way. As Polanyi clearly claimed, his theory of society was deeply influenced by Aristotle's notions of 'household' and 'community' (Aristotle 1992; Polanyi 1957, 1977). Polanyi wrote:

> Aristotle taught that to every kind of community (*koinōnia*) there corresponded a kind of good-will (*philía*) amongst its members which expressed itself in reciprocity (*antipeponthos*) (...) In our terms this implies a tendency in the larger communities to develop a multiple symmetry in regard to which reciprocative behaviour may develop in the subordinate communities.
>
> (Polanyi 1957; 253)[40]

The central role of reciprocity in the economic relationship, as well as the use of Aristotle's analysis as a starting point to discuss the nature of the economy, led Polanyi to describe substantive economic behaviour in a way that was much closer to Hayek's perspective[41] as well as to his brother's (Polanyi 1951),[42] and in opposition to the neoclassical outlook, as in Becker's economic approach (see Chapter 2).

On economic rationality. Polanyi versus Becker

In order to describe the behaviour of neoclassical economic agents, Polanyi introduced the notion of *economistic rationalism* (Polanyi 1957; 1977). According to Polanyi, however, economic rationalism is a myth: the complexity of social interrelations amongst individuals does not allow a simple mechanism of choice like the one described in neoclassical economics. Economic rationalism implies that an individual's behaviour is a mechanism of maximization of an expected utility function in a context of scarcity of means and given ends. Polanyi always underlined that the way of seeing individuals as economic agents in neoclassic economics had reached a dominant position, and it is a crucial aspect of economics imperialism (Khalil 1996), in opposition to the real nature of human beings that is to be socially embedded individuals (Beckert 2003; Davis 2015).

Although in Polanyi's writings there are no direct references to Becker, his definition of economic rationalism, i.e. the logical and mental procedures of the human beings that lived and worked in a market society is very similar to the definition of economic rationality *á la* Becker. Becker defined the economic approach as:

> a comprehensive one that is applicable to all human behaviour, be it behaviour involving money prices or imputed shadow prices, repeated or infrequent decisions, large or minor decisions, emotional or mechanical ends, rich or poor persons, men or women, adults, or children, brilliant or stupid persons, patients or therapists, businessmen or politicians, teachers or students.
>
> (Becker, 1976, 8)

Polanyi was the strongest opponent of the reduction of individuals to rational economic agents in this way.

The transformation of individuals into rational agents has been applied to every single aspect of individual private lives as well as to the public aspect of societies:

> rational action, as such, is the relating of ends to means; economic rationality, specifically, assumes means to be scarce. But human society involves more than that. What should be the end of man, and how should he choose his means? Economic rationalism, in the strict sense, has no answer to these questions, for they imply motivations and valuations of a moral and practical order that go beyond the logically irresistible, but otherwise empty, exhortation to be 'economical'.
>
> (Polanyi 1977, 13)

Economic rationalism had gradually denied the true nature of humankind through the camouflage of an irresistible logic.[43] In fact, according to Polanyi, the main reason for the successful performance of economic rationalism is the fact that it has been regarded as natural. The reduction of labour into a *fictitious* commodity reinforced this process,[44] but:

> the social philosophy erected on such foundations [economic rationalism and fictitious commodities] was as radical as it was fantastic. To atomize society and make every individual atom behave according to the principles of economic rationalism would, in a sense, place the whole of human

existence, with all its depth and wealth, in the frame of reference of the market. This, of course, would not really do – individuals have personalities and society has a history.

(Polanyi 1977, 14)

Neoliberalism is to be intended as the final and complete application of Polanyi's definitions of the formal meaning of economic and economic rationalism (Cangiani 2012). One of the worst consequences of this process has been the gradual lack of control of individual liberty, which has revealed the counterrevolutionary aspect of neoliberalism in opposition to the emancipatory aspect of the old classical liberalism.

On individual freedom. Polanyi versus neoliberalism

Polanyi's critique on economic rationalism is directly linked with the discourse on individualism that he introduced in the 1930s, when he explained his interpretation about the origin of the fascism in Europe (Polanyi 1935, 1937). In his definition of fascism, Polanyi included the Italian dictatorship, German Nazism and Soviet bolshevism.[45] According to Polanyi, fascism was intended to be 'the most virulent result of industrial capitalism' in spite of the fact that for a few decades (from the general introduction of universal suffrage to the First World War), capitalism and democracy had been flourishing at the same time. The dramatic economic and social crisis, which followed the end of the First World War, revealed the weakness of capitalism. Democracy was sacrificed in order to preserve the economic order of capitalism, and fascism arose as a new political movement: either gradually (Italy) or brutally quickly (Germany and in Russia), either legally (Italy and Germany) or after a revolution (Russia), fascism destroyed the democratic system.

Polanyi considered fascism as the natural development of capitalism. When the economic system started to collapse, fascism emerged as the political consequence of the presence of a disembedded economy during the late phase of capitalism. Politics was reduced to slavery by economy and the democratic system was dramatically changed into a mere tool to preserve capitalism. This happened in Italy, spain and Germany: fascist dictators were colluding with big capitalists, and liberal democracy was sacrificed in order to defend the capitalistic society.

The same process, in Polanyi's interpretation, occurred in the Soviet Union: Stalinism was a form of fascism which destroyed democracy in order to save a centralized form of economy, based on the same theoretical principle (formal economics) and on the same anthropological dimension (economic rationalism) (Polanyi 1937). Furthermore, according to Polanyi, fascist systems shared the same concept of society, intended as a 'totality': every aspect of human life has to be ruled and subjugated to the leadership, and individuals are just regarded as servants of the state, and individual freedom is no longer a value *per se* (Polanyi 1935). The annihilation of individuality is the most massive antidemocratic feature of any form of fascism, which denies the true nature of humankind.

The reduction of individual freedom into economic agents' ability to maximize a utility function suffers two faults. First, individuals are reduced to commodities through the alienation of labour, hence, not only freedom, but also happiness, are identified with the capacity of individuals to be rational economic agents. Second, the idea that the mechanism of a self-regulated market was natural provoked a huge social gap between individuals, who are educated to believe in the authenticity of that mechanism and, consequently, were forced to obey what Polanyi called 'our obsolete market mentality' (Polanyi 1947b).

Polanyi's individualism is based on a concept of individual freedom that requires an authentic connection amongst individuals and between individuals and their community.[46]

Polanyi's thesis on the rise of fascism was explicitly opposed to Hayek's idea as it was set out in Hayek's *Road to Serfdom* (Hayek 1944). According to Hayek, socialism reduces individual liberty (in fact socialism is the road to serfdom either for individuals or for the society as a whole), and fascism has emerged as the most dangerous political consequence of socialism.

Although Hayek and Polanyi diverged on the interpretation of the rise of fascism, their philosophical distance should be slightly revised. First, when Hayek talked about socialism, he was referring to communism as developed in Soviet Russia; while in Polanyi's thought socialism is connected with Christianity and has nothing to do with Soviet communism, being rather close to Owenism (Polanyi 1944). Second, both Hayek and Polanyi had considered Soviet communism as a form of fascism. Third, Hayek and Polanyi shared the same concept of individualism. Their individualism was based on the Scottish tradition (from Smith's invisible hand to Carl Menger) that exalts the role of individuals. Furthermore, they shared the same aversion for the 'false individualism' (in Hayek's words) or 'political rationalism' (in Polanyi's formulation) that had generated neoclassical economic rationalism (Hayek 1948; Polanyi 1977).[47]

The real divergence between Polanyi and Hayek centred on the nature of the market. Hayek was much more oriented toward a definition of a self-regulated market, even though in a way that was very different from neoclassic economics; not a system able to integrate individual choice, by following a static performance based on efficiency, but a dynamic system of the individual's interconnections based on negative-feedback (Petsoulas 2001). Polanyi regarded the market as a form of integration between the economy and other social institutions,[48] along with reciprocity and redistribution, historically and culturally determined, not naturally pre-determined (Polanyi 1944, 1957, 1977).[49] In this framework, Polanyi's anticipatory critique of neoliberalism can be defined as, namely, what kind of freedom for individuals is possible in a society where human behaviour is regarded as rational only if it follows the rules of economic determinism. What Polanyi prophesized was the radical change of the meaning of individual freedom in a neoliberal society: the classical concept of freedom has been brutally replaced by a new form of freedom, based on the radical transformation of individuals into rational agents. Along with this process, human society has been shaped into a model of economic rationality, born into economic departments, and massively sponsored by scholars, politicians, and the press, especially in the last two decades.[50] Polanyi's concern about the possible consequences of the application of what he called the formal meaning of economics to any single aspect of humanity is similar to the present dilemma about the nature of a neoliberal society.

Notes

1 The first theorem has been considered as the modern version of Adam Smith's invisible hand (Arrow and Hahn 1971; Hahn 1973).
2 The main contribution on the passage from an individual utility function to a social utility function is Arrow's impossibility theorem (Arrow 1951). He assumes that individual preferences as well as social choices are complete and transitive. Following development of Arrow's work, we are focused on the idea that social evaluations are determined by a weighty sum of individual evaluation based on the principle that the satisfaction of individual preferences constitutes social welfare (Harsanyi 1977; Hausman and McPherson 2009)
3 For a short and useful story on the use of revealed preferences after Samuelson, see Mas-Colell (1978).
4 Becker dedicated his book to 'Milton Friedman, H. Gregg Lewis, T. W. Schultz, and George Stigler, from whom I learned about the economic approach' (Becker 1976, 1).
5 Without a valid explanation, Mill claimed that: 'it is quite compatible with the principle of utility to recognize the fact, that some *kinds* of pleasure are more desirable and more valuable than others' (Mill 1871, 11).
6 Hedonism considers pleasure and pain as mental states. A current debate on the return of hedonism to economics is taking place (Kahneman and Sudgen 2005; Layard 2005; Frey and Stutzer 2010).
7 As it is well known, Menger's subjectivism goes beyond the explanation of the theory of the consumer: intermediate goods (input) as well as final goods (input) are considered a means to satisfy an indirect need (a higher degree need).
8 There are some objections about the fact that Pareto did actually drop cardinal measurements out of the description of indifference curves (Bruni and Guala 2001; Weber 2001).
9 Becker received his Ph.D. in 1955 in Chicago, moved in 1957 to teach at Columbia University, and finally returned to Chicago in 1968.
10 Becker's human capital directly derived from his concept of discrimination in the marketplace as rational (Becker [1955] 1971). Furthermore, the interest in human capital was not alien to economists in Chicago (Teixeira 2014). Knight mentioned it in a discussion on the relationship between economic freedom and human capital (Knight 1941). Friedman used the concept in two different papers (Friedman 1943, 1953). In the 1950s, Schultz introduced the topic among the programme at the Department of Economics, and, in 1960, he dedicated his Presidential Speech to the American Economic Association to human capital (Schultz 1961).
11 'The economic approach implies that there is an "optimal" expected length of life, where the value in utility of an additional year is less than the utility foregone by using time and other resources to obtain that year' (Becker, 1976, 9).
12 'A person decides to marry when the utility expected from marriage exceeds that expected from remaining single or from the additional search for a more suitable mate' (Becker 1976, 10).

13 'Persons only choose to follow scholarly or other intellectual or artistic pursuits if they expect the benefits, both monetary and physic, to exceed those available in alternative occupations' (Becker 1976, 11).

14 'Discrimination by any group W[hites] reduces their own incomes as well as N [egroes]' (sic.), and thus retaliation by N makes it worse for N rather than better' (Becker 1976, 17).

15 Given the differences between an ideal democracy and the actual one, as well as the imperfection of government behaviour, it is preferable not to regulate economic imperfections (i.e. monopolies) 'rather than to regulate them and suffer the effects of political imperfections' (Becker 1976, 38).

16 'The method used formulates a measure of the social loss from offenses and finds those expenditures of resources and punishments that minimize this loss' (Becker 1976, 40).

17 'Children are viewed as durable goods, primarily a consumer's durable, which yields income, primarily psychic income, to parents. Fertility is determined by income, child costs, knowledge, uncertainty, and tastes. An increase in income and a decline in price would increase the demand for children, although it is necessary to distinguish between the quantity and quality of children demanded. The quality of children is directly related to the amount spent on them' (Becker 1976, 193).

18 On a related note, the link between Austrians and Ordoliberals has been recently studied (Vanberg 2004; Kolev 2015).

19 This is not to be intended as a sort of comparison between the two schools regarding different economic issues (Skousen 2005). This comparison should be regarded as an inquiry around methodological and theoretical differences between them, around themes that involve the individual's rationality, the role of the market, and the meaning of freedom (McKenzie 1983; Caldwell 2011). Conclusions are close to Aranzadi's book on the differences between Mises' vision and Becker's (Aranzadi 2006) and Huerta de Soto's book on order and creativity as peculiar to the Austrian school (Huerta de Soto 2008).

20 The role of Mises in this story is complex. Mises' apriorism, as well as his rejection of inductivism, made him a founder of a new Austrian approach that is close to the Chicagoans' perspective (Aimar 2009). Contrary to this interpretation, Caldwell considered many parts of Mises' *opus magnum* (Mises 1949) as an enriched development of Menger's thought (Caldwell 1990).

21 Aside from these differences, an ambiguity persists: some scholars consider both the Austrians and the Chicagoans as forerunners of libertarianism, due to their similar position about policy (Huebert 2010). Furthermore, other scholars point out a relevant reciprocal influence between the Austrian and Chicago schools of economics within the Virginia school of economics (Boettke 1987; Brady 2010).

22 Schumpeter's definition of economic analysis as 'the analytic or scientific aspect of economic thought' is close to Menger's theoretical economics (Schumpeter 1954).

23 The Walras-Pareto tradition includes the formalization of a human behaviour based on preferences as well as the formalization of a system of general economic equilibrium that is able to describe the rational functionality of a society. This approach made economics closer to physics, and it includes mathematical economics and econometrics, both developed in the past century. The main critique on the use of the method of physics in social sciences derives from Hayek, who called this attitude 'scientism' (Hayek, 1952).

24 Weber's notion of a *Wertfreiheit* of science was the gateway for the formalization of politics, laws, economics, and social sciences in general. Weber's approach allows excluding a historical sense of contingency from those disciplines that can finally reach a scientific status. As is well known, Talcott Parson first introduced

Weber's work as well as Pareto's sociology (Parsons 1949) to the American audience (Scaff 2011). A possible influence of Weber's work into the Chicago school came from Knight (Emmett 2009). According to Kirzner, Weber's *Wertfreiheit* was still present in Mises' methodology and has been upheld by Mises and Robbins (Kirzner 1976). According to Lachmann, Weber had a central role in the Austrian economics, too: Weber's conception of *Verstehen* (understanding) can be regarded in Menger's subjectivism, in Mises' *Human Action* and in Hayek's dynamics of plans coordination (Lachmann 1970).

25 As Kirzner wrote, it was Gunnar Myrdal who first described the Austrians 'as being the rare nineteenth-century economists who did not inject political motives into their economics' (Kirzner 1990, 96).

26 The role of realism in Menger and other Austrian economists was first introduced by Mäki (1990); more recently Salerno (2010).

27 'The conception of economic activity as maximizing behavior suffers from two weaknesses. On the one hand, it involves setting up such an ultimate end, with the presumption that it can be meaningfully "maximized"; on the other hand, it ignores the multiplicity of intermediary ends and the effect that their very number has on the allocation of resources' (Kirzner 1960, 116).

28 The allocation of scarce resources among competitive ends.

29 About the economists' *hybris* in the omniscience of 'efficiency', Buchanan wrote: 'Efficiency in the sense of maximizing a payoff or outcome from the use of limited resources is meaningless without some common denominator, some value scale, against which various possible results can be measured. To the individual decision maker the concept of an 'efficiency criterion' is a useful one, but to the independent observer the pitfalls of omniscience must be carefully avoided. The observer may introduce an efficiency criterion only through *his own estimate of his subjects' value scales*. Hence the maximization criterion which the economist may employ is wholly in terms of his own estimate of the value scales of individuals other than himself. *Presumptive efficiency* is, therefore, the appropriate conception for political economy' (Buchanan 1959, 126).

30 In *The Constitution of Liberty* (Hayek 1960), Hayek promoted an urgency to go back to the values of classical liberalism (the Rule of Law), and he reformulated his idea of spontaneous order as a natural order where free individuals can make their plans possible, according to Hayek's theory of knowledge.

31 One year later, Posner went further on, and claimed that according to Stigler, liberty is seen as 'the size of the individual opportunity set' (Posner 1979, 140). According to Posner, the wealth-maximization principle embeds morality because individuals cannot prosper without benevolence and empathy (Posner 1979). His consideration of wealth maximization as an ethical attractive norm in common law has been further explained in another article where he claimed that the wealth maximization is supported by the principle of consent so that efficiency has an ethical and political basis (Posner 1980).

32 A possible explanation for the rise of the Chicagoans' neoliberalism could be the opposition to Dewey's liberalism that was becoming very popular in the United States during the 1950s. Dewey's liberalism was the American version of social democracy and a welfare state (Dewey [1935] 1987). In Dewey's system, the political sphere – democracy – is supposed to dominate the economic sphere; in Friedman's approach, a value-free economics rules.

33 A massive secondary literature underlines how Karl Polanyi had anticipated many aspects of the social and cultural transformation of our present age (Polanyi Levitt 2013; Hillenkamp and Laville 2013; Maucourant 2013; Thomasberger 2012; Cangiani 2011; Standing 2010). Recently, some heterodox economists have extensively applied Polanyi's categories to describe: (a) 'ways of mapping' society (Schaniel and Neale 2000); (b) the so-called 'third sphere' (Adaman and Yahya

2002); (c) alternative approaches to the informal sector (Özveren 2005); (d) aspects and defects of the political systems in a young market economy as in Russia (Sanchez-Andres and March-Poquet 2002); (e) lack of participation in democratic processes as happens in the United States (Champlin and Knoedler 2004). With the only exception of Thomasberger (2012) and Polanyi Levitt (who explicitly talked about neoliberalism as a counterrevolutionary movement), these contributions are broadly focused on Polanyi's foresight in understanding the present process of globalization and the present tensions between capitalism and democracy (Polanyi Levitt 2013).

34 Polanyi's main thesis in his *The Great Transformation* was that nineteenth century civilization had been destroyed by the collapse of the economic and political equilibrium that still persisted before the First World War. This equilibrium was rooted in four institutions: military balance amongst European states and the United States; the gold standard; the general acceptance of a self-regulating market; and classical liberalism. Polanyi wrote: 'the fount and matrix of the system was the self-regulating market. It was this innovation that gave rise to a specific civilization. The gold standard was merely an attempt to extend the domestic market system to the international field; the balance-of-power system was a superstructure erected upon and, partly, worked through the gold standard; the liberal state was itself a creation of the self-regulating market' (Polanyi [1944] 2001, 3). This broken equilibrium led to fascism in the interwar, to the financial crash in 1929, and to the Second World War. According to Polanyi, along with this transformation, a spontaneous movement had been developing within society in order to protect itself against the mechanism of capitalism, which transformed humanity and nature into mere commodities, and divided the political sphere from the economic sphere, formerly united. Polanyi defined 'double movement' as a combination of destruction and self-defence. This mechanism of self-defence has been compared to some current social forces fighting against neoliberalism (Gillis 2008; Sandbrook 2011; Dale 2012; Levien and Paret 2012).

35 The concept derives from the expression *naturalistic fallacy*, a methodological mistake from a wrong logical deduction. From a mere fact to a norm, human economy in general is identical with one of its particular forms – the market form based on the supply-demand-price mechanism (Polanyi 1977). According to some literature about Polanyi and the rise of neoliberalism, Polanyi's economic fallacy is the proper starting point to understand the nature of a neoliberal society (Block and Somers 1984; Schram 2015).

36 According to Polanyi, the second meaning of 'economic' (founded on the physical character of production, and free from any link with scarcity of means) already appeared in the posthumous edition of *Grundsätze* (Menger 1923; Polanyi [1958] 1971), and Menger used it in order to restrict the application of the formal meaning of 'economic' to the sole modern exchange economy (Cangiani 2010; Becchio 2014).

37 Polanyi introduced the idea of fictitious commodities in *The Great Transformation:* 'self-regulation implies that all production is for sale on the market and that all incomes derive from such sales. Accordingly, there are markets for all elements of industry, not only for goods (always including services) but also for labour, land and money, their prices being called respectively commodity prices, wages, rent, and interest' (Polanyi [1944] 2001, 72).

38 Polanyi had introduced the distinction between the two meanings of economic in 1948 while he was teaching economic history at Columbia University, and it will be the focus of his following research project on the Economic Aspects of International Growth for the Ford Foundation (1953–58).

39 Interaction is undertaken in order to achieve material result in terms of survival by local movements (production, transportation, transaction and dispositions of

goods) and appropriation movements ('the legal acquisition of property', of material or non-material objects, 'administration and circulation of goods, distribution of income, tribute and taxation') (Polanyi 1977).

40 Aristotle's household is 'an association of persons, established according to nature for the satisfaction of daily needs' and its aim is to satisfy the well-being of any member of the community, likewise in Polanyi's notion of embedded economy (Somers 1990; Booth 1991).

41 On the complex connection between Hayek and Polanyi around the nature of economy, starting from an Aristotelian conception of political economy, see O'Neill (1995, 1998).

42 On a reciprocal influence between Hayek and Michael Polanyi (Polanyi 1951) on catallaxy and spontaneous order, see Gray (1984); Allen (1998); Jacobs (2000); and Klein (2012), to name but a few.

43 Polanyi's definition of 'moral dilemma' in a neoliberal society is that individuals are sacrificed to the self-regulating system, in which individuals can not control their real conditions of life. (Polanyi 1941–42, unpublished).

44 Like money and land, labour is '*obviously* not [a] commodity; the postulate that anything that is bought and sold must have been produced for sale is emphatically untrue in regard of [it]. In other words, according to the empirical definition of a commodity [it is] not a commodity. Labour is only another name for a human activity which goes with life itself, which in its turn is not produced for sale but for entirely different reasons, nor can that activity be detached from the rest of life, be stored, or mobilized' (Polanyi [1944] 2001, 75).

45 This notion is similar to what Hannah Arendt later presented in her work on the origin of totalitarianism (Arendt 1951). For further links between Polanyi and Arendt about the distortion of individual freedom within the market society, see Hallowell (1974), Fenichel Pitkin (1998), Somers (2006), Azam (2009).

46 Polanyi's individualism was based on what he defined 'Christian socialism'. Even though Polanyi's understanding of Christianity was definitely heterodox (Dale 2010), he insisted on the similarities between Christianity and socialism, both grounded on the principles of equality and equity (Polanyi 1935).

47 In contrast to the possibility of finding some convergence between Hayek and Polanyi around a possible critique of neoliberalism, see especially Filip (2012), Polanyi Levitt (2012), and Block, who defined Hayek as 'the father of neoliberalism' (Block 2001, xx).

48 As brilliantly explained by the anthropologist Chapman (1980), Polanyi's analysis of the market contains a major ambiguity (Polanyi 1957, 1977): it is essential not to assimilate the exchange form of integration and its dominance (self-regulated market), with markets which exist in many societies, but which are not price-making markets, even though the prices in these markets may fluctuate by supply and demand conditioned by religious, social, political or socio-economic factors that are beyond the economy. Many other scholars consider Polanyi's exchange as a form of integration to be intended implicitly as market exchange (Maucourant and Plociniczak 2013). It would be much better to use the word 'household' to define what Polanyi had in mind when he talked about markets outside the domain of 'exchange market' or 'market economy', as suggested by McCloskey (1997).

49 Polanyi wrote: 'normally, the economic order is merely a function of the social, in which it is contained. Neither under tribal, nor feudal, nor mercantile conditions was there a separate economic system in society' (Polanyi [1944] 2001, 71).

50 Polanyi proposed to go beyond market economy, by introducing a system based on the idea of 'community', and that implies a collective ownership of the means of

production, free management, and democracy (Polanyi 1957, unpublished). Polanyi's model was utopian in many respects. From an economic point of view, a planned production is technically impossible without any control over distribution. From a sociological point of view, this society implies a ruling group of managers who easily will be operating in the same way as they operate a capitalist system. From a philosophical point of view, communities are usually closed groups with rigid internal rules, often tacit, but still well fixed, and individual freedom of those who do not accept communitarian rules is inevitably constrained.

References

Adaman, F. and Yahya, M. (2002) 'Theorizing the "Third Sphere": A Critique of the Persistence of the "Economistic Fallacy"', *Journal of Economic Issues*, Vol. 34:4, pp. 1045–1078.

Aimar, T. (2009) 'The Curious Destiny of a Heterodoxy: The Austrian Economic Tradition', *Review of Austrian Economics*, Vol. 22:3, pp. 199–207.

Aimar, T. (2014) *The Economics of Ignorance and Coordination: Subjectivism and the Austrian School of Economics.* Cheltenham, UK: Edward Elgar.

Allen, R. (1998) *Beyond Liberalism: The Political Thought of Friedrich von Hayek and Michael Polanyi.* New Brunswick, NJ: Transaction.

Aranzadi, J. (2006) *Liberalism against Liberalism: Theoretical Analysis of the Works of Ludwig von Mises and Gary Becker.* New York: Routledge.

Arendt, H. (1951) *The Origin of Totalitarianism.* New York: Schocken Books.

Aristotle (1992) *The Politics.* London: Penguin Books.

Arrow, K. (1951) *Social Choice and Individual Values.* New York: Wiley.

Arrow, K. and Hahn, F. (1971) *General Competitive Analysis.* San Francisco: Holden-Day.

Azam, G. (2009) 'Hannah Arendt and Karl Polanyi: Economic Liberalism, the Political Collapse, and Mass Society', *Revue du MAUSS*, Vol. 34:2, pp. 321–335.

Barnett, C. (2010) 'Publics and Markets: What's Wrong with Neoliberalism?', in Smith, S., Marston, S., Pain, R. and Jones, J. (Eds) *The Sage Handbook of Social Geographies.* New York: Sage, pp. 269–298.

Barry, N. (1982) 'The Tradition of Spontaneous Order', *Literature of Liberty*, Vol. 5:4, pp. 5–18.

Becchio, G. (2014) 'From Social Needs to Social Goods in Carl Menger's Final Work' *History of Political Economy*, Vol. 46:2, pp. 247–264.

Becker, G. [1955] (1971) *The Economics of Discrimination.* Chicago: University of Chicago Press.

Becker, G. (1962) 'Irrational Behavior and Economic Theory', *Journal of Political Economy*, Vol. 70:1, pp. 1–13.

Becker, G. (1964) *Human Capital: a Theoretical and Empirical Analysis, with Special Reference to Education.* Chicago: The University of Chicago Press.

Becker, G. (1965) 'A Theory of the Allocation of Time', *The Economic Journal*, Vol. 75:299, pp. 493–517.

Becker, G. (1976) *The Economic Approach to Human Behavior.* Chicago: Chicago University Press.

Becker, G. (2014) 'Gary S. Becker – Facts'. Nobel Media AB: Nobelprize.org.

Beckert, J. (2003) 'Economic Action and Embeddedness: How Shall we Conceptualize Economic Action?', *Journal of Economic Issues*, Vol. 37:3, pp. 769–787.

Bentham, J. (1789) *An Introduction to the Principles of Morals and Legislation.* Oxford: Clarendon Press.

Blaug, M. [1961] (1997) *Economic Theory in Retrospect.* Cambridge: Cambridge University Press.

Block, F. (2001) 'Introduction', in Polanyi, K. *The Great Transformation: The Political and Economic Origins of Our Time.* Boston: Beacon Press, pp. xviii–xxxviii.

Block, F. and Somers, M. (1984) 'Beyond the Economistic Fallacy: the Holistic Social Science of Karl Polanyi', in Skocpol, T. (Ed.) *Vision and Method in Historical Sociology.* Cambridge: Cambridge University Press, pp. 47–84.

Block, F. and Somers, M. (2014) *The Power of Market Fundamentalism.* Cambridge, MA: Harvard University Press.

Boettke, P. (1987) 'Virginia Political Economy: A View from Vienna', *Market Process,* Vol. 5:2, pp. 7–15.

Böhm-Bawerk, E. [1881] (1962) 'Whether Legal Rights and Relationships are Economic Goods', in *Shorter Classics of Böhm-Bawerk*, Vol. 1. South Holland, IL: Libertarian Press, pp. 30–138.

Booth, W. (1991) 'The New Household Economy', *The American Political Science Review,* Vol. 85:1, pp. 59–75.

Borch, K. (1973) 'The Place of Uncertainty in the Theory of the Austrian School', in Hicks, J.R. and Weber, W. (Eds), *Carl Menger and the Austrian School of Economics.* Oxford: Clarendon Press, pp. 61–74.

Bowles, S. and Gintis, H. (1993) 'The Revenge of Homo Economicus: Contested Exchange and the Revival of Political Economy', *Journal of Economic Perspectives,* Vol. 7:1, pp. 83–102.

Brady, G. (2010) 'The Chicago Roots of the Virginia School', in Emmett, R. (Ed.) *The Elgar Companion to the Chicago School of Economics.* Cheltenham, UK: Edward Elgar, pp. 233–252.

Bruni, L. and Guala, F. (2001) 'Vilfredo Pareto and the Epistemological Foundation of Choice Theory', *History of Political Economy,* Vol. 33:1, pp. 21–49.

Buchanan, J. (1959) 'Positive Economics, Welfare Economics, and Political Economy', *The Journal of Law and Economics,* Vol. 2:1, pp. 124–138.

Caldwell, B. (1990) 'Introduction', in Caldwell, B. (Ed.) *Carl Menger and his Legacy in Economics.* Durham, NC: Duke University Press, pp. 3–14.

Caldwell, B. (2011) 'The Chicago School, Hayek, and Neoliberalism', in Mirowski, P. and Van Horn, R. (Eds) *Building Chicago Economics.* Cambridge: Cambridge University Press, pp. 301–334.

Cangiani, M. (2010) 'From Menger to Polanyi: The Institutional Way', in Hagemann, H., Ikeda, Y. and Nishizawa, T. (Eds) *Austrian Economics in Transition.* Houndmills, UK: Palgrave Macmillan, pp. 138–153.

Cangiani, M. (2011) 'Karl Polanyi's Institutional Theory: Market Society and its "Embedded" Economy' *Journal of Economic Issues,* Vol. 44:1, pp. 177–197.

Cangiani, M. (2012) 'Freedom in a Complex Society', *International Journal of Political Economy,* Vol. 41:4, pp. 34–53.

Champlin Dell, P. and Knoedler, J. (2004) 'Embedded Economies, Democracy, and the Public Interest', *Journal of Economic Issues,* Vol. 38:4, pp. 893–907.

Chapman, A. (1980) 'Barter as a Universal Mode of Exchange', *L'Homme,* Vol. 20:3, pp. 33–83.

Dale, G. (2010) *Karl Polanyi and the Limits of the Market.* Cambridge: Polity Press.

Dale, G. (2012) 'Double Movements and Pendular Forces: Polanyian Perspectives on the Neoliberal Age', *Current Sociology*, Vol. 60:3, pp. 3–27.

Davis, J. (2015) 'The Conception of the Socially Embedded Individual', in Davis, J. and Dolfsman, W. (Eds) *The Elgar Companion to Social Economics*. Cheltenham, UK: Edward Elgar, pp. 116–130.

De Martino, G. (2000) *Global Economy, Global Justice. Theoretical Objections and Policy Alternatives to Neoliberalism*. London: Routledge.

Dewey, J. [1935] (1987) 'Liberalism and Social Action', in Boydston, J. (Ed.) *The Papers of John Dewey: The Later Works, 1925–1953*, Vol. 11. Carbondale, IL: Southern Illinois University.

Edgeworth, F. (1881) *Mathematical Physics: an Essay on the Application of Mathematics to the Moral Sciences*. London: Kegan Paul.

Edgeworth, F. (1889) 'The Mathematical Theory of Political Economy. The Address of the President of Section F – Economic Science and Statistics – of the British Association, at the Fifty-Ninth Meeting, Held at Newcastle Upon Tyne, in September 1889', *Journal of the Royal Statistic Society*, Vol. 52:4, pp. 538–576.

Emmett, R. (2008) 'New Perspectives on Chicago School', in *The New Palgrave: A Dictionary of Economics Online*. London: Macmillan.

Emmett, R. (2009) *Frank Knight and the Chicago School in American Economics*. London, UK: Routledge.

Emmett, R. (Ed.) (2010) *The Elgar Companion to the Chicago School of Economics*. Cheltenham, UK: Edward Elgar.

Fenichel Pitkin, H. (1998) *The Attack of the Blob: Hannah Arendt's Concept of the Social*. Chicago: University of Chicago Press.

Filip, B. (2012) 'Polanyi and Hayek on Freedom, the State, and Economics', *International Journal of Political Economy*, Vol. 41:4, pp. 69–87.

Frey, B. and Stutzer, A. (2010) 'Happiness and Public Choice', *Public Choice*, Vol. 144:3, pp. 557–573.

Friedman, M. (1943) 'The Spending Tax as a Wartime Fiscal Measure', *American Economic Review*, Vol. 33:1, pp. 50–62.

Friedman, M. (1951) 'Neo-liberalism and Its Prospect', *Farmand*, Vol. 60:7, pp. 89–93.

Friedman, M. (1953) 'Choice, Chance, and the Personal Distribution of Income', *Journal of Political Economy*, Vol. 61:4, pp. 277–290.

Gillis, B. (2008) 'The Swinging of the Pendulum: the Global Crisis and Beyond', *Globalization*, Vol. 5:4, pp. 513–522.

Gray, J. (1984) *Hayek on Liberty*. New York: Basic Blackwell.

Hahn, F. (1973) 'The Winter of Our Discontent', *Economica*, Vol. 40:159, pp. 322–330.

Hallowell, J. (1974) 'Liberalism and the Open Society', in Germino, D. and Beyme, K. (Eds) *The Open Society in Theory and Practice*. The Hague: Martinus Nijhoff, pp. 121–141.

Harsanyi, J. (1977) *Rational Behaviour and Bargaining Equilibrium in Games and Social Situations*. Cambridge: Cambridge University Press.

Harvey, D. (2005) *A Brief History of Neoliberalism*. Oxford: Oxford University Press.

Hausman, D. and McPherson, M. (2009) 'Preference Satisfaction and Welfare Economics', *Economics and Philosophy*, Vol. 25:1, pp. 1–25.

Hayek, F. (1937) 'Economics and Knowledge', *Economica*, Vol. 4, pp. 33–54.

Hayek, F. (1944) *Road to Serfdom*. London: Routledge.

Hayek, F. (1945) 'The Use of Knowledge in Society', *American Economic Review*, Vol. 35:4, pp. 519–530.

Hayek, F. (1948) *Individualism and Economic Order*. London: Routledge.

Hayek, F. (1952) *The Counter-Revolution of Science*. Glencoe, IL: The Free Press.

Hayek, F. (1960) *The Constitution of Liberty*. London: Routledge.

Hayek, F. [1966] (1967) 'The Principles of a Liberal Social Order', in Hayek, F. *Studies in Philosophy, Politics and Economics*. Chicago: University of Chicago Press, pp. 160–177.

Hayek, F. (1967) *Studies in Philosophy, Politics, and Economics*. Chicago: University of Chicago Press.

Hayek, F. (1973) *Law, Legislation and Liberty*, Vol. I, 'Rules and Order'. Chicago: University of Chicago Press.

Hayek, F. (1976) *Law, Legislation and Liberty*, Vol. II, 'The Mirage of Social Justice'. Chicago: University of Chicago Press.

Hayek, F. (1978) *New Studies in Philosophy, Politics and Economics*. London: Routledge and Kegan Paul.

Hayek, F. (1979) *Law, Legislation and Liberty*, Vol. III, 'The Political Order of a Free People'. Chicago: University of Chicago Press.

Hayek, F. (1994) *Hayek on Hayek*. London: Routledge.

Heilbroner, R. (1953) *The Worldly Philosophers: The Lives, Times, and Ideas of the Great Economic Thinkers*. New York: Simon & Schuster.

Herfeld, C. (2013) 'The Many Faces of Rational Choice Theory', *Erasmus Journal for Philosophy*, Vol. 6:2, pp. 117–121.

Hillenkamp, I. and Laville, J.L. (2013) *Socioéconomie et démocratie*. Paris: Erès.

Hodgson, G. and Knudsen, T. (2010) 'Generative Replication and the Evolution of Complexity', *Journal of Economic Behaviour and Organization*, Vol. 75:1, pp. 12–24.

Huebert, J. (2010) *Libertarianism Today*. Santa Barbara, CA: Praeger.

Huerta de Soto, J. (2008) *The Austrian School: Market Order and Entrepreneurial Creativity*. Cheltenham, UK: Edward Elgar.

Hume, D. [1739–1740] (1896) *A Treatise on Human Nature*. Oxford: Clarendon Press.

Hutcheson, F. (1755) *A System of Moral Philosophy*. London: A. Millar and T. Longman.

Ingrao, B. and Israel, G. (1990) *The Invisible Hand: Economic Equilibrium in the History of Science*. Cambridge, MA: The MIT Press.

Jacobs, S. (2000) 'Spontaneous Order: Michael Polanyi and Friedrich Hayek', *Critical Review of International Social and Political Philosophy*, Vol. 3:4, pp. 49–67.

Jevons, W. (1871) *The Theory of Political Economy*. London: Macmillan & Co.

Kahneman, D. and Sudgen, R. (2005) 'Experienced Utility as a Standard of Policy Evaluation', *Environmental and Resource Economics*, Vol. 32:1, pp. 161–181.

Khalil, E. (1996) 'What is Economic Action? From Marshall and Robbins to Polanyi and Becker', *Journal of the History of Economic Thought*, Vol. 18:1, pp. 13–36.

Kirzner, I. (1960) *The Economic Point of View*. Menlo Park, California: The Institute of Human Studies.

Kirzner, I. (1976) 'Philosophical and Ethical Implications of Austrian Economics', in Dolan, E. (Ed.) *The Foundation of Modern Austrian Economics*. Kansas City, KS: Sheed and Ward, pp. 75–88.

Kirzner, I. (1990) 'Liberalism and the Austrian School', in Caldwell, B. (Ed.) *Carl Menger and his Legacy in Economics*. Durham, NC, Duke University Press, pp. 93–106.

Klein, D. (2012) *Knowledge and Coordination: A Liberal Interpretation*. Oxford: Oxford University Press.

Knight, F. (1934) 'Economic Science in Recent Discussion', *The American Economic Review*, Vol. 24:2, pp. 225–238.

Knight, F. (1941) 'The Role of the Individual in the Economic World of the Future', *Journal of Political Economy*, Vol. 49:6, pp. 817–832.

Kolev, S. (2015) 'Ordoliberalism and the Austrian School', in Boettke, P. and Coyne, C. (Eds) *The Oxford Handbook of Austrian Economics*. New York: Oxford University Press, pp. 419–444.

Lachmann, L. (1970) *The Legacy of Max Weber*. London: Heinemann.

Lavoie, D. (1989) 'Economic Chaos or Spontaneous Order? Implications for Political Economy of the New View of Science', *Cato Journal*, Vol. 8:3, pp. 613–635.

Lavoie, D. (1990) 'Understanding Differently: Hermeneutics and the Spontaneous Order of Communicative Processes', in Caldwell, B. (Ed). *Carl Menger and his Legacy in Economics*. Durham, NC: Duke University Press, pp. 359–378.

Layard, R. (2005) *Happiness: Lessons from a New Science*. New York: Penguin.

Levien, M. and Paret, M. (2012) 'A Second Double Movement? Polanyi and Shifting Global Opinions on Neoliberalism', *International Sociology*, Vol. 27:1, pp. 1–21.

Lewis, P. (2012) 'Emergent Properties in the Work of Friedrich von Hayek', *Journal of Economic Behavior and Organization*, Vol. 82:2–3, pp. 368–378.

Maas, H. (2009) 'Disciplining Boundaries: Lionel Robbins, Max Weber, and the Borderlands of Economics, History, and Psychology', *Journal of the History of Economic Thought*, Vol. 31:4, pp. 500–517.

Mäki, U. (1990) 'Mengerian Economics in a Realist Perspective', in Caldwell, B. (Ed.) *Carl Menger and his Legacy in Economics*. Durham: Duke University Press, pp. 289–310.

Mas-Colell, A. (1978) 'On Revealed Preferences Analysis', *The Review of Economic Studies*, Vol. 45:1, pp. 121–131.

Maucourant, J. (2013) 'Unité et pluralité du capitalisme: une perspective institutionnaliste', in Diemer, A., Borodak, D. and Dozolme, S. (Eds) *Heurs et malheurs du capitalism*. Toulouse, France: Editions Oeconomia, pp. 41–63.

Maucourant, J. and Plociniczak, S. (2013) 'The Institution, the Economy, and the Market: Karl Polanyi's Institutional Thought for Economists', *Review of Political Economy*, Vol. 25:3, pp. 512–531.

McCaffrey, M. and Salerno, J. (2014) 'Böhm-Bawerk's Approach to Entrepreneurship', *Journal of the History of Economic Thought*, Vol. 36:4, pp. 435–454.

McCloskey, D. (1997) 'Other Things Equal. Polanyi Was Right, and Wrong', *Eastern Economic Journal*, Vol. 23:4, pp. 483–487.

McGuian, J. (2016) *Neoliberal Culture*. New York: Palgrave Macmillan.

McKenzie, R. (1983) *The Limits of Economic Science*. Boston: Kluwer.

Menger, C. (1871) *Grundsätze der Volkswirtschaftslehre*. Vienna: Braumuller.

Menger, C. [1883] (1985) *Investigations Into the Method of the Social Sciences with Special Reference to Economics*. New York: New York University Press.

Menger, C. (1923) *Grundsätze der Volkswirtschaftlehre. Zweite Auflage mit einem Geleitwort von Richard Schüller aus dem Nachlass herausgegeben von Karl Menger*. Vienna and Leipzig: Hölder-Pichler-Tempsky.

Michael, R. and Becker, G. (1973) 'On the New Theory of Consumer Behavior', *The Swedish Journal of Economics*, Vol. 75:4, pp. 378–396.

Mill, J.S. (1871) *Utilitarianism*. London: Longmans, Green, Reader, and Dyer.

Mirowski, P. (2013) *Never Let A Serious Crisis Go to Waste: How Neoliberalism Survived the Financial Meltdown*. London and New York: Verso.

Mises, L. [1927] (1985) *Liberalism in the Classical Tradition*. Irvington-on-Hudson, NY: The Foundation for Economic Education.

Mises, L. (1949) *Human Action*. Yale, CT: Yale University Press.

Mises, L. (1957) *Theory and Society*. Yale, CT: Yale University Press.

Mises, L. (1960) *Epistemological Problems of Economics*. Princeton, NJ: Van Nostrand.

Nell, E. and Errouaki, K. (2013) *Rational Econometric Man: Transforming Structural Econometrics*. Cheltenham, UK: Edward Elgar.

Oakeshott, M. (2006) *Lectures in the History of Political Thought*. Exeter, UK and Charlottesville, VA: Imprint Academic.

O'Driscoll, G. and Rizzo, M. (2015) *Austrian Economics Re-Examined: The Economics of Time and Ignorance*. London: Routledge.

O'Neill, J. (1995) 'Essences and Markets', *The Monist*, Vol. 78:3, pp. 258–275.

O'Neill, J. (1998) *The Market: Ethics, Knowledge and Politics*. London: Routledge.

Özveren, E. (2005) 'Polanyi, Chayanov, and Lessons for the Study of the Informal Sector', *Journal of Economic Issues*, Vol. 39:3, pp. 765–776.

Pareto, V. (1896) *Cours d'Economie Politique*. Geneve: Droz.

Pareto, V. (1900) 'Sunto di Alcuni Capitoli di un Nuovo Trattato di Economia Pura del Prof. Pareto', *Giornale degli Economisti*, Vol. 20:11, pp. 216–235.

Pareto, V. (1906) *Manuale di Economia Politica*. Milano: Società Editrice Libraria.

Parsons, T. (1949) *The Structure of Social Action*. Chicago: Free Press.

Petras, J. and Veltmeyer, H. (2013) *Extractive Imperialism in the Americas: Capitalism's New Frontier*. Leiden and Boston: Brill.

Petsoulas, C. (2001) *Hayek's Liberalism and its Origins. His Idea of Spontaneous Order and the Scottish Enlightenment*. London: Routledge.

Polanyi, K. (1935) 'The Essence of Fascism', in Lewis, J., Polanyi, K. and Kitchin, K. (Eds) *Christianity and the Social Revolution*. London: Victor Gollancz Ltd, pp. 359–396.

Polanyi, K. (1937) *Europe Today*. London: Workers Educational Trade Union Council.

Polanyi, K. (1941–42, unpublished) *The Moral Values Underlying Social Organization in the Political, Economic and Cultural Field*. Montreal, Canada: Bennington College, Karl Polanyi Archive, Concordia University.

Polanyi, K. [1944] (2001) *The Great Transformation. The Political and Economic Origins of Our Time*. Boston: Beacon Press.

Polanyi, K. (1947a) 'On Belief in Economic Determinism', *The Sociological Review*, Vol. 37:1, pp. 96–112.

Polanyi, K. (1947b) 'Our Obsolete Market Mentality. Civilization Must Find a New Thought Pattern', *Commentary*, Vol. 3:1, pp. 109–117.

Polanyi, K. (1953, unpublished) *Origins of Economic Theory*. Montreal, Canada: Columbia University Council for Social Research in the Social Sciences, Karl Polanyi Archive, Concordia University.

Polanyi, K. (1957, unpublished) *Freedom in a Complex Society*. Montreal, Canada: Karl Polanyi Archive, Concordia University.

Polanyi, K. [1958] (1971) 'Carl Menger's Two Meanings of 'Economics'', in Dalton, G. (Ed.) *Studies in Economic Anthropology*. Washington, DC: American Anthropological Association, pp. 16–24.

Polanyi, K. (1977) *The Livelihood of Man*. New York: Academic Press.

Polanyi, K., Arensberg, C. and Pearson, H. (Eds) (1957) *Trade and Market in the Early Empires. Economies in History and Theory*. Chicago: Henry Regnery Company.

Polanyi, M. (1951) *The Logic of Liberty*. Chicago: University of Chicago Press.

Polanyi Levitt, K. (2012) 'The Power of Ideas: Keynes, Hayek, and Polanyi', *International Journal of Political Economy*, Vol. 41:4, pp. 5–15.

Polanyi Levitt, K. (2013) *From the Great Transformation to the Great Financialization*. London: Ferwood Publishing.

Posner, R. (1979) 'Utilitarianism, Economics, and Legal Theory', *Journal of Legal Studies*, Vol. 8:2, pp. 103–140.

Posner, R. (1980) 'The Ethical and Political Basis of Efficiency Norm in Common Law Adjudication', *Hofstra Law Review*, Vol. 8:1, pp. 487–508.

Rizzo, M. (2015) 'The Problem of Rationality. Austrian Economics between Classical Behaviorism and Behavioral Economics', in Boettke, P. and Coyne, C. (Eds) *The Oxford Handbook of Austrian Economics*. New York: Oxford University Press, pp. 364–392.

Robbins, L. (1932) *Essay on the Nature and Significance of Economic Science*. London: Macmillan.

Rosser, B. (2012) 'Emergence and complexity in Austrian Economics', *Journal of Economic Behavior and Organization*, Vol. 82:1, pp. 122–128.

Salerno, J. (2010) 'Menger's Causal-realist Analysis in Modern Economics', *Review of Austrian Economics*, Vol. 23:1, pp. 1–16.

Samuelson, P. (1937) 'A Note on Pure Theory of Consumers' Behavior', *Economica*, Vol. 5:17, pp. 61–71.

Samuelson, P. (1948) 'Consumption Theory in Term of Revealed Preferences', *Economica*, Vol. 15:60, pp. 243–253.

Samuelson, P. (1950) 'The Problem of Integrability in Utility Theory', *Economica*, Vol. 17:68, pp. 355–385.

Sanchez-Andres, A. and March-Poquet, J. (2002) 'The Construction of Market Institutions in Russia: A View from the Institutionalism of Polanyi', *Journal of Economic Issues*, Vol. 34:3, pp. 707–722.

Sandbrook, R. (2011) 'Polanyi and the Post-Neoliberalism in the Global South: Dilemmas of Re-embedding the Economy', *New Political Economy*, Vol. 16:4, pp. 412–443.

Scaff, L. (2011) *Max Weber in America*. Princeton, NJ: Princeton University Press.

Schaniel, W. and Neale, W. (2000) 'Karl Polanyi's Forms of Integration as Ways of Mapping', *Journal of Economic Issues*, Vol. 34:1, pp. 89–104.

Schmidt, V. and Thatcher, M. (2013) (Eds) *Resilient Liberalism in Europe's Political Economy*. Cambridge: Cambridge University Press.

Schram, S. (2015) *The Return of Ordinary Capitalism: Neoliberalism, Precarity, Occupy*. New York: Oxford University Press.

Schultz, T. (1961) 'Investment in Human Capital', *American Economic Review*, Vol. 51:2, pp. 1–17.

Schumpeter, J. [1908] (1980) *Methodological Individualism*. Brussels: Institutum Europaeum.

Schumpeter, J. (1934) *The Theory of Economic Development. An Inquiry into Profits, Capital, Credit, Interest, and the Business Cycle.* Cambridge, MA: Harvard Economic Studies.

Schumpeter, J. (1942) *Capitalism, Socialism and Democracy.* New York: Harper and Brothers.

Schumpeter, J. (1954) *History of Economic Analysis.* New York: Oxford University Press.

Shaftesbury, A. (1737–38) *Characteristicks of Men, Manners, Opinions, Times.* London: J. Purser.

Skousen, M. (2005) *Vienna and Chicago: Friends or Foes? A Tale of Two Schools of Free Market Economics.* Washington, DC: Capital Press.

Smith, A. (1759) *The Theory of Moral Sentiments.* London: A. Millar.

Smith, A. (1776) *An Inquiry into the Nature and the Causes of the Wealth of Nations.* London: Edwin Cannan.

Smith, G. (2013) *The System of Liberty: Themes in the History of Classical Liberalism.* Cambridge: Cambridge University Press.

Somers, M. (1990) 'Karl Polanyi's Intellectual Legacy', in Polanyi-Levitt, K. (Ed.) *The Life and Work of Karl Polanyi.* Montreal: The Black Rose Books, pp. 152–158.

Somers, M. (2006) 'Citizenship, Statelessness, and Market Fundamentalism: Arendtian Right to Have Rights', in Bodeman, Y. and Yurdakul, G. (Eds) *Migration, Citizenship, Ethnos.* New York: Palgrave Macmillan, pp. 35–62.

Standing, G. (2010) *Work after Globalization. Building Occupational Citizenship*, Cheltenham, UK: Edward Elgar.

Stedman Jones, D. (2012) *Masters of the Universe: Hayek, Friedman, and the Birth of Neoliberal Politics.* Princeton, NJ: Princeton University Press.

Stigler, G. (1972) 'The Adoption of the Marginal Utility Theory', *History of Political Economy*, Vol. 4:2, pp. 571–586.

Stigler, G. (1978) 'Wealth, and the Possibly Liberty', *Journal of Legal Studies*, Vol. 7:2, pp. 213–217.

Stigler, G. (1982) *The Economist as a Preacher, and Other Essays.* Chicago: Chicago University Press.

Stigler, G. and Becker, G. (1977) 'De Gustibus Non Est Disputandum', *American Economic Review*, Vol. 67:2, pp. 76–90.

Stiglitz, J. (2001), 'Foreword', in Polanyi, K. *The Great Transformation. The Political and Economic Origins of Our Time.* Boston: Beacon Press, pp. xii–xviii.

Streissler, E. (1973) 'Menger's Theories of Money and Uncertainty – A Modern Interpretation', in Hicks, J.R. and Weber, W. (Eds) *Carl Menger and the Austrian School of Economics.* Oxford: Clarendon Press, pp. 164–189.

Teixeira, P. (2014) 'Gary Becker's Early Work on Human Capital – Collaboration and Distinctiveness', *IZA Journal of Labor Economics*, Vol. 3:12, pp. 1–20.

Thomasberger, C. (2012) 'The Belief of Economic Determinism, Neoliberalism, and the Significance of Polanyi's Contribution in the Twenty-First Century', *International Journal of Political Economy*, Vol. 41:4, pp. 16–33.

Vanberg, V. (2004) 'The Freiburg School: Walter Eucken and Ordoliberalism', wp. http://hdl.handle.net/10419/4343/.

Van Overtveldt, J. (2007) *The Chicago School: How the University of Chicago Assembled the Thinkers who Revolutionized Economics and Business.* Chicago: Agate.

Weber, C. (2001) 'Pareto and the 53 Percent Ordinal Theory of Utility', *History of Political Economy*, Vol. 33:3, pp. 541–576.

Weintraub, R. (2002) *How Economics Became a Mathematical Science.* Durham, NC: Duke University Press.

Witzum, A. (1997) 'Distributive Considerations in Smith's Conception of Economic Justice', *Economics and Philosophy,* Vol. 13:2, pp. 241–259.

Wright, J. (2003) *The Ethics of Economic Rationalism.* Kensington, NSW: UNSW Press.

Zouboulakis, M. (2014) *The Varieties of Economic Rationality: From Adam Smith to Contemporary Behavioral and Evolutionary Economics.* London: Routledge.

4   Turning the world into a firm

In this last chapter the diffusion of the organizational structure of government, which is to be found both within enterprises and state bureaucracies, will be taken into consideration so as to explain how the neoliberal mindset had the opportunity to reach the widespread diffusion that can be observed almost everywhere today. The entrenchment of the neoliberal mentality in the concrete practice of government that is carried on within firms and public agencies is to be understood neither as an extension of the logic of the market, nor as an extension of what happens within firms and into the realm of public institutions. The point is that every collective form of life represents itself in those terms that have been articulated by the neoliberal organization theory: the self-understanding of individuals whose action is framed by the organizational discourse is, in fact, largely dependent on the spread of a specific set of assumptions about the meaning and scope of collective actions. Thus, a change in collective mindsets should be preceded by a modification of how the dominant discourse within the theory of organizations represents the institutional construction of human action.

4.1 Neoliberalism and the political role of the firm

Imagine a group of old, close friends gathered together around a table, who, now famous scholars, remember the time spent at university and the subsequent beginnings of their academic careers. Almost all of them have reached a prominent position within economics, a discipline that each of them contributed, albeit in different degrees, to change substantially. A scene like this does not belong to fiction, however: it describes exactly what happened in Los Angeles at the Law and Economics Center at Emory University on 21 to 23 March 1981. The chair of the discussion was John Moore, but the organizer of the meeting was Edmund Kitch, who also transcribed and edited it (Kitch 1983). Among the participants in the dialogue there were names that belong to the history of economic thought: Milton Friedman, Gary Becker, George Stigler, Ronald Coase, Richard Posner, Aaron Director, Robert Bork, and Harold Demsetz.

The reader of the dialogue can learn a lot about informal ways of communicating and sharing experiences within American academia – or, to put it differently, about the construction and reinforcement of a shared team spirit within an academic discipline. The reported conversation is often interrupted by laughter that comes after a joke, and the speakers participate in the discussion paying careful attention to the hierarchy that determines the position occupied by each of them – no matter whether this hierarchy refers to the seniority or to the scientific weight of each scholar. However, this is not the reason why we want to draw attention to Kitch's transcription of the informal colloquium held at the Law and Economics Center at the beginning of the 1980s. All the participants in the conversation praised one of the colleagues who sat at the table, Aaron Director. As Kitch observes, one of the purposes pursued by the meeting was precisely to pay a tribute of honour to Director, the founder of the *Journal of Law and Economics* in 1958, which he co-edited with Ronald Coase. Therefore, and not surprisingly, part of the conversation revolved around the inner story of the Chicagoan Law and Economics movement to which this journal has given voice since the beginning of its existence. It is to be noticed – and highlighted – why everybody among the participants was so prone to show their own gratitude to Director: he was the first to develop ideas about the meaning of anti-trust that would later become part of the core doctrine taught at Chicago. In addition, those ideas became so influential that it could be plainly said that they changed world history. What was at stake, in fact, was not simply a change in American legislation about the boundary between state and enterprise activity. At stake was the whole of the neoliberal political project.

In this regard, the colloquium organized by Kitch had also the aim to celebrate the first great victory that the Chicago School had achieved at the beginning of its long scientific and political history. The general tone of the introductory and conclusive parts of the article written by Kitch are structured upon the rhetoric of the challenges and the efforts made to win it, or, better, upon the rhetoric of a fight that has been won. The enemies that have been defeated are twofold: on the one hand, ignorance of the truth as regards the sound functioning of the market, and, at the same time, ignorance of the ethical merits of capitalism. On the other hand, a more concrete feature of the enemy, namely all those who oppose the political and social welfare of the United States – and an implicit syllogism suggests that those contrary to the improvement of the American economy are at the same time enemies of human liberty, since the political and economic well-being of the United States is the presupposition for global well-being.

At the beginning the ideas shared by the first Chicagoans spread among the economic discipline; then, through a series of rulings delivered by the Supreme Court, they took root in American policy. This has been possible partly because important works that exposed the Chicagoan thought in matters of anti-trust began to be quoted as authoritative sources by members of the Court, partly because an increasing number of judges appointed to deal with economic issues all over the United States had received a legal education that was more affected by the Chicagoan conceptual framework and less influenced by the traditional point of view on the matter, with its bulwark in Harvard. During the years following the publication of seminal works such as Posner (1976) and Bork (1978) one would have said that the shift introduced by the proponents of the Chicagoan paradigm has been accomplished. This explains the celebrative tones used by almost all the participants in the meeting and by Kitch himself. After all, nobody would have ever imagined that the one hour course that Director held at the Chicago Law School starting in 1946 – a course that was part of Edward Levi's weekly class on antitrust legislation – would have represented the beginning of a revolution both within the history of economic thought and within the public policies concerning antitrust and concurrence issues. Nevertheless, what the students experienced thanks to Aaron's teaching was – to use Bork's expression – no less than a 'religious conversion' (Kitch 1983, 183). Moreover, such deep changes in mentality, usually, lead people to act vigorously to spread the gospel of truth they have been touched by.

Still, what was so revolutionary in Director's ideas about antitrust? Briefly, it was about applying price theory to the analysis of legal issues. This is not simply related to the general commitment of the Chicago School to the neoclassical model. The programme developed by the Chicago School was far from being a matter of epistemology. The point was, since the beginning, to figure out – and to create – a social world governed by looking at those behavioural schemes that the neoclassical model has contributed to pose as definitive of human rationality in general, as if they had a normative character as well as a descriptive one. Neoliberalism – and this case shows it in a way that should be clear to everyone – is about governing people in a new way.

If one turns to the traditional anti-trust doctrine, which, as far as the United States are concerned, received its first legal consecration in the Sherman Act of 1890, the point stands out more sharply. The idea that underpinned antitrust policies carried out by liberally oriented authors and legislators was very simple: if one wants to guarantee the existence of a market based on concurrence, there must be rules that put some restraints on the agency of market actors, namely on their capability to take advantage from idiosyncratic elements that constitute their mode of being. It could be said that any antitrust procedure entails a certain degree of discretion. There are cases in which it might be not so easy to pinpoint where lies the boundary that separates a correct market behaviour from a behaviour motivated by the will to take advantage from the position one occupies as a market actor. However, the principle was simple: if a market actor does something that could impinge upon the other actors' rights, then the first actor must be stopped, by imposing a penalty, or by reducing the range of the advantage it has acquired. As is evident, the liberal view about the meaning and scope of antitrust procedures rests upon an overarching principle, which does not pertain to the economic realm per se: what such procedures should preserve, in fact, is the liberty of each actor – no matter whether it deals with an enterprise or an individual – when it trespasses the threshold of the market. This liberty is hence to be considered as a propriety that defines the actor independently from what it will do as an economic agent. Here it is not difficult to ascertain the persistence of a concept of agency construed by looking primarily at the agency of human individuals as a model – a concept, thus, whose origin goes back to the possessive individualism that makes out the main feature of liberalism (Macpherson 1962). This is a deficiency, perhaps, of this conception, which can be overcome, however, by considering the fact that groups such as organizations or institutions can be considered also as intentional agents – and intentionality, to a certain extent, can be viewed as the core of the agency.

Be that as it may, the point is that antitrust means, within the liberal worldview, to create an environment that not only allows for concurrence, but also, in a certain way, forces the actors to behave competitively. If public interventions modify the size of a company, or punish it for its misbehaviour, this means that the state is interested in preserving the intangibility of the market as the only site where it makes sense for an agent to act competitively. In sum, all the ingredients of the liberal way of conceiving of the relationship between the market and the state are to be found here: administrative and legal means are used to assure the good functioning of the market, and this occurs in the name of the market itself, assuming that it needs to be protected from possible failures due to individual behaviours that can endanger concurrence.

The principle according to which concurrence is not only a positive feature of market oriented behaviours, but also the very essence of the market as a site of human interaction is thus seen as a principle that can claim to be universal only within the economic realm, which is a separate realm in comparison to the political one. This explains the kind of antitrust measures previous to the beginning of the neoliberal era, which, taken as a whole, aimed essentially at preserving an environment where firms had the incentive to behave competitively. Antitrust legislation was about punishing illegal behaviours like tying arrangements, vertical integrations, exclusive dealing, and price-fixing agreements. Still, its main concern was – rather obviously – to fight against monopolistic tendencies, namely to impede mergers and acquisitions from leading to concentrations of economic power that *de facto* hamper competition. The point is not to make monopoly illegal, but to prevent the abuse that derives from a monopolistic position, as, for example, when one firm excludes another from entering into a market. However, consumers' rights too were to be upheld according to classical conceptions of antitrust legislation: when the market power of a firm is too big, then the risk grows that consumers' power may diminish. Therefore, judicial interventions are necessary to prevent unfair transfers of wealth from purchasers to firms with market power. Further, it must be also added that, from a liberal viewpoint, too big corporations are also seen as entities capable of threatening democracy: their dimension could lead them to gain power not only as economic, but also as political actors. A very important aspect of the issue has been well captured by Hayek (1960) who pointed out the dangers related to a situation in which firms are interlocked with each other because one firm is allowed to possess the stocks of another one. Such a situation is favourable to the emergence of a power concentration in the hands of those managers who sit on the board of more than one enterprise. When this elite of top managers can act unleashed, claiming, moreover, to be called to give answers to questions that lie far beyond their competence, then democracy itself can be endangered.

The scenario changes completely within neoliberally oriented antitrust legislation. What counts, here, is market efficiency, not concurrence per se. This does not mean that concurrence ceases to be important, or that it disappears from the way in which the neoliberal discourse articulates the meaning of market behaviours. Now the focus of policy is on the consequences that legislation has upon the efficiency of the market. Moreover, this focus entails a completely new way of conceiving of the concept of competition among actors. From a liberal point of view, competition should be protected and, if needed, improved. From a neoliberal one, concurrence is an intrinsic property of any market; what should be improved and assured, then, is the efficiency of the market.

Efficiency, however, could be defined as an 'essentially contested' concept, to use an expression current within epistemology (Gallie 1955–56). This means that efficiency is so multifaceted a concept that much about its definition – if not everything – depends on the perspective from which the subject of science looks at its extension. But the Chicago School succeeded in creating a very precise and technical definition of what efficiency should be, so that any political implication of it could remain hidden – or, better, so that it became possible to prevent first the scientific community, then decision-makers from perceiving the political project that the Chicagoan concept of market efficiency pre-supposed. Furthermore, this was a true stroke of genius. In fact, efficiency, since then, has become a property of the total welfare, which can be perceived thanks to the readability offered by neoclassic models. In other words: if the outcome of an action induces the aggregate of all producers to reduce the total amount of goods they produce, then this outcome is to be held as inefficient – and only the occurrence of this circumstance should compel the judicial power to intervene.

Of course, there might be – and, *de facto*, there are – other definitions of efficiency (Fox 2008). A firm can pursue efficiency by its efforts to produce and distribute goods at the lowest feasible cost. The allocation of resources can be understood as efficient when, taking account of buyers' willingness to achieve them at their lowest cost, they are sold at the highest price. The aim to more efficiency leads the effort to diffuse knowledge or technological innovation within an organization as well as within the market through cross-fertilization among firms. Finally, we can speak of efficiency with respect to consumer welfare; in this case, attention must be drawn to whether an economic behaviour can cause a shrink in consumers' surplus.

Now, maintaining that the consumer's welfare was not a central concern for those Congress members who voted for the Sherman Act would be possible only if one wanted to deny the historical truth. The same commitment to historical truth invites the observer to admit that, if one casts a glance at the history of the American Court decisions, it cannot be said that attention to the well-being of consumers has totally disappeared and that the suggestions coming from Chicago have thoroughly deprived the original meaning of the Sherman Act. There have been cases, in fact, in which defendants who wanted to overcome the presumption that a proposed acquisition or merger would lessen competition were invited by the courts to demonstrate that the intended acquisition would result in significant economies and that these economies would ultimately benefit competition and, finally, consumers (Kirkwood and Lande 2008). Single officials too, who were particularly devoted to their duty, played an important role in contrasting the anticompetitive effects of those behaviours that were at odds with the antitrust legislation. As long as the Nixon Administration was convinced of the opportunity to restrain the tendency toward vertical and horizontal mergers, Richard W. McLaren – just to mention one example among others – while serving in the Antitrust Division from 1969 to 1971 demonstrated great zeal in applying the antitrust legislation (Fligstein 1990). Nevertheless, as soon as the Chicagoan paradigm came into the foreground, oppositions to big concentrations of economic power have been removed not only from the economic discourse, but also from the public policy practice.[1]

One could be tempted to see in the shift of paradigm introduced by Chicago's ideas about market efficiency, and in their influence on the current conception of antitrust policies, the proof that neoliberalism aims at depriving the political and legal sphere of their autonomy. Nevertheless, if we consider the reasons why market efficiency is what the legislator and the judge are supposed to improve, then we can perceive that the scenario we are confronted with is rather different. According to Chicago's doctrine, efficiency is not meant any more as an attribute of given outputs that can be observed and then inserted into a broader analytical model. The concept of efficiency the Chicago School talks about has a normative character that encompasses the activity of all possible actors involved in any social interaction under the assumption that their behaviour is the result of a maximizing attitude. Efficiency does not even deserve to be measured, even if the term still evokes the necessity of measurement. Efficiency, in fact, presupposes equilibrium, because the interaction among maximizing actors, according to neoclassic assumptions, will always produce an equilibrium outcome. Within the same context, a new conception of competition comes into the foreground. Competition does not deserve regulation in order to be improved or tamed. Competition is already there where agents interact, no matter whether they do it outside or inside the market. Competition, thus, acquires a political significance, in the sense that it becomes the state of affairs by referring to which the governmental action is supposed to acquire its own legitimacy.

If it is referred to the antitrust issue, then, this view leads to the conclusion that it is not necessary to intervene in order to put constraints of whatsoever kind upon agents. This conclusion entails as a corollary that the emergence of monopolistic behaviours is not to be prevented as such. This aspect might be seen as a sort of unintended consequence of a strain of arguments that stems from a rigorous application of the neoclassical idea of market equilibrium. That the willingness to adhere ruthlessly to the neoclassic paradigm is an important feature of the Chicagoan frame of mind is undeniable. But, as Van Horn (2009) has shown with sufficient accuracy, those who gave birth to the Law and Economics movement were also aware of what was at stake in providing a theoretical framework that had to lie at the feet of state policies. Their 'conversion' to a new model of antitrust policy occurred within a short lapse of time between the end of the 1940s and the beginning of the 1950s. Prior to this time, scholars like Director, Levi or Friedman were concerned about the disruptive effects of big concentrations of market power, as Simons had been before them. Then they came to a conclusion that, at first sight, might sound rather astonishing: given a regime of competition, monopolistic tendencies end up compensating for each other. It might be true that barriers to entry, price fixing, horizontal or vertical mergers, a firm's growth in size can amount to situations in which the advantage gained by one competitor causes damage to another competitor. However, it must be proven case by case whether these situations are such as to affect efficiency or to restrain trade. In other words, the rule of reason is enough of a criterion that helps decide whether to adopt legal measures against a firm.

The rationale behind this way of considering the question of monopoly was that corporations had suddenly become, in the eyes of all the Chicagoans, those institutions that at best approximated the impersonal ideal of the market (Van Horn 2009, 208), a circumstance that could be expressed just as well by saying that the corporation had risen to the status of a giant that can never fail to do the right thing as a maximizing agent. Therefore, corporations, when confronted with environments whose extension – not only in the geographical sense of the term – encourages the concentration of power, are compelled to rise in size: within such environments economies of scale seem to be a necessary precondition for survival. Of course, it is easy to imagine that the effort made to reach economies of scale can entangle monopolistic effects, or that this effort can lead competing firms to come to agreements and arrangements, a situation that is usually termed as an oligopoly. Now, since both the tendency to grow in size and the resulting convenience to establish agreements with partners of comparable size are the outcome of rational behaviour, it is illogical to cast a negative judgement upon this state of affairs: if looked at according to the Chicagoan perspective, the situation just described offers a typical example of the maximizing attitude that characterizes agents that strive to survive and, in the long run, succeed in surviving.

The argument keeps close to being circular, but is nonetheless typical of the Chicagoan way of presenting the conclusions drawn from neoclassical assumptions. It recalls Friedman's effort to lay the ground for an epistemic foundation of what would have later become mainstream economics

(Friedman 1953). In the present context, however, it is Stigler's way of dealing with the issue of economies of scale that one has to bear in mind. In Stigler (1958) this issue is cast within a framework that is supposed, initially, to take into consideration the importance of the problem both for economic analysis and for the public decision maker who has to stand over the social and political relevance of organizations like enterprises. Hence, the decisive move consists in leaving unanswered the question about what size a firm is supposed to have with respect to its social function. Economic analysis, so Stigler's argument goes, can tell us what comes into the foreground when we look at enterprises facing problems related to labour relations, rapid innovation, government regulation, and unstable foreign markets. If, instead, questions arise that are related to monopoly power, undesirable labour practices, or discriminatory legislation, then the economic science restrains itself from casting a judgement upon the given state of affairs. Neutral as it must be as a science, economics provides an answer only to the question of efficiency.

Traditionally, determining the optimum size of an enterprise was, first, a matter of comparative evaluation of resources. Yet, the compound of average costs and rates of return referred to firms of similar size operating within the same environment cannot yield the desired final result, namely which of them has the optimal size. If historical cost evaluation of resources is taken into consideration, the observer should be able to evaluate an amount of data that can be barely processed by the human mind, and if the evaluation is based on expected earnings, the situation is not so different, in the sense that the observer should be an omniscient subject. The second method used to solve the problem, based on the evaluation of the costs due to technological investments, had to face similar difficulties and was of scarce utility. What Stigler proposes is a new method of evaluation, which he calls the 'survivor technique'. It is based on the postulate that 'the competition of different sizes of firms sifts out the more efficient enterprises' (ibid., 55).

Does this argument explain why certain enterprises have successfully overcome all the environmental challenges in the fight for survival? In a way, it does not: on the one hand, enterprises can win the competition because they are efficient, and, on the other, enterprises can show the degree of efficiency they have reached because they have won the competition – because, to use Stigler's terms, they have been 'sifted out'. But, as strange as it may sound, this argument fails, in effect, to bring an explanation: since enterprises are maximizing agents and the optimal size of an enterprise has been the outcome of a decisional process aimed at maximizing, the fact that the enterprise with the optimal size stands out as a 'survivor' rests on the pertinence of the choices made by the enterprise itself in order to win the competition with rivals of similar size.[2]

It would be a great mistake, thus, to overlook that the Chicagoan way of looking at the political question connected to the influence that corporations might achieve if their size grows too much constitutes precisely the core of the neoliberal project. Apparently, what stands out here is a sound separation between realms – the social function of corporations on one side, on the other their economic performances within a market which sifts out only those enterprises that are best equipped for competition. We suggest, on the contrary, that it is not a sort of commitment to the neutrality of scientific analysis that motivates the apparent disregard of the unintended consequences that an antitrust policy not directed toward the limitation of monopolistic effects could have on democracy. A precise conception both of society and of the power devices that govern it underpins the Chicagoan conception discussed up to this point.

While Simons in his *Positive Program for Laissez Faire* (an article issued in 1934, which can be rightly considered as a sort of manifesto of declining classical liberalism) was still deeply convinced that '*the great enemy of democracy is monopoly, in all its forms*' (Simons 1948, 43; author's emphasis) for the great concentration of power it allowed, all the Chicago scholars who came after him had no fear of the increasing power of an elite involved in the government of society by virtue of the positions it occupied both within the corporate world and within public institutions. It was the elite observed with great concern by a liberal sociologist like Mills late in the 1950s[3] – and it is, apart from the obvious historical differences, the elite that popular simplifications of distribution of global power vividly captures through the image of the '1 %'.

Thanks to Chandler (1977), scholarship became acquainted with the fact that, starting at least from the last decaying days of the nineteenth century, market practices and tendencies toward the establishment of oligopolistic relationships among big corporations are strictly related to each other and can well coexist within the same historical context. Bearing this in mind is important in order to understand the genesis of neoliberal ideas. Precisely when Chicagoan economists began to reject the previous conception that posed the image of a well functioning market in opposition to the image of a market infected by oligopolistic tendencies, American big corporations were gaining the confidence of public opinion in their effort to present themselves as the bulwark of American identity.

The path that led to this result had been long and arduous, as Marchand (1998) shows in a detailed manner. In the age of robber barons, people of different political orientation and belonging to different social classes shared a general criticism against the power of big corporations. Starting from *Santa Clara County v. Southern Pacific Railroad*, a sentence issued in 1886, which proclaimed that the legal status of a person can be ascribed to a corporation, the American corporation began to seek for a soul that could justify its new status as a 'person', that is its ever more growing role as a social actor. The need for a soul implied the commitment to values that could be felt by stakeholders as the expression that the corporation was not simply a gigantic monster uniquely devoted to increase its profits on behalf of shareholders. In other words, this quest for cultural acceptance led the corporation to undertake all possible efforts to discard the impression that its unique scope was to maximize profits at the cost both of those who worked for it and of the rest of society.

The large size of the giant business corporation was perceived as proof of its ruthlessness, aloofness, coldness. It thus became necessary to build a collective imagery that allowed public opinion to consider the presence of the corporation as a familiar one. This task could be accomplished only by reducing the distance between the ordinary milieu within which most people spent their lives and the impersonal force of a business that had its material staple in a chain of production dispersed all over the country or even overseas. The discursive machinery brought about to achieve this goal poured its persuasive force into both the inside and outside of the corporation itself. Two contributing factors, which were to experience an increasing growth concerning their cultural and social significance during the same period of time, helped the corporation to delete its old image of a soulless giant. On the one hand, the diffusion of new communication medias and, on the other, the establishment of a specific form of knowledge the scope of which was to understand, first, how collective mindsets work, and, second, how they could be steered and driven in this or that direction. Once acquainted with works like Bernays (1928), both advertisers and those who managed the human resources of enterprises quickly understood that a well-constructed propaganda machine could influence every aspect of human behaviour.

Those who engaged themselves in the effort to build the new corporate image were the chief executives of big enterprises that Berle and Means (1932) described as the new leading force within American business. They played a pivotal role in promoting the creation of an entrepreneurial ethos that had the function to transform the corporation into a community, which was supposed to enter a dialogue with other communities, firstly with the local groups where plants were settled, secondly with the entire nation. At the local scale, the corporation sought to address the needs of the environment surrounding workplaces. This was an important move in order to face the reproach that organizations of huge size were not only anonymous and rootless, but also able to endanger the cohesion of social ties. At the national scale, the effort was directed toward the construction of a corporate image able to embody the main traits of the American worldview. Not surprisingly, in the foreground stood the freedom of enterprise meant as the core of the whole system of values upon which America was supposed to rest. The system of laws set up by America's Constitution exists, after all, in order to secure all forms of individual liberty, and the freedom of enterprise is surely not one of the less relevant among them.

The necessity to present the corporation as an individual whose personhood was not simply the result of a judicial ruling required also the strengthening of the internal ties that made the corporation an effective unity. There is no need to say that the rhetorical efforts in this direction brought another advantage, surely not less important, namely the softening of the degree of internal conflicts. In particular, during the historical period when American unionism was able to mobilize large parts of public opinion, generating a 'we' solidarity that would unite labour and management in loyal service to a

single goal became a priority for corporate America. Strategies for implementing the internal communications were deployed by management in
order to make clear that the enterprise was able to take care of individual
needs and vulnerabilities. The latter acquired an increasing visibility as soon
as scientific management became the main tool for generating self-reflection
within the organization. Becoming aware of the internal processes and collecting
information upon both what fosters motivation and what engenders frustra-
tion or dissatisfaction became part of the executives' tasks. At the same time,
a narrative that underscored the family-like character of the enterprise served
the purpose both to compensate the distance that actually existed between
employer and worker and to fulfil with content the rhetoric of industrial
democracy.

If we consider how obvious is the idea that American mentality and the
tradition of liberalism are bound up in an indissoluble unity, it is worth
remembering that the political and cultural fate of corporate America could find
a strong counterpart in a cultural movement that surely shared with liberalism
the commitment to democracy, but was also prone to hand the management
of democracy over to the corporation. In his most influential work, *The Process
of Government*, Arthur Bentley states without hesitation that 'the corporation is
government through and through' (Bentley 1908, 268). Such a statement
should not arouse surprise if one perceives the corporation as one instantiation,
among others, of a group of individuals that bear different interests and seek
to compose them in a sustainable way. This is a perspective that allows one to
compare the different forms of governing the corporation with the different
state forms of government that have been identified by political science.
Bentley goes so far as to consider the corporation as a sovereign entity, as can
be acknowledged by looking at the following passage:

> Certain technical methods which political government uses, as, for
> instance, hanging, are not used by corporations (...). The difference in
> technical methods, the fact that political governments control corporations,
> even the fact that corporations sometimes control political governments,
> does not suffice to throw their processes out of the range that must be
> included in the same word that is used to cover the phenomena of political
> government.
>
> (Bentley 1908, 268)

In a way that resembles Foucault's definition of the political as the art of
government, Bentley's description of the processes of government aims at
analysing all the possible forms of adjustment of those conflicts that unavoidably charge the encounter of groups of different size and nature. The fact
that he welcomes the increase of the social and political relevance assumed by
the corporation rests on the idea that the corporation is supposed to guarantee
social harmony and democracy better than the state bureaucracy, which is
always about to infect the good functioning of political life because of the

private interests of those who work as bureaucrats.[4] Based on an elitist-democratic model of government, which is technical in its deepest nature, the corporation is deprived of populism, racism, demagogy, statism, namely of all those deficiencies that flaw the public government.

Other figures belonging to the cultural American landscape at the beginning of the last century are worth being mentioned here, albeit fleetingly. The anti-capitalism of the utopian writer Edward Bellamy developed a stance that was not contrary to the corporation per se, while a political thinker like Herbert Croly, who was strongly committed to the Progressive movement, was convinced that, if conveniently tamed (which could mean even nationalized, if necessary) and if managed in such a way that the Unions had the right to voice opinions different from those of the executive, the corporation could serve the scope of fostering both democracy and nationalism. Assuming that a merely Jeffersonian conception of democracy lacks the ingredients that are necessary to improve a strong sense of collective life, Croly, rather consistently, suggests that the corporation should be entrusted with the task of educating the nation for defending American values (Croly 1909). Not surprisingly, Croly was a great admirer of Marcus Alonzo Hanna, the perfect personification of a tycoon who did not hesitate to interlace his entrepreneurial activity with the political life of the nation. Furthermore, among the supporters of *The New Republic*, a magazine created by Croly in 1914, we find Willard Straight, whose diplomatic activity in the Far East was combined with his political engagement aimed at convincing the political elite that it was necessary for the United States to develop a more expansive foreign policy in Asia. Straight's ideas, as well as Lippmann's, who joined the group of intellectuals gathered around *The New Republic*, did not call for an aggressive and imperialistic stance: the goal to acquire a dominant position should have been achieved by fostering the emergence of an international order that would have enabled the American corporation to win the economic competition with foreign enterprises.[5] In this sense, both Croly and his friends and supporters were prone to see no difference between the capability that both public institutions and corporations had to shape the inner life of the nation as well as its foreign policy. Competition, at an international scale, is competition among nations, but the range of the agency of each nation state coincides with the range reached by its corporations.

It is worth noting that the birth of corporate America is a historical phenomenon that can be compared with analogous developments that took place in other parts of the world at almost the same time. On the other side of the Atlantic corporatism became part of the political programme of Italian Fascism. The latter was a multifaceted movement that succeeded in creating a totalitarian society not only by employing violence and by those repressive methods that are typical of dictatorial regimes, but also by deploying a propaganda machine within which corporatism played a pivotal role. It must be noticed, however, that it also harboured anti-capitalistic oriented fringes whose main commitment was to develop an organic society (in the sense Tönnies used this term) that should have had its cornerstone in an innovative way of managing the enterprise by developing forms of partnership between ownership and labour. More generally, all the social planning programmes that the Fascist regime developed in order to create a welfare state were carried on under the flag of corporatism (Ben-Ghiat 2001).

Even if in different forms, Nazi Germany too made great efforts toward the creation of corporate environments within which the consolidation of specific forms of interaction between labour forces and management was supposed to foster both the enforcement of German industry and the new identity the Nazi movement wanted to give the German nation. The *Büro für die Schönheit der Arbeit* (Bureau for the Beauty of Labour), created in 1934, had the mission to convince patrons and executives of German enterprises to ameliorate the material conditions of life at the workplace – but accomplishing this mission was also instrumental in the diffusion and consolidation of the Nazi regime (Rabinbach 1976).

Even if the list of examples could be continued, the point we want to make is already clear. During the first half of the last century, modern industrial societies experienced the emergence of similar phenomena related to the increasing importance of the corporation. The similarity consists in the fact that, even if the corporate elite and the political elite may have pursued different goals, they were able to find a common ground by considering the corporate culture as a good means either to improve the construction of strong national identities, or to consolidate the political and cultural acceptance of big business by public opinion.

Now, if one considers the role played by management both in totalitarian regimes and in democratic countries within this process, one could be tempted to affirm that Burnham (1941) was right, at least to a certain extent. Animated by a strong libertarian ethos after the abandonment of his previous radical leftist positions, Burnham targeted the power exerted by a new class of technocrats that, both in democratic America and in Soviet Russia, were prone to assume the role of educators of the entire nation. According to Burnham, it would be misleading to focus only on the value system that they sought to mobilize. Much more important was the power position they were assigned. By taking advantage from this position they soon demonstrated the capability to shape political agendas whose range was far beyond the mere advocacy of corporate interests. Burnham's discourse leans on the analysis carried on by Berle and Means, but the goal he pursued went far beyond the desire to accomplish a sociological survey of what was going on during his time, which would have been ambitious enough. *The Managerial Revolution* is rather a dystopic vision animated by the willingness to denounce the ominous fate of both Western democracies and the communist system. Such an ambition deprives the work of any scientific significance. Nevertheless, if it is still worth referring to it, this occurs because it contributed to grasping a phenomenon that must be taken into account if one wants to understand the context within which neoliberalism emerged: namely, to make clear that what happens within the boundary of an enterprise has to do not only with the production, sale and, consequently, profits, but also with culture, values, and politics – or, to use a Foucauldian term, biopolitics. In other words, looking at Burnham's ideas serves to create a useful point of contrast: what threatened Burnham was precisely what the proponents of the Chicago school welcomed unconditionally. Instead of denouncing the problematic feature – to say the least – of a market structure endangered by the presence of few, big competitors, the proponents of the neoliberal programme gave their scientific support to the new born corporate America.

Actually, the period immediately subsequent to the Second World War saw the triumph of efforts made to convince American public opinion of how strictly intertwined was the destiny of the United States with the success of its big business enterprises. During the war American business could still any criticism directed toward the egoistic goals it was supposed to pursue by showing an unquestionable commitment to victory against the enemy. Not surprisingly, this commitment made itself visible not only by adapting the productive system to the war needs, but also by constructing a rhetoric that had the function of presenting corporate values as those values for which the American soldier fought at the front. As Alfred Sloan, CEO of General Motors, remarked in 1939, it was hard to recognize any difference between the interests of the corporation and the interests of the nation (Marchand 1998, 317).

However, the engagement of corporate America during the war did not imply an unconditioned compliance with the set of policies adopted by the American government. Managers and chief executives insisted on how essential the freedom of enterprise was to the American identity, and made every effort to put in the foreground the fact that precisely the freedom of enterprise would have collapsed, or would have even disappeared, if America had lost the war. The struggle for victory against the Axis was thus meant as a struggle for liberty, both for the United States and for the world. This rhetoric justified the reproach against those policies that the Roosevelt administration began to endorse during the New Deal. These policies implied the adoption of forms of regulation that were seen as unbearable and, above all, as contrary to the development of a sound economic system based on the freedom of enterprise. It would seem that, the necessity of sustaining the military effort of the nation might have induced toleration for a certain degree of centralized regulation in the economic field, but nonetheless, the message that corporate America was willing to launch was rather clear: it makes no sense to fight against totalitarian systems that deprive individuals of liberty if America itself is not convinced of the fact that limiting the freedom of enterprise constitutes an inexcusable attack on individual liberty.

In conclusion, during the Second World War and in the immediate aftermath corporate America had the unique opportunity to kill two birds with one stone. First, it succeeded in persuading public opinion that the moral values in the name of which the war had been fought were the same values that big business was contributing to radiate across the nation. In this way, the previous image of the soulless corporation could be removed from the collective discourse. Second, it went on, now undisturbed, with its campaign against those 'socialist' forms of regulation that would have ended up with encumbering the economic prosperity of the nation.

Yet, this is only one part of the story. The truth is that American corporations took enormous advantages from the economic policies that characterized the war period, and, furthermore, learned how comfortable it was to pursue their own interests by operating in an environment that not only provided for, but also demanded the mutual interaction between big business and governmental agencies. Since then this intertwinement kept on saturating the political landscape, in the sense that it became more and more difficult to forge any policy without considering the strategic weight of corporate America concerning internal as well as foreign policy issues. The result has been a win-win situation for all the actors involved. It is even possible to use the term corporatism in order to describe the peculiar architecture of the relations between the public sphere and the network formed by big business corporations. It is true that the commonly shared discourse has always forbidden even the use of the term 'corporatism' with regard to the way in which public agencies and big corporations are interlocked. 'Interest group liberalism' is the only expression that seems to be accepted. It is true as well that the United States has never had a manifest authoritarian corporatism that could be compared with the one that characterized European history during the twentieth century. The institutional architecture of the country, with its large administrative-state regulatory apparatuses, has hence allowed the emergence of a specific form of corporatism, which grew in a creeping way at the beginning, and then became coextensive with the governmental structure. In this regard, the difference between democratic and republican administrations is rather minimal. Eisenhower, for instance, who coined the term 'corporate commonwealth' with reference to his own politic agenda, pursued a vision of society in which pluralism and liberalism were able to go hand in hand with a pragmatic, voluntary and incremental form of corporatism, which emphasized social harmony and class collaboration. If one disregards the proclamation of principles, however, the policies carried out during his administration stand out for their similarity with those carried out during Roosevelt's one. Generally speaking, the two brands of corporatism, the republican and the democratic one, did not differ substantially from each other, both bringing the same result, namely the blurring of private groups and public agencies (Wiarda 1997). In no way and in no time, after the Second World War, corporate America ceased to be considered the most appropriate partner of whatsoever governmental action tending to improve the presence of the United States as a global player. The repeal of the Glass-Steagall Act, which occurred during the Clinton administration in 1999, is just one example among others, worth being mentioned for the enormous consequences it had on a global scale.[6]

Yet, it would be misleading to reduce neoliberalism to a form of corporatism. The latter helps surely define an important aspect of what neoliberalism is about. It is a sort of truism that the theory of market efficiency developed by the Chicago School dovetails its main assumptions about firm behaviour within a competitive market with the need big corporations have to justify their tendency to occupy quasi monopolistic positions. Moreover, it is true as well that neoliberal economics at Chicago grew up within a cultural and political context that was deeply charged by the intrusive presence of corporations, which had just succeeded in making their interests coincide with the interests of the whole nation. However, the neoliberal economic theory carries ambitions that reach far beyond ex-post justifications for what big corporations do when acting in a monopolistic way.

The idea that promoting a certain economic order constitutes not only a step toward the strengthening of national culture, but also a necessary premise for the self-positioning of the nation state within the geopolitical arena is, per se, alien to the main tenets of neoliberalism. Of course, in order to understand why neoliberalism took root firstly in the United States before spreading all over the world, it is important to bear in mind how tight have always been the bonds between governmental agencies and private business. Nevertheless, by doing so we simply remind ourselves that pointing out broad cultural and social contexts is a sound premise for the historical location of the observed phenomena. More precisely: might it be opportune, on the one hand, to consider the presence of these bonds as a justification for saying that the United States has been – and still is – a corporatist country, and then the observer should be simply induced, on the other, to pose the question whether the United States has been more vulnerable to embracing a neoliberal point of view about policy issues or not. Hence, it seems too hasty, we argue, to subsume the relation between corporatism and neoliberalism under a causal schema.

It seems plausible to affirm, however, that neoliberalism came into existence in a historical moment that was favourable to an economic theory whose aim was to reduce the weight of the free market (meant in terms of *laissez-faire*) and to underscore the positive role played by public institutions in shaping actively the context within which economic actors operate. In this sense, the Chicago School met exactly the Zeitgeist – but at the same time proposed a model for the government of the economic and the political sphere that went far beyond the mere necessity to interlace the two spheres with each other.

Generally speaking, if a nation state embraces a nationalist stance or undertakes a foreign policy devoted to acquire a hegemonic position within the global arena (or both), and if it does so by adopting a specific set of measures that make it possible for their enterprises to play a dominant role, this is a state of affairs that may reveal motivations of a different nature – it could reveal, for example, the willingness to increase its own prestige. The neoliberal model of rationality limits itself to suggest a certain ratio between means and goals, but this model aims at presenting itself as neutral with regard to the results one can eventually reach by adopting a neoliberal agenda. There are, thus, different sets of values to which corporatism is prone to give advantage – elitism, or nationalism, for example – but none of them is necessarily close to the neoliberal *Weltanschauung*. For the supporters of neo-liberalism, it was of pivotal importance, however, to pose the enterprise as a subject able to embody pure market rationality. And corporate America did not need to be asked twice: after having fought – and won – its own war against what was supposed to represent a culture of state centralism and state regulation, it kept on holding high the banner of the freedom of enterprise, and it did so even in the presence of continuous, blatant proof of state interference in favour of American big business.

4.2 The neoliberal theory of organizations

One could now raise the following question: if one of the major tenets of neoliberalism is about the market space to be constructed in order to let big corporations thrive and flourish, how could it happen that the neoliberal discourse has been – and still is – perceived as an uncompromised defence of the free market? Not only those scholars belonging to the ideological field of Marxism, but the informed citizen too (once one would have said 'the average man') have no hesitation in making neoliberalism coincide with a political programme whose unique aim is to destroy public institutions and substitute the services offered by the latter with services offered by firms. This substitution is perceived – and feared – as the triumph of the free market.

It is true that the public image of a neoliberal world is interwoven with the rhetoric of the free market, and it is also true that this image has dominated – and is still dominating – the battlefield within which opponents and supporters of neoliberalism have been fighting since the beginning of the neoliberal era. Yet, the market here in question is not simply the institution where exchanges take place, but is above all and foremost a god that stands out against both the flow of cash that floods in the pits where traders buy and sell derivatives of all sort, and the flow along which mortals like us spend their lives.

Religious aspects of the market rhetoric that characterizes neoliberalism have been actually observed within the community of traders (Zaloom 2006). Members of the latter tend to attribute to a hypostatized image of the market ominous properties – a sort of agency, one could say. Far from being cold and rational calculators, or cyborgs deprived of any feeling, traders usually let personal desires and convictions flow into their evaluations and judgment about the value fluctuations the financial products undergo in the course of the day. This lack of emotional neutrality engenders a narrative about the behaviour of the market tinged with religious undertones. During the online exchange the traders' normal day is made of, the market places itself between buyers and sellers and, in this state of in-betweenness, it acquires a sort of personal autonomy that induces one to get forgetful of the abstract shape of Pareto's indifference curve. If interviewed, traders not infrequently refer to the market with religious tones that betray their mystical engagement in what they are doing.[7]

Furthermore, this narrative goes in hand with a specific form of practice, which can be well described in terms of ascesis. As the market is supposed to always do the right thing, it is thus rather obvious that one has to conform oneself to how the market expresses its will by determining the direction of the flow of prices. Of course, it is important to be self confident, and to rely on oneself – this is an essential part of traders' discipline too. However, one must learn how to decipher the protean will and mercurial moods of the market, being the latter the highest authority from which one can expect punishment or reward. Furthermore, the market is given another trait that is usually part of the endowments of divine figures, namely atemporality. From a trivial empirical perspective, one cannot perceive any beginning or end of the activity of financial markets: while the trading day approaches its end in Tokyo, traders sit in front of their screens in the City, and when they begin to move to the next pub, their mates are going to begin the working day in Wall Street. However, apart from this, what really matters here is, once again, a peculiar narrative that induces one to perceive the market's tendency toward a state of equilibrium as if the latter were the internal movement of a divine substance that is not related to the human experience of time and space. The work of the trader consists in grasping these movements and capturing their fleeting appearance, well aware of the fact, however, that the market, in itself, does not move nor suffers any temporal change (Miyazaki 2003).

Yet, it would be a sort of wishful thinking to assume that only those who work in the financial sector share such a view of the market. A sort of 'market populism' (Frank 2000) has been dominating the collective imaginary for decades. In addition, this conveys the image of the market as a powerful god too. It is a god that cannot be restrained by any state power, and the narrative market populism is based on promises that all the inhabitants of earth will benefit precisely from the absence of any restriction. Not everybody, of course, shares this faith in the omnipotence of the market, but even sceptics and heretics share the narrative according to which the market is what moves everything in the world. That this narrative could conform to the truth is an impression reinforced by the fact that, within a market that is as big as the global space, giant corporations do what they want, unleashed and outside any control. Metanational corporations (Doz, Santos and Williamson 2001) such as Glencore, Accenture, Exxonmobil, Dutch Shell, just to name a few of them, have their legal domicile in one country, corporate management in another, financial assets in a third, and administrative staff spread over several more. Just tracking the many sources of their revenues in order to turn them into compliant tax-payers has become impossible. Before them citizens fear that what still remains of the collective rights conquered during the Glorious Thirty is going to be eroded by privatizations of public services that are perceived as a gift made to transnational firms.

In short, this is the well-known story that depicts the free market as the greatest blessing that could ever occur in human history – or as the greatest curse, it depends on the viewpoint from which one considers the matter. Now, considering the global diffusion of this narrative it seems not so inappropriate to speak of a stroke of genius as regards how neoliberalism succeeded in convincing the global audience that everything is about the free market, and not about a revolution in the art of governing people through both enterprises and public institutions. The premise for this has been to promote a conception of antitrust that could leave room for the willingness of big corporations to develop themselves by taking advantage of governmental protections. The neoliberal discourse, thus, passes as a theory of the free market what is in reality a very sophisticated theory of government that calls for the entrenchment of both corporate and state power thanks to their mutual partnership.

It is a pity – but this is said ironically – that Friedman's attack against the very idea of *laissez-faire* passed thoroughly unobserved. We refer to Friedman (1951), a short text already considered in Chapter 2 of this volume. This article could be well considered as a sort of manifesto of neoliberalism, which, must be admitted, has been then obscured, not surprisingly, by his later, and more famous, *Capitalism and Freedom* (Friedman 1962). At the beginning of the glorious history of the Chicago School (Friedman was appointed there in 1943) Friedman takes stance in an unequivocal manner against any form of *laissez-faire* policy. Of course, among the enemies that Western civilization must fight we find mentioned communism too. While the latter, sooner or later, is going to be defeated, Friedman deems much more important to draw attention to the wrong idea that the state has nothing to do as regards the improvement of the economic order within which individual life can thrive and prosper. For a long time, *laissez-faire* policies have been an appropriate means to improving the freedom of individuals. Now, so argued Friedman in 1951, time has come to recognize that the state itself must intervene in order to construct those spaces of interaction within which individuals can compete with others. An artificially constructed competitive order, where competition is the normal form of interaction among producers, consumers, employers and enterprises: this is the outspoken prospect of the coming neoliberal era that Friedman foretells and wishes at the same time. In short, what the reader finds here is nothing less than the project of governing individuals by compelling them to compete with each other no matter within which space of interaction they find themselves and which social or institutional role they play. One point to note is the social Darwinian connotation that Friedman's discourse possesses – a connotation that was not alien to Stigler (1958) too.[8] Much more important, however, is the complete detachment from the classical liberal tradition, which Friedman refuses by opposing it with a conception of the market that, we dare say, is purely nominal.

It is rather clear that the informed citizen would have not so easily taken notice of a text such as Friedman (1951) in order to become acquainted with how the first proponents of neoliberalism had dreamed of a new world dominated by a generalized competition that should have been regulated if not imposed upon by state power. Nonetheless, it would have been perhaps a little bit easier to observe the development of the economic world during the last twenty to thirty years. In this way, it would have been possible to see how strong has always been not only the commitment of states toward monopolistic or oligopolistic actors, but above all the willingness these actors had to be helped, sustained and supported by public agencies in order to avoid the competition that characterizes a free market. Scholars who have devoted attention to this issue bring enough evidence of the uninterrupted bargaining process in which corporations get involved when they have to either avail themselves of state aids, or eschew national norms they find inconvenient (Levy and Prakash 2003). Rules are needed when operating on a global scale, and these rules are the result of negotiation between a corporation and one or more states. We understand this fact better if we consider that the geopolitical play is made by the interaction of several members that strive for a hegemonic position. Within this game, multinational corporations are interested in forming alliances with states, either with those states where they are rooted, or with states of equal weight in the case of metanational corporations. The existence of international standards is, for example, a great advantage for creating economies of scale. On one hand, firms with production – or distribution – units spread across many countries find everywhere the same standards; on the other, they know that concurrent firms will be subject to these standards as well. Furthermore, the appeal to international standards allows the opportunity to bypass the standards imposed by states that want to preserve their autonomy for this or that reason. Finally, litigations appealing to international courts, which supervise the application of international standards, appear to be more convenient than dealing with courts in single countries. These standards are not, however, the creation of companies, but are often the result of negotiation between the needs of companies and those of states. International rules for the protection of patents offer another opportunity that companies have learnt to exploit to their advantage. Were the market of intellectual property free, it would be rather complicated for big corporations to defend themselves from developing countries producers.

The point that should not be missed, here, is that the supranational regimes that constitute the backbone of global governance do not exist for the sake of corporations. The latter can participate – and, *de facto*, do participate – in the process that leads to the definition of regulatory regimes (a process, it must be added, that involves the presence of NGOs too). If corporations are important actors in the formation of governance regimes, this happens because corporations are aware that regulatory regimes have – at least potentially – the function to constrain some aspects of corporate activity, and have not simply the function to create new market opportunities for them. For this reason, it is crucial for corporations to maintain open channels of communication and negotiation with public agencies, which, in their turn, are eager to find in them reliable partners in order to define and manage what now has become commonsensical to term 'global governance'.[9]

In this vein, some have interpreted even the complex institutional architecture that sustains the European Union as the result of a set of policies whose scope was – and still is – to create spaces of exception with regard to a free market in order to foster multinational corporations (Davies 2013).

As scholarship has shown in the last few decades, the boundary between corporations, states and supranational agencies is porous. It would be misleading, thus, to conceive of the relation among these entities as if the goal that states have to pursue in order to defend their sovereignty were to build fences that should impede the movements of corporations, while the latter are supposed to float undisturbed in the impalpable ether of global markets.[10] What can be observed is a multifaceted interconnection between companies and state agencies. If the final result of this interconnection is a mutual benefit, it is the state, however, the actor that determines the condition of possibility of any undertaking whose nature is worth defining as 'economic'. This sounds like a truism: who would come to the idea that property rights emerged without the intervention of the state, or at least state-like institutions, whose aims and scopes are, by definitions, of a political nature? Nevertheless, once again, it is one thing to build a legal and jurisdictional frame that allows economic actors to behave within their domain, assuming, at the same time, that outside the economic sphere there is room for forms of human interaction that do not depend on economic rationality. A different state of affairs occurs when both public institutions and firms obey the same model of rationality and contribute, albeit in different degrees and using different institutional tools to govern individual behaviour, to realize the neoliberal society Friedman foresaw at the beginning of the 1950s.

The point becomes clearer if we draw attention to how economic theory has dealt with the role played by companies within the broader social context. As soon as one delves into this question, one can perceive the institutional character of the market, its embeddedness in broader cultural and political frameworks; in short, one feels in a certain way forced to reconsider the epistemic status of economics. Perhaps such a shift goes not so far as to suggest that economics should turn itself into anthropology, but surely it invites one to place economics again where the Austrians suggested it should stay, namely within the Humanities. At any rate, what comes to the surface, then, is the set of anthropological presuppositions that stays behind both the economic behaviour of individuals and the economic theory that claims to explain it.

When mainstream economics approaches the institutional aspect of economic theory, it does it, instead, by drawing from the same toolbox that contains the price theory. There is enough space in this toolbox (even if it is not infinite), thus there is nothing wrong in it, were it not that the result of this epistemological move brings about an understanding of the role played by institutions that is far from being satisfactory. A critique of neoliberalism necessitates a deconstruction of how the neoclassic approach to institutions became dominant to the point that even decision makers who operate within the public sphere ended up with embracing it.

First of all, it is opportune to take into consideration the conception of the firm we find in Coase (1937), a seminal work that, from a genealogical perspective, lies at the roots of how neoliberalism approaches the question of institutions. For Coase, firms exist because market transactions are too expensive in order to achieve what is needed to make the organizational machine work properly. This machine needs coordinating, but coordination, to be effective, needs, in its turn, the availability of information: without the latter, managing an organization would be impossible. As the neoclassic model invites one to assume, price movements are clear enough indicators to direct entrepreneurial strategies within the market. Exchange transactions, as if they were a set of moves in a game, generate the information needed to build a strategy – how much to produce, at which costs, and so on. Furthermore, the information generated this way offers itself to the observer: acquiring it is free. Exchange transactions, however, take place within the environment outside the firm. Inside the firm, instead, coordination occurs thanks to decisions taken by managers. These decisions supersede the price mechanism, because the latter, if introduced in order to regulate the internal organization of the firm, would entail too high costs. If the organization coincided with a market, it would be necessary to negotiate and conclude separate contracts for each exchange transaction with the owners of the factors of production. One single contract, thus, substitutes for this series of contracts. This one contract implies that whoever owns a certain factor of production agrees 'to obey the directions of an entrepreneur *within certain limits*' (Coase 1937, 391)

Coase's contribution to the solution of the problem of why firms exist was as simple as it was genial. Moreover, it fitted – indeed not surprisingly – very well to the neoclassical model. It was the first time that the economic science cast a glance into the organization. Moreover, for a long time Coase's explanation of why firms exist at all – describing them like islands that communicate to each other by navigating in the sea of the market, though remaining distinct from it – was the only one for which mainstream economics had been feeling the need. Neoclassical economics did not explain the boundary of a firm – but also did not want to do it. Nevertheless, decades later a shift took place in the direction of a better understanding of how to relate what happens outside the firm with what happens inside it (to put it in very trivial terms). The shift consisted in drawing attention, first, to the transaction costs that affect all the possible interaction between the organization and its environment; and, second, to the hierarchical distribution of power within the organization. Yet, this was not a real and effective paradigm shift: the notion of transaction costs was already to be found (in a more or less explicit form) in Coase's text (Langlois 1998) and, what is more, an analysis of the function of institutions that still avails itself of the neoclassical model of rationality reveals itself to be insufficient in order to explain how power relations lie at the core of all forms of organized interaction (Dunn 1992).

Transaction costs stand separate from and in addition to ordinary production costs; they are related, more specifically, to the functioning of the economic system taken as a whole. A firm has to face transaction costs when searching for information as regards the availability of goods, requirements, technological devices, human resources, and when it compares the relative prices of them. When, once it has found what is needed, it draws up a contract, which is an operation that implies costs too, mainly related to the bargaining process. Finally, the firm has to consider the costs that would arise in case a legal action should take place because the other party did not stick to the terms of the contract. Oliver Williamson, to whom the scientific community owes a great deal for the most important contributions to the subject, compares transaction costs to the frictions in a physical system (Williamson 1985, 19). While the neoclassical model envisages a system of exchanges where there is no friction, namely where the price mechanism works undisturbed, the transaction costs theory aims at taking into consideration the real economic process where the occurrence of various forms of friction is the norm. This adherence to how organizations behave is supposed to entail a great methodological advantage compared with neoclassical economics, in the sense that transaction economics does not need to make unrealistic assumptions, as the latter has to do.

Williamson accomplishes the goal to obtain more realistic descriptions of the economic system thanks to two main conceptual tools. First, transaction costs theory assumes that individuals act as free riders if they can. Hence the importance of systems of control that make it possible if not to prevent, at least to compensate for the costs stemming from opportunism. This train of thought, if followed consistently, should enable a satisfying explanation not only of the existence of firms, but also of organizations in general: the latter came to exist in order to tame the potentially disruptive behaviour of free riders (North 1990).[11]

Second, human beings act under the constraints imposed by bounded rationality. That the exercise of human rationality is bound by both cognitive and environmental constraints was the achievement of Simon's investigation upon the grounding structures of decision making (Simon 1955, 1956), which led him to his seminal analysis of the nature and scopes of organizations (Simon and March 1958). Simon's theory of bounded rationality claimed to offer a viable alternative, at least as far as descriptive power was concerned, to the neoclassical rational choice theory.[12] Thus, it refused the main assumptions of the neoclassical schema. According to the latter, decision makers have a well-defined utility function, and hence they can assign a cardinal number as a measure of their liking of any particular scenario of future events; decision makers are confronted with a well-defined set of alternatives to choose from; decision makers will choose the alternative that will maximize the expected value, in terms of their utility function, of the set of events consequent on the choice. Simon is opposed to this conception that individuals are used to draw attention only to the problems they can effectively confront and cope with. Attention is, in fact, a scarce resource, as well as the time one needs to convey attention to this or that problem. It is the environment where human beings live that constrains them to 'focus on dealing with one or a few problems at a time, with the expectation that when other problems arose there would be time to deal with those too' (Simon 1983, 20). It is also worth underscoring that both human beings and other animals share this dependence on environmental constraints, being a result of the evolutionary process. Tied to our evolutionary history as well is the role played by emotional mechanisms, which ordinarily help us direct our attention to the most urgent needs. On a superior level human beings are able to generate alternatives in order to orient themselves in the environment. Finally, they are capable of collecting facts about the environment, and this is too an important element of the process that leads to the finding of viable alternatives and to the assessment of their probable consequences. In sum, Simon proposes a conception of human rationality that equates it with a set of problem solving procedures. The theoretical gain Simon expects from his model of rationality consists of a closer adherence to the effective behaviour of human beings. By the same token, the result should consist of a definitive abandonment of the neoclassical model that posits optimization as the final goal of the human action: according to Simon, actors, because of the cognitive constraints imposed on their rationality, can come to solutions that are not optimal, but are 'satisficing' – to use the term he coined. Instead of standing in front of the subject as a kaleidoscopic, but nevertheless transparent set of infinite possibilities to be pondered and compared to each other, the world Simon's theory depicts is a set of models, whereas each of them offers a partial and fragmentary image of reality. These models, nonetheless, are more than enough as to allow human beings to cope with the various affordances of the world. Were it not so, our species would have disappeared a long time ago.

Combining these two assumptions, namely opportunism and bounded rationality, transaction costs theory claims to be able to offer a consistent explanation of how organizations interact with an environment where other organizations and institutions too are present; how organizational change is possible and for what reasons it takes place; and why specific changes both inside and outside organizations may make the establishment of monopolies opportune. Moreover, it claims to do it by constructing a theoretical frame that is:

> (1) more micro analytic, (2) is more self-conscious about its behavioural assumptions, (3) introduces and develops the economic importance of assets specificity, (4) relies more on comparative institutional analysis, (5) regards the business firm as a governance structure rather than a production function, and (6) places greater weight on the ex post institutions of contract, with special emphasis on private ordering.
>
> (Williamson 1985, 18).

Nobody would deny the positive impact that transaction costs theory has had on our insight into how organizations work and engage with their environment. Nevertheless, it would be undeniable as well that this theory cannot go beyond the epistemic limits that characterize the neoclassical model. First, Williamson too upholds the partition between cost of production and transaction costs. This partition prevents perception of organizations as actors that are not motivated solely by the goal of maximization. If we consider the explanation given of why hierarchies exist, we find a similar allegiance to the neoclassical model. The agent Williamson talks about, which must be kept in its place and whose loyalty is always on the brink of vanishing, is nothing more and nothing less than a rational agent with guile. Thus, Williamson's insistence on the unavoidability of opportunism shares with the rational choice model of human action the same presupposition, namely that human beings act in a non-cooperative way unless either they are induced to cooperate, or they find it convenient to do it.

Truly, institutional analysis stemming from Williamson's model does state that the context of action counts in so far as the latter is precisely what elicits – or prevents – selfish and opportunistic ways of conduct. This point has been underscored enough by evolutionary biology. Within this discipline, scholars have devoted a lot of their energy in investigating the evolutionary causes of cooperation and its opposite, at least since Hamilton (1963) and Williams (1966). For a long time, supporters of the primacy of non-cooperative over cooperative behaviours, which were then to be seen as late by-products of evolution, have been challenged by their opponents. More recently, a consensus seems to have arisen that both cooperative and non cooperative behaviours are necessary, while sustaining the prevalence of one over the other would be misleading (Sober and Wilson 1998; Wilson 2015). In particular, it would imply a dismissal of the context that frames individual attitudes and effective behaviours. Here we come to the point: Williamson's account suggests, rather, that organizations exist so as to subdue individual opportunist behaviour, which, in its turn, is supposed to pre-exist individual interactions within groups of peers.

Equally questionable, we argue, is the idea shared by Simon and Williamson that the bounded rationality theory constitutes an effective alternative to the rational choice theory. Describing individuals – or organizations – as actors constitutively bound by and to their limited capability of assessing the environment means to complete the neoclassical model and not to exceed it. Sen, who cannot be reproached for defending naively the neoclassical model, puts it bluntly: 'Simon's formulation of "satisficing" behaviour, connected with his important idea of bounded rationality, can be accommodated *within* a general maximizing framework, eliminating the tension between satisficing and maximizing' (Sen 2002, 193; author's emphasis).

Moreover, even the supporters of mainstream economics have ended up with acknowledging that not all the choice of alternatives are given, that the consequences of alternatives are not perfectly known with respect to the certainty, risk or uncertainty that are attached to each of them, and, finally, that rational individuals have to produce in some way the criteria for representing the ordering of the utility functions related to each of the possible alternatives. An example of this circumstance, which could be defined as a self-immunization of rational choice theory, can be found in the Lecture given by Gary Backer in Stockholm while receiving the Nobel Memorial Prize in Economic Sciences in 1992:

[a]ctions are constrained by income, time, imperfect memory and calculating capacities, and other limited resources, and also by the available opportunity in the economy and elsewhere. These opportunities are largely determined by the private and collective actions of other individuals and organizations.

(Becker 1993, 385)

Crucial, thus, is not the place that institutions have within the environment where individuals and firms pursue their goals. What makes the difference, rather, is how to conceive of the multi-layered and complex bundle of social and cultural ties that contribute to form the architecture of choices. If one assumes that organizations – and, in North's analysis, institutions too – result from the advantage individuals have in imposing on themselves a set of constraints that facilitate individual and collective processes of decision making, one is not so far from begging the question. At the bottom line, by following this train of thoughts one is *de facto* assuming that actors choose to gather together in order to maximize the advantage that derives from operating within ordered forms of collectives. Individuals are then regarded as 'unconscious maximizers'. As if they were guided by nature itself in choosing specific organized forms of life, human beings are supposed to be not aware of the consequences that derive from living within hierarchical and ordered groups; nonetheless, their engagement with the latter brings a positive trade-off. The course of evolution, within which human social behaviours are to be placed, is thus attributed the role of explaining why maximizing is a good strategy.

In a deep and consistent attempt to investigate the virtues and vices of the model of rationality that restricts the latter to the relation between means and goals, Nozick (1993) goes so far as to assimilate the rational behaviour of individuals to the matter of fact that a living being must adapt itself to the environment. The move seems to be rather consistent if one considers the formal character that both rational choice theory and the biological concept of adaptation have in common. From the point of view of mainstream economics, preferences are exogenous and the fact that they may change in the course of time should not disturb the goal economists pursue, namely to explain how individuals adapt themselves to price modifications.[13] Nozick, nevertheless, does not conceal the limits of instrumental rationality, and his investigation is, in fact, an attempt to find convincing arguments for a theory of the substantive rationality of goals and desires.

From the point of view of those biologists who tend to interpret any step within the path of evolution as a form of adaptation, individual choices are to be measured and evaluated by considering the improvement of the fitness their results bring about, no matter what constitutes the content of the choice itself. Here again, Nozick carries on his analysis with an opportune philosophical prudence: he does not embrace this position without caution and, not surprisingly, he refers to Gould and Lewontin (1979), a work that pointed out the reductionism implicit in the adaptationist paradigm, which considers natural selection as an optimizing agent. Thus, when Nozick considers rationality as an instrument evolution provided to human beings in order to augment the fitness of the species, he does it by avoiding any form of reductionism and makes an effort to preserve the conceptual grounds on which individual freedom can be justified.

If we have been reminded, albeit fleetingly, of Nozick's contribution, this is for the reason that it offers a good example of what is needed to frame conceptually a theory of rationality that aims both at explaining the relations among individual choices, emergence of institutions and evolutionary drives, and at showing the role individual freedom plays in this context. The neoliberal discourse about the relations that tie individuals to the organizations and institutions they belong to, seems, on the contrary, to pursue the scope of offering a rather simplified schema for the explanation of why individuals choose to adhere to various forms of organized life. Within this schema both individual needs and collective forms of life, such as organizations and institutions, are related to the mechanism of adaptation – an assumption that can be hardly denied. What is questionable, however, is the idea that contributing to their maintenance reveals the rationality of a choice that is always consistent with the individual drive of adaptation.

The strength of the neoliberal discourse seems to lie precisely in this majestic picture of human sociability, where everything seems to fall into place. Nevertheless, something seems to be left out from this picture: in fact, only two of three options envisaged by Hirschman (1970) are present here, namely loyalty and voice (to be noticed: when one chooses the latter, the result, even unintended, is an improvement of the collective), while the option exit seems, rather worryingly, to be absent. As Foucault did not fail to notice, the neoliberal subject is 'someone who accepts reality', while economics reduces itself to be the 'science of the systematic nature of responses to environmental variables' (Foucault 2008, 269). What then remains overlooked is twofold: at the micro level, it is the network of power relations that characterizes how individuals negotiate their position within institutions and organizations; at the macro level, it is the fact that the various forms which the intertwinement of institutions and organizations take cannot be reduced to the pursuit of efficiency.

4.3 Institutions, evolution and the frame of individual choices: or, farewell from the neoclassic nuts and bolts

It may be true that instrumental rationality is the only form of rationality that human beings can avail themselves of. Good reasons stemming from the consideration of how human beings have developed intergroup relations in the course of evolution seem to lead to this conclusion. Yet, transferring concepts that come from the domain of evolutionary biology in order to promote a political programme is dangerous. This has been the case between the nineteenth and the beginning of the twentieth century, both in Europe and in the United States (Maasen, Mendelsohn and Weingart 1995; Haraway

1989). More recently, Edward Wilson's socio-biology has been a further example of this attitude (Kitcher 1985). The economic theory that underpins the neoliberal project is to be seen as a form of naturalization of the political too. Significantly, the last chapter of Becker (1976) takes into consideration the great affinity existing between the economic theory and Wilson's conception of human nature. Becker draws the conclusion that the two disciplines not only deal with the same subject matter, namely human behaviour, but also share common goals and common presuppositions: 'both economics and sociobiology would gain from combining the[ir] analytical techniques', because the economic representation of human preferences 'may be largely explained by the selection over time of traits having greater survival value' (ibid., 294).

The willingness to find in the realm of biology those conceptual tools that serve the scope of naturalizing a social science is not wrong per se. What makes the difference is the epistemic frame within which the project of this naturalization should take place. To say the least, the conceptual tools provided by the neoliberal discourse about human behaviour and the basic forms of human interaction are rather coarse. On the contrary, the debate that has characterized the self-understanding of biology in recent decades has aimed – and still aims – at building a complex explanatory frame that can help understand how individual behaviours and institutions co-evolve in the course of history.

It is a 'deep history' (Smail 2008) which comes to the foreground once the biologist follows the path that goes from the present back to the origins of mankind. The point that must not be missed here is twofold. First, biology itself is a historical discipline (Mayr 2004). Second, the deep history investigated by the biologist has not yet ended (Eldredge 1995, 1999). In the absence of these two assumptions, the quest for the origin pursued by biology would amount to a justification of the present state of affairs that affects the world we live in.

This point becomes clearer if one takes into consideration parallel developments which have occurred within the humanities in the last few years. Continental philosophers like Derrida (1976, 1982) devoted much of their efforts to show the problematic implications, whose nature is never simply theoretical, of any attempt to define the task of the philosophical foundation in terms of a univocal determination of what constitutes the origin. Such a metaphysical shift is, in most cases, a projection: the discourse that claims to establish once and for all the origin of being meant as both the ultimate constituent of reality and the source of universal meaning articulates the transfer of elements that belong to the present into a past that ends up taking on a mythical significance. Moreover, the latter works as a pivotal element of a narrative that validates the forms of symbolic violence that traverse society. Outside the disciplinary field of philosophy, the rhetorical construction of the origin has become the target of several research programmes too. At stake is the historical and cultural process that allows for the formation of individual and collective identities. On the one hand, the narratives that underpin identity structures have to be consistent enough to enable a clear and unambiguous recognition of the boundary that encloses the sphere of shared meanings and values. This boundary recognition cannot avoid the emergence of specific images of what is perceived as 'other' and belongs to a sphere that is placed out of the regime of normality, obviousness, common sense. On the other hand, these narratives have to be open enough so as to prevent the process of identification from undergoing a sort of contraction and, therefore, reducing itself to the exclusion of what belongs to the sphere of otherness. This oscillation between openness and closure is attributed an enormous significance as regards the possibility for a group to allow for shared patterns of communication that sustain democracy, tolerance, cultural diversity, minority rights and so on. Attention has been drawn, thus, to the mechanism of exclusion that underpins the internal cohesion of groups (Tajfel 1981), the construction of national identities (Anderson 1983; Hobsbawm 1990), the self-definition of the western identity by creating specific images of the subordinated and colonized other (Said 1978, 1993; Spivak 1999), the establishment of separate gender identities by ascribing a positive value only to manhood and heterosexuality (Butler 1993) – just to mention few works that now count among the classics within the humanities. Not by chance the latter has widened the range of its own research field to such an extent: by devoting their efforts to the investigation of the discursive structure that generates the emergence of collective and individual identities, these disciplines can at best serve one of their main functions, namely to improve the spread of the open-mindedness that sustains a democratic society (Nussbaum 2010).

Now, this decennial work of deconstruction carried on within different disciplinary fields has amounted to a common result: an identity structure characterized by a strong closure, which means at the same time foreclosure of the other (may it be the underdog, strangers deprived of citizenship rights, women and homosexuals), is always based on a rhetoric of the origin that naturalizes specific elements of human culture. This naturalization constitutes in so far a pivotal element of a reactionary political project as it detaches symbolic elements that belong to the realm of culture and poses them into the realm of nature, whereas the latter is represented as the source of what cannot change in the course of human history (Douglas 1986). What counts more in the present context is that, for a long time, the discipline that studies the relation of living organisms with their natural environment, namely biology, has provided several cues for those who aimed at creating a reactionary discourse based on a naturalization of the social. The critical work done internally to evolutionary biology itself occurred during the last few years and has led to a deep revision of the conceptual tools that serve to both articulate methods and goals of the discipline and define its objects. Some seminal endeavours in this direction like Rose, Lewontin and Kamin (1984) has been motivated, at least in part, by the willingness to attain a sort of ideological purification of the discipline so as to prevent further abuses of how biologists conceive of the relationship between human behaviour and natural evolution. However, it has been a refinement of the conceptuality used to define the object of the discipline which has contributed more deeply to change the traditional image of the nature/nurture pair (Oyama 1998; Mitchell 2003). At present, thus, it would be difficult for either social sciences or political discourses to transfer notions deriving from biology into a narrative that, for example, hypostatizes the role of genetic influences in order to explain human behaviours. The adaptationist programme has turned into a representation of evolution that has detached itself from any form of biological determinism (Oyama, Griffiths and Gray 2001; Orzack and Sober 2001).

Difficult, but not impossible. The research programme of evolutionary psychology, for example, had continued, more or less overtly, to propagate the conception of human behaviour that has been carried on by socio-biology (Barkow Cosmides and Tooby 1992). Within this perspective, a line divides the biological development of our species and the cultural process that led mankind to leave the open spaces of the savannah, spread all over the planet, and give birth, then, to what we are used to calling human civilization. This line, however, is not insurmountable. Albeit biological evolution is supposed to have ended, it still affects how individuals behave and how they interact. Here we meet precisely a rhetorical construction that functions as a myth of origin: a set of events which occurred in the past of our evolutionary history is attributed an explanatory power as regards cultural processes that occur in the present. Following this model can be very problematic when it comes to explain, for example, compliance with norms and codes, selfishness, altruism and cooperation. The picture of human behaviour that evolutionary psychology conveys intends, *de facto*, to justify a biological determinism that leaves no room even for a description of the network that ties together genes, individuals and the institutions that have become part of the environment where individuals operate.

Dupré (2001) has given an accurate account of how the main lines of the research programme carried on by evolutionary psychology have been privileged by mainstream economics. Dupré's critique of the latter is persuasive because his goal does not consist in reproaching the economist's willingness to cooperate, on an epistemological level, with biologists. It does not reproach biology for pursuing a reductionist programme. There may be strong or weak forms of reductionism, but reductionism can be a good methodological premise to which the entire scientific undertaking is committed, especially when the need for an interaction between social and natural sciences comes into the foreground.[14] That said, the unease concerning economics is about the unhappy choice of which biological theory to interact with. This choice is unhappy not only for epistemological reasons: it can hardly conceal the interest that economics has in presenting human beings as decision makers that cannot really avoid depending on some fundamental drives that originate from their evolutionary past.

The suggestion that can be drawn – a suggestion that any deconstruction of the neoliberal conception of organizations and institutions has to take into account – is that economics should begin a dialogue with those research programmes within the biological discipline whose aim is to understand the relation between individuals and the environment as a reciprocal action (as a '*Wechselwirkung*', to use a German term, which is, perhaps, more suitable here).

The concept of 'niche', for example, provides a fruitful insight into how living organisms and their environment modify each other through interactions that occur in the course of evolution. This does not entail an attempt to minimize the role played by natural selection – or, worse, to withdraw it. The point is to understand how niche construction and natural selection work together and give room to two distinct causal processes: while natural selection is responsible for genetic inheritance, niche construction adds to the later ecological inheritance. The crucial point is that the two causal processes are not separate: the present transformations of the niche where a species lives comprise the previous genetic modifications caused by niche construction itself. This research programme amounts to a better understanding of how genes and culture co-evolve. If one focuses only on genetic modifications induced by the combination of variation and selection, then it becomes a very hard undertaking to look at phenomena like cultural diversity and cultural transformations over time from a biological perspective. The niche construction paradigm, instead, allows for considering culture as a selective force in human evolution. The reliance of our species on resources not only of a physical but also a semantic nature which we have been creating during the last 100,000 years or so must be, thus, taken into consideration within the image of mankind provided by biology (Odling-Smee, Laland and Feldman 2003; Kendal, Tehrani and Odling-Smee 2011).

It is worth mentioning, too, the constructivist approach to human cognition, which is a research programme developed within neurosciences presenting some epistemic affinities with the niche construction theory. This approach consists in considering human cognition as something that cannot be exhaustively explained if one looks at it without looking, at the same time, at the environment. According to those who advocate neural constructivism, cognition – meant as the ensemble of all representational features of brain cortex – emerges from the interaction between neural growth and environmentally derived neural activity. If one assumes that this interaction is indispensable for eliciting cognition, then the brain turns out to be something different from a network of pre-existing areas whose power to act becomes effective only as a specific response to given problem domains. By embracing a constructivist approach the neuroscientist can thus explain the process of learning in a way that differs radically from the way proposed by evolutionary psychology. The latter, in fact, cannot account for the flexibility that characterizes human cognition. The consequence is that not only cognitive skills but also social and political attitudes are but the expression of genetically coded responses to present external pressures. In contrast, the constructivist approach is able to explain how environmental factors shape the brain's structure. The latter result is thus characterized by a strong flexibility, which depends not only on the possibility our brain has to produce neural cells after birth, but above all on the synaptic plasticity. The human – but not only human, it must be added – learning process can then be described as a continuous process of accommodation of what has been learnt with the ongoing emergence of new representations in the course of experience (Quartz and Sejnowski 1997).

This emphasis on brain flexibility does not lead to the idea, however, that human nature is indefinitely malleable. The point is to understand the role played by those constraints that derive from the social construction of a world that co-evolve with individuals, being at the same time created by them, and is able to influence their cognitive performances. Starting from the seminal article by Clark and Chalmers (1998), scholars have become acquainted with the idea that the scaffolding of culturally relevant data is an important element to be taken into consideration to understand cognition.[15] Human beings lean on external support whenever a cognitive process is going on. Language, technological devices, from pen and paper to personal computer, external media in general play an active causal role in triggering the cognitive process. The brain and these external entities create a coupled system that determines any behavioural competence of individuals. This does not amount to say that mental representations of the world are outside the brain; the point is to understand if it makes any sense at all to speak of cognition without considering the interaction between the brain and those external features that complete our representation of the world. When we act in order to modify a state of affairs in the world, the line that divides the latter from the agent is rather clear. On the contrary, when our action has an epistemic value, when, in other words, we want to expand our knowledge, this line vanishes, because we give then some credit to information data that are already available in the environment and has become part of the cognitive process.

The discussion about Clark's active externalism has reached a huge dimension. Different positions contend for the most appropriate assessment of the balance between what is external and what is internal in cognition. Hutto – just to mention an extreme, but seemingly fruitful stance within the current debate – claims that social neuroscience can now take the place of previous research programmes based solely on the definition of a good theory of mind. The individual's engagement with shared narrative practices is an essential part of human behaviour. Thank to this engagement, humans develop and refine how they respond to the affordances of their environment. This means that individual cognitive skills depend on dynamic frameworks where knowledge is distributed. The acquisition of knowledge, thus, is totally embodied in the interactions among humans. This approach aims at explaining how human beings make sense of actions without sticking to the old paradigm of cognitivism, which was incapable of abandoning its representationalist assumptions (Hutto and Myin 2013; Hutto and Kirchhoff 2015).

Hutto's view, according to which encultured neural patterns both enable and are enabled by the active construction of the niche where humans live, has been welcomed by those phenomenologists who strive to define intersubjectivity within the paradigm of a naturalized phenomenology. In Gallagher and Bower (2014), for example, enactivism goes so far as to take into consideration not only an individual's sensory-motor responses to various world affordances, but also how affective aspects of embodiment contribute to the rise of cognitive processes. Here, again, neural processes are not supposed to respond to external changes as if they were the control centre of a computing machine; instead, their role in processing information and, thus, in creating meaning is conceived as a part of a larger embodied system. Within the latter the individual experience of the shared world that phenomenology used to subsume under the concept of intersubjectivity arises. Gallagher's naturalized phenomenology helps better recast our understanding of not only bodily skills and habits that serve to steer the intentional response to external objects, but also the individual history of personal experiences and, finally, how individuals react to social codes and norms stemming from institutional practices.

Both ontology (Smith 2003) and – not surprisingly – evolutionary biology (Griffiths and Stotz 2000) have begun a productive and still ongoing dialogue with those theories that, albeit in different forms, advocate an enactivist conception of how knowledge arises, is produced and re-produced among groups and, finally, transmitted from one generation to the next. Only economics seems to have failed the opportunity to enlarge its own epistemic horizon concerning how to frame the relations among individual decisions, institutional codes and evolutionary constraints. A theoretically poor – and, ultimately, not so easily defensible any more – conception of the latter keeps on playing the role of a mythical foundation of the selfishness that the rational choice theory suggests to be the main trait of human behaviour (even though this theory presents its model of rationality as if it were a typical instantiation of the Weberian Wertfreiheit).

The impression arises that mainstream economics sustains a model of decision making that offers a rather narrow picture of the interrelation of human choices and institutional frameworks in order to better defend one of its central dogmas, namely the exogenous character of preferences. Otherwise it seems difficult to explain why, when it comes to building a theory of firms, organizations and institutions, it keeps on sticking to the model based on the rational choice theory. It is easy to understand, however, that there is a strategic reason that induces the community of economists to consider the exogeneity of preferences as a powerful bulwark able to guarantee the methodological solidity of the discipline. Any conception aiming at enlarging the perspective within which individual choices are taken would entail, at the same time, the introduction of evaluations of an ethical and political nature into the economic discourse, which is precisely what the community of economists wants to avoid. As long as the individual studied by economics remains a 'rational fool' (Sen 1982), economics can thus keep on serving the neoliberal purpose to establish guidelines for the government that present themselves as merely technical in their nature.

The point is as grave as astonishing. Penrose (1959) is not, in fact, a work belonging to a discipline different from economics. Its influence on the economic discourse, however, has been relatively modest. Nelson and Winter (1982) too has been, in a certain way, foreclosed by the mainstream discourse. Speaking of foreclosure in the present context is not a form of compliance with a postmodern vogue: these two scientific contributions are well known, but their content has been made uninfluential. Starting from these works, it is possible to understand, in a rather different way, phenomena like economic growth, technological innovation and, above all, how the motivation for competing arises within the frame given by organizations. In addition, from an epistemological perspective, it would be possible to bring economics closer with those forms of 'generalized Darwinism' (Stoelhorst 2008; Hodgson and Knudsen 2008, 2010) that are promisingly conferring a new feature to the dialogue between natural and social disciplines.

Much more astonishing, however, is that the organizations theory that stems from Simon's thought would have well provided a theoretical framework within which factors that are not strictly connected with maximization can receive the visibility they deserve.[16] The critical remarks above about Simon's claim that his conception of bounded rationality can constitute a viable alternative to the rational choice theory remain valid. Nonetheless, it is true that Simon's insights into how the management of organizations entails specific forms of distributing power, governing the lives of individuals, monitoring events outside and inside the organization itself, give enough clues to understanding organizations as entities that are primarily directed toward the goal of reproducing themselves and surviving in an environment that is potentially hostile. It may be true that some of Simon's intuitions are not totally original, being anticipated, to a certain extent, by Barnard (1938). Looking at organizations as the site where a group of individuals held together by the common goal to survive despite the power conflicts that may arise in the course of time, is, however, the first step toward understanding organizational life in a way that cannot be reduced to the interpretive paradigm based on the neoclassical model. In this sense, Simon and March (1958) remains a work on which it is worth reflecting time and again if one's aim is to investigate the origin of neoliberal governmentality.

At this point, two ways are open, both logically and historically. The first leads to critical discourses and practices that aim at putting in question the biopolitics of organizations. The second leads to a refinement of those discourses and practices that contribute to shape the processes of subjectivation that take place in a neoliberal society.

The beginning of the first can be identified with March (1962). Here some intuitions already present in the book he co-authored with Simon undergo a sort of radicalization, in the sense that the observer's gaze becomes more acute. This refinement of the gaze brings into the foreground what remained silent in Coase (1937), namely the fact that 'to obey the directions of an entrepreneur *within certain limits*' is a political issue. No group can avoid the emergence of internal conflicts as the preferential dispositions among sub-systems of the organization differ from one another. The composition of the conflict is of vital importance for any organization. In order to reach this goal two conditions must be fulfilled: it is necessary, first, to set a stable goal and, second, this goal must be meaningful. It may be the case that maximizing profits comes to be the goal an organization attributes to itself. Firms usually adopt this solution. Theories of the firm inspired by the neoclassical model are content with acknowledging this fact and do not have any further question to pose. A critical standpoint toward how firms come to the solution of internal conflicts considers, instead, the decision to attribute a peculiar meaning to maximization as a strategy among others. The next step is much more illuminating: emphasizing the rationality of the decisions taken to improve the growth of the firm is a strategic choice too – better, it is a choice that has a ritual function, in the sense that gathering information in order to take those decisions that are supposed to improve the performance of the organization is perceived as the best way to manage the organization itself. This means that staging the decision-making process counts more that the results expected by the process itself. As Feldman and March (1981, 177) put it:

> decision making in organizations is more important than the outcomes it produces. It is an arena for exercising social values, for displaying authority, and for exhibiting proper behavior and attitudes with respect to a central ideological construct of modern western civilization: the concept of intelligent choice. (…) The gathering of information provides a ritualistic assurance that appropriate attitudes about decision making exist. Within such a scenario of performance, information is not simply a basis for action. It is a representation of competence and a reaffirmation of social virtue. Command of information and information sources enhances perceived competence and inspires confidence.

March's analysis focuses on the symbolic meaning of the decision process that takes place within an organization and, thus, it transforms thoroughly not only the standpoint of the observer, but above all the observed object. The firm, in Coase's description, was a black box: once the necessity of its hierarchical structure and the presence of contracts in order to justify the fact that intrafirm relations do not follow the rule of the market is explained, the economic discourse kept from questioning how power relations within the firm effectively work. Following the path inaugurated by March it has become possible to look at the firm as a form of organization among others, within which the observer can identify a set of constant patterns. First, the omnipresence of communication. Nothing within an organization is mute, even the physical spaces, the architectural design of them, and the many devices and work tools that are touched, manipulated and used for a certain purpose contribute all together to make the organization a talking landscape charged with meanings (Clegg and Kronberger 2005; Latour 2005; Dale and Burrell 2008). The flux of communication within this landscape is uninterrupted, and it is not the content of what is communicated that is of worth, but the process of communicating in itself.[17] Should the organization not consist of a bundle of performative utterances, there would be – rather obviously – no production and circulation of information about internal and external states of affairs. Moreover, the hierarchical distribution of power – and this is the crucial point – could not be properly anchored to ensure internal stability, no shared narrative could ever emerge and, consequently, the sedimentation of identity structures would be impossible.

Second, the intrinsically negotiated nature of all the decisions taken within the organization. This second aspect of organizational life is strictly related to the first: negotiating is possible only if specific communication channels are open in order to allow the bargaining process. Emphasizing the pivotal role of negotiation, however, amounts to saying that vital issues like who controls whom, who says what to do to whom, who, in general, sets the agenda for the things to do, cannot be decided merely by imposing guidelines or giving orders. This happens because the exercise of power elicits counter reactions and various forms of resistance that must successively be embedded into the flow of the organizational life. Every communicative performance is subject to interpretation, distortion or abuse, as happens, for example, when individuals strive to create spaces of freedom; or, conversely, it can be directed toward the exhibition of prestige, authority, force. In other words, participants in the communicative process are concerned by the maintenance of their position as well as by the willingness to produce an alteration in the current state of affairs by describing it differently.

The literature that shows how fruitful it is to analyse the firm as a specific form of organization that does not differ substantially from other ones has grown consistently – going from Pfeffer (1981) and Perrow (1986) to Clegg, Courpasson and Phillips (2006) and Fleming and Spicer (2007), just to mention two classics and a representative couple of works belonging to the recent literature – allowing for a clear understanding of the extent to which what happens within firms is not so much about maximizing profits and is much more about the government of human life.

No less important has been the scientific contribution coming from those sociological and anthropological works that, using an ethnographic approach, have captured in a very concrete manner how organizations recruit their future members, motivate them to stay within the organization, offer them the opportunity to build not only a career but above all a project of life, and listen to their needs and desires – in other words, how organizations succeed in modulating, attuning, influencing or simply shaping the levels of aspirations of their members, which is, according to March and Simon (1958), the quintessence of managerial activity (Jakall 1989; Kunda 1992; Knorr Cetina and Preda 2005; Ho 2009). Participant observers who describe how power is exerted within organizations and how the instauration of specific discursive regimes, which are shaped thoroughly by the economic rationality, coalesces with the exercise of power itself offer precious and rare insights into neoliberal biopolitics, even when their epistemic toolbox contains none of the conceptual tools stemming from the Foucauldian analysis of neoliberalism. By close looking at how individuals behave within the organizational boundary – be it only symbolic – the ethnographer's gaze catches how deeply the organizational regime affects the body of men and women. Executives and managers for whom Simon wrote and whom he also described had to face one central problem, namely how to safeguard the internal stability of the organization; accomplishing this task meant paying attention to those factors that would have led to conflict – it meant, in short, to work in order to achieve loyalty, reduce voice and disincentive exit. The manager who lives in the neoliberal era has still to deal with this task, to which a new one is, however, to be added, namely the creation of a psychic landscape that makes possible for the members of the organization to compose the cognitive dissonance generated by destructive competition and aspiration to self-realization. In fact, as maximizing behaviours are supposed to be proper not only to the organization, but also to its members, who are invited to assume the role of partners of the organization, thus acting as if they were an autonomous enterprise, competition is the main trait of personal interactions among members of the organization. Overall present, the rhetoric of competition is there to guarantee that individual self-realization can grow only during the continued execution of those exercises that lead one to shape one's own personality in compliance with values like selfishness, resilience, greed, indifference – whereas the latter results to be, perhaps, the virtue that the organization appreciates more (Herzfeld 1992). The cognitive dissonance here at stake arises as soon as the everyday experience teaches that cooperation is preferable both to create an organizational atmosphere that generates a sense of well-being and to make possible for the organization itself to strive for success, prestige, and survival within a competitive society.

If observed narrowly, thus, organizations are but the mise-en-scene of the neoliberal rationality. Each aspect of the organizational life serves the scope to train individuals in order to make them acquainted with a specific *Weltanschauung*, whose narrative core consists of conferring a mythical feature onto the economic model of rationality. This mise-en-scene can avoid, normally, the deployment of coercion, threat, subtle propaganda machineries. Foucault was right in underscoring that the neoliberal society is a post-disciplinary one: the discourse of the enterprise needs not to be imposed from the top, so to say; it is, rather, a discourse that permeates every single corner of organizational life. This explains – and perhaps it is the only way to explain it – the omnipresence of the neoliberal mindset. Public institutions, as far as they constitute a collective that gathers individuals who otherwise would never spend so much time together, do not differ from any other form of organization (March and Olsen 1989). Hence, they, too, have to define a goal, or a set of goals, in order to work – in order, better, to build those narratives either granting internal cohesion, or justifying their presence in the eyes of other institutions and organizations. Now, if the goal pursued by public institutions is substantially the same as organizations like firms pursue, namely efficiency, which means, in the case of institutions, being accountable not in order to offer a moral or political justification of their existence, but to justify the chosen ratio between costs and benefits within the policy adopted, then there is no way out from neoliberalism.[18]

Such a social and cultural development can be analysed in a critical way by adopting an epistemic stance like the one outlined so far. For those who share this stance it not only provides a critical analysis of how organizations and institutions shape the frame within which contemporary processes of sub-jectivation take place. The idea that underpins this critical work is, explicitly or implicitly, that a deconstruction of how the biopolitical regime that affects individuals should provoke, albeit indirectly, a distancing from, or a suspen-sion of the compliance with the neoliberal mentality to which more or less all of us are induced by simply spending so much time within organizational or institutional boundaries. Such an act of distancing is surely not easy to be undertaken because neoliberalism is embedded in any act of government within both organizations and institutions. Furthermore, the neoliberal discourse was able to spread so diffusely through society also because the rhetoric that sustains neoliberal narratives within organizational and institutional arrange-ments depends largely on the knowledge about the functioning of organiza-tions that the theory of organizations itself has contributed to achieve. We come back, finally, to the aforementioned point: the seminal work of Simon – taken here as a dividing line within the epistemic realm whose object of investigation is the decision-making process – can set off, on the one hand, a critical discourse aiming at showing that the economic order of organizations is about politics, reproduction of power, government and control of life, and, on the other hand, its exact opposite, namely a discourse that presents the existing order of things as the best of both possible worlds.

When Critical Management Studies came to exist as a subdiscipline of the theory of organizations, it was already possible to figure out that any critical discourse whose aim was to challenge the power structure of organizations would have been hooked into the same discourse that sustained the logic of an efficient management of organizations (Nord and Jermier 1992).

Some years later, Boltanski and Chiapello (1999) turned this suspicion into certainty. This book contained the results of a monumental investigation of how the managerial discourse has increasingly focused itself on the personal satisfaction of those who work within an organization. The authors' scope was to demonstrate that this rhetoric of personal satisfaction was the result of the latest transformation of the capitalist system of production. Having to cope with the wave of anti-capitalistic feelings that went through the Western world during the 1960s and 1970s, the entrepreneurial attitude toward the logic that is called to underpin the legitimation of the capitalist mode of production has been revealed to be surprisingly open. This openness was, however, a strategic move. This means that the rhetoric of management had absorbed and

184 Turning the world into a firm

assimilated those forms of critique that reproached capitalism for being inhumane, alienating, and incapable of allowing for individual self-realization. Hence the insistence on the valorization – and self-valorization – of human capital, on the positive value of instability, flexibility and innovation, on the necessity to blur the boundary between labour time and free time, on the career as a life plan, on the coincidence of the main traits of individual personality with those skills and competences that are needed to accomplish a given task within the organization.

The book was issued at a time when Europe had begun to be swept over by the new managerial discourse, which was already well rooted in the world of American enterprises. It has thus the merit to record both the changes that were taking place in the workplace almost everywhere in Europe and the sense of unease that followed these changes. The collection of data, which consist of a very well documented analysis of the managerial discourse, is a means to a very clear end, namely to demonstrate that the new management has chosen deliberately and consciously to elaborate a response to the critique against capitalism by showing how capitalism could be, on the contrary, attractive and human. The question about what else should a manager do but motivate persuasively their employees is not raised. The authors seemingly think that they share with their audience the conviction that capitalism is a bad affair but somebody must defend it, and the best supporters of it are necessarily those who take advantage of its existence. Managers find themselves precisely in that position. A sort of fascination for capitalism pervades the book too: even when given up for dead, capitalism can rise from its ashes because of the spirit that pervades it. The rhetorical structure of contemporary managerial discourse seems to be the clothes that the spirit of capitalism has chosen to wear to make itself visible. In sum, Boltanski and Chiapello's account of how individuals are put to work within the contemporary firm is a good example of how the critique of ideologies can help analyse social phenomena. In this sense, this work is not really useful if one aims at carrying on a critique of neoliberalism – notoriously, from the viewpoint of the critique of ideologies neoliberalism is only one of the various shapes that capitalism can take. Nevertheless, Boltanski and Chiapello's description of the efforts made by contemporary management in order to be convincing that organizations can be the site where individuals come to self-fulfilment and self-realization is rather interesting. This description seizes very well, in fact, one important point, which is to be seen not as a characteristic of capitalism but as a point of the force of neoliberalism. When the rhetoric of management aims at persuading that creativity is needed at the workplace, or that a stakeholder's values are as important as a shareholder's ones, and so on, this happens because of the virtually indefinite translatability of the neoclassical model. The latter, in fact, does not find in the theory of organization a mere complement. The theory of organization and the neoclassical model of rational choice, being, epistemologically speaking, two of a kind, it is more opportune to consider organization theory as a translation of the neoclassical model.

Organization theory can acquire an autonomous status only if it radically detaches itself from the presupposition according to which organizations and institutions exist because transaction costs must be reduced and embraces, instead, an ecological conception of the various forms of interaction between human beings: the narratives they share in order to make sense of their living together (including the scientific theories that have the function to provide descriptions of human behaviour that are supposed to be true), and the institutional frame that generates and is generated by the same interaction among individuals. Such an ecological conception would allow for understanding an aspect of institutional and organizational life that should not be missed by any possible deconstruction of neoliberalism, namely that any economic theory is always a theory of the political too.

Notes

1 It is also worth remembering that the tendency toward expansion of big corporations could hardly be held in check by the existing legislation. The Celler-Kefauver Act, passed in 1950 and meant to reinforce the Clayton Antitrust Act of 1914, had the scope to prevent vertical and horizontal mergers. This led here to a perverse effect, in the sense that corporations, in order to escape judicial prosecutions, moved toward the acquisition of societal assets of firms operating in completely different sectors. As Fligstein (1990) shows in a detailed manner, starting from the 1960s there had been a huge increase in corporate diversification strategies. Here are to be found the roots of the financial conception of corporate control that characterizes the contemporary global economy.

2 A decade after the publication of this article, Stigler was appointed to preside over a commission installed by the Nixon Administration so as to clarify whether the antitrust legislation in effect at that time was sufficient or not to regulate mergers and similar issues. The commission found that it would have been counterproductive to embitter the existing antitrust legislation, and insisted on the idea that the creation of conglomerate companies could not have anticompetitive effects. Thus, Stigler, during his career, was also given the opportunity to make his opinion heard beyond the walls of academia and into the public domain. (See *Congressional Record*, vol. CXV, 17 June 1969, pp. 1812–2346).

3 See Mills (1956). How unsatisfactory might have been Mills' approach if considered from a Marxist perspective appears clearly in Sweezy (1956). This review of Mills' book did not spare compliments but was also very critical as regards the presuppositions that lay at the root of Mills' analysis. One should not forget that Mills was a Wobbly, after all.

4 This is a way of thinking with deep roots in the American political tradition. One of its first formulations can be found in Chapter X of *The Federalist* (2003), authored by Madison, where it is suggested that the risks deriving from the possibility that one or more power groups endangers the normal course of democratic life should not be avoided by enlarging the space of manoeuvre of the central government.

5 Orozco (1987) provides an interesting and rather complete reconstruction of the American political thought within which the idea of the corporation as a political actor has been developed.

6 The Glass-Steagall Act of 1933, which restricted affiliations between banks and security firms, was repealed by the Gramm-Leach-Bliley Act of 1999. It is well known that the repeal of the Glass-Steagall Act triggered the explosion of the financial market – see for example Held, McGrew, Goldblatt and Perraton (1999).

However, it is also important to highlight the tie between this explosion and the successful effort made by the United States to acquire a hegemonic position thanks to the role played by Wall Street as a global hub of financial exchange – on this, see Cox (2012).

7 This can be interpreted as well as a symptom of mental disease, which typically affects individuals who have lost contact with reality (Tuckett 2011). Considering that financial assets are different from other kinds of assets because of how they are perceived and represented, Tuckett suggests that the encounter with them elicits an amount of emotions that the trader can hardly keep at bay. Financial assets are volatile, abstract and difficult to be evaluated; therefore, the great instability of the context within which decisions to buy or sell are to be taken causes a psychological pressure that goes far beyond the uncertainty described by Kahneman and Tversky. Financial assets, then, turn into objects of desire, thus acquiring a phantasmatic nature. Tuckett defines a *phantastic object* as a 'mental representation of something (or someone) which in an imagined scene fulfils the protagonist's deepest desires to have exactly what she wants when she wants it' (ibid., 17). This psychological state compensates, on one hand, for the absolute lack of transparency that characterizes the financial environment. However, on the other, it provokes a perception of the financial market that equates the latter with a gambling game. The danger related to this is patent, especially if one considers the weight financial markets have within the whole of the world economy.

8 In their attempt to complete Foucault's analysis of neoliberalism Dardot and Laval (2013) are right in pointing out how much the neoliberal discourse owes to the tradition of social Darwinism. However, while acknowledging the importance of their contribution, we do not share the general perspective that gives sense to their analysis, which we consider an endeavour to bend the Foucauldian stance into a Marxist frame.

9 The term 'governance' covers perfectly the transformations the art of government has undergone during the neoliberal era. As a mixture of best practices and accountability, all the interventions subsumed under the concept of governance are instantiations of one of the most pervasive traits of neoliberalism, namely the idea that democracy means efficient management of controversial issues. The term governance tends to eschew a precise definition, but precisely this indeterminacy seems appropriate to give expression to the indefinite sphere where the practice of governance takes place: it is the sphere where public agencies work together with private ones in attempting to give room to decision making processes that are supposed to lead to optimal outputs after an accurate evaluation of the costs and benefits at stake. On this, see Andronico (2012).

10 A representative example of that kind of approach was Boyer and Drache (1996).

11 See also North (2005). North's work contributed to enlarge the perspective of transaction costs theory in two important directions: first, toward an explication of the relationship between institutions and firms, and, second, toward the understanding of economic processes and their changes.

12 Indeed, within the early discussions about the cognitive biases of rational choices Simon's contributions as well as Kahneman's and Tversky's have been often welcomed as they could represent an alternative to the neoclassical model (Hogarth and Reder 1986).

13 The point has been made very clearly in Stigler and Becker (1977), a milestone on the path that led neoclassical economics to underpin the neoliberal project – and perhaps rarely has a title sounded more suitable to the matter dealt with: *De gustibus non est disputandum.*

14 Caution is needed, however, when the metaphysical question arises about what is to be reduced to what, namely when the ontological levels of reality that science wants to connect to each other are at stake. On this, it is still worth referring to Dupré (1983).

15 See also: Clark (2003; 2011); Rupert (2009); Menary (2010).
16 Mirowski (2002) has shown rather convincingly how complicated it may be to
    place Simon's figure within mainstream economics in a univocal way. This diffi-
    culty is related to some aspects of Simon's own personality as well as to some traits
    of his thought.
17 Casting a glance into the deep history of our evolutionary past can be fruitful in
    this case too. Once verbal language has emerged, the practice of gossip has super-
    seded the practice of grooming thus playing the function of the latter, which is the
    reinforcement of group ties (Dunbar 1996).
18 A good example to make this point clear is the case of the allocation of vital
    resources among entitled citizens by public institutions. When the discussion about
    principles of justice becomes impossible because no agreement on the latter seems
    to be in sight, or is simply judged to be too onerous, then recourse to solutions
    oriented by a cost-benefit analysis is unavoidable because of the reduction of
    complexity it brings about. On this, see Elster (1992).

References

Anderson, B.R.O'G. (1983) *Imagined Communities. Reflexions on the Origin and
Spread of Nationalism.* London and New York: Verso.

Andronico, A. (2012) 'The Dark Side of Governance', in Heritier, P. and Silvestri, P.
(Eds) *Good Government, Governance, Human Complexity. Luigi Einaudi's Legacy
and Contemporary Societies.* Florence: Olschki.

Barkow, J.H., Cosmides, L. and Tooby, J. (Eds) (1992) *The Adapted Mind. Evolutionary Psychology and the Generation of Culture.* Oxford and New York: Oxford
University Press.

Barnard, C.I. (1938) *The Functions of the Executive.* Cambridge, MA: Harvard
University Press.

Becker, G. (1976) *The Economic Approach to Human Behavior.* Chicago and London:
University of Chicago Press.

Becker, G. (1993) 'Nobel Lecture: the Economic Way of Looking at Behavior', *Journal
of Political Economy*, Vol. 101:3, pp. 385–409.

Ben-Ghiat, R. (2001) *Fascist Modernities. Italy, 1922–1945.* Berkeley and Los
Angeles: University of California Press.

Bentley, A.F. (1908) *The Process of Government. A Study of Social Pressures.* Chicago:
The University of Chicago Press.

Berle, A.A. and Means, G.C. (1932) *The Modern Corporation and Private Property.*
New York: Macmillan.

Bernays, E.L. (1928) *Propaganda.* New York: Horace Liveright.

Boltanski, L. and Chiapello, E. (1999) *Le nouvel esprit du capitalisme.* Paris: Gallimard.

Bork, R.H. (1978) *The Antitrust Paradox: A Policy at War with Itself.* New York:
Basic Books.

Boyer, R. and Drache, D. (Eds) (1996) *States against Markets. The Limits of Globalization.*
London: Routledge.

Burnham, J. (1941) *The Managerial Revolution. What Is Happening in the World.* New
York: The John Day Company.

Butler, J. (1993) *Bodies That Matter. On the Discursive Limits of "Sex".* New York:
Routledge.

Chandler, A. (1977) *The Visible Hand. The Managerial Revolution in American Business.*
Cambridge, MA and London: Harvard University Press.

Clark, A. (2003) *Natural Born Cyborgs. Minds, Technologies and the Future of Human Intelligence*. Oxford: Oxford University Press.

Clark, A. (2011) *Supersizing the Mind. Embodiment, Action and Cognitive Extension*. New York: Oxford University Press.

Clark, A. and Chalmers, D. (1998) 'The Extended Mind', *Analysis*, Vol. 58:1, pp. 7–19.

Clegg, S.R. and Kronberger, M. (Eds) (2005) *Space, Organizations and Management Theory*. Malmoe-Copenhagen: Libris and Copenhagen Business School Press.

Clegg, S.R., Courpasson, D. and Phillips, N. (2006) *Power and Organizations*. London: Sage.

Coase, R. (1937) 'The Nature of the Firm', *Economica*, Vol. 4:16, pp. 386–405.

Cox, R.W. (2012) 'Corporate Finance and US Foreign Policy', in Cox, R.W. (Ed.), *Corporate Power and Globalization in US Foreign Policy*. London and New York: Routledge, pp. 11–30.

Croly, H. (1909) *The Promise of American Life*. New York: Macmillan.

Dale, K. and Burrell, G. (Eds) (2008) *Spaces of Organization and the Organization of Space. Power, Identity and Materiality at Work*. Basingstoke, UK: Palgrave Macmillan.

Dardot, P. and Laval, C. (2013) *The New Way of the World: On Neoliberal Society*. London and New York: Verso.

Davies, W. (2013) 'When a Market Is not a Market? 'Exemption', 'Externality' and 'Exception' in the Case of European States Aid Rules', *Theory Culture & Society*, Vol. 30:2, pp. 32–59.

Derrida, J. (1976) *Of Grammatology*, trans. by Spivak, G.C. Baltimore, MD: Johns Hopkins University Press.

Derrida, J. (1982) *Margins of Philosophy*, trans. by Bass, A. Chicago: University of Chicago Press.

Douglas, M. (1986) *How Institutions Think*. Syracuse, NY: Syracuse University Press.

Doz, Y., Santos, J. and Williamson, P. (2001) *From Global to Metanational. How Companies Win in the Knowledge Economy*. Boston, MA: Harvard Business School Publishing Corporation.

Dunbar, R. (1996) *Grooming, Gossip and the Evolution of Language*. London: Faber and Faber Ltd.

Dunn, M. (1992) 'Firms, Markets and Hierarchies. A Critical Appraisal of Ronald Coase's Contribution to the Explanation of the 'Nature of the Firm'', *Ordo*, Vol. 43:7, pp. 193–204.

Dupré, J. (1983) 'The Disunity of Science', *Mind*, Vol. 92:367, pp. 321–346.

Dupré, J. (2001) *Human Nature and the Limits of Science*, Oxford: Oxford University Press.

Eldredge, N. (1995) *The Great Debate at the High Table of Evolutionary Theory*. New York: John Wiley & Sons.

Eldredge, N. (1999) *The Pattern of Evolution*. New York: Freeman.

Elster, J. (1992) *Local Justice. How Institutions Allocate Scarce Goods and Necessary Burdens*. New York: Russell Sage Foundation.

Feldman, M.S. and March, J.G. (1981) 'Information in Organizations as Signal and Symbol', *Administrative Science Quarterly*, Vol. 26:2, pp. 171–186.

Fleming, P. and Spicer, A. (2007) *Contesting the Corporation. Struggle, Power and Resistance in Organizations*. Cambridge and New York: Cambridge University Press.

Fligstein, N. (1990) *The Transformation of Corporate Control*. Cambridge, MA and London: Harvard University Press.

Foucault, M. (2008) *The Birth of Biopolitics: Lectures at the Collège de France, 1978–1979*, edited by Senellart, M., trans. by Burchell, G. Basingstoke, UK and New York: Palgrave Macmillan.

Fox, E.M. (2008) 'The Efficiency Paradox', in Pitofsky, R. (Ed.) *How the Chicago School Overshot the Mark: The Effect of Conservative Economic Analysis on U.S. Antitrust.* Oxford: Oxford University Press, pp. 77–88.

Frank, T. (2000) *One Market Under God. Extreme Capitalism, Market Populism, and the End of Economic Democracy.* New York: Doubleday.

Friedman, M. (1951) 'Neo-liberalism and its Prospects', *Farmand*, Vol. 40:7, pp. 89–93.

Friedman, M. (1953) *Essays in Positive Economics.* Chicago: The University of Chicago Press.

Friedman, M. (1962) *Capitalism and Freedom.* Chicago: The University of Chicago Press.

Gallagher, S. and Bower, M. (2014) 'Making Enactivism Even More Embodied', *Avant*, Vol. 5:2, pp. 232–247.

Gallie, W.B. (1955–56) 'Essentially Contested Concepts', *Proceedings of the Aristotelian Society*, Vol. 56:1, pp. 167–198.

Gould, S.J. and Lewontin, R.C. (1979) 'The Spandrels of San Marco and the Panglossian Paradigm: A Critique of the Adaptationist Programme', *Proceedings of the Royal Society of London*, Series B, Vol. 205:1161, pp. 581–598.

Griffiths, P.E. and Stotz, K. (2000) 'How the Mind Grows: A Developmental Perspective on the Biology of Cognition', *Synthese*, Vol. 122:1/2, pp. 29–51.

Hamilton, W.D. (1963) *The Evolution of Altruistic Behavior.* Chicago: The University of Chicago Press.

Haraway, D. (1989) *Primate Visions: Gender, Race and Nature in the World of Modern Science.* New York and London: Routledge.

Hayek, F. (1960) 'The Corporation in a Democratic Society: In Whose Interest Ought It and Will It Be Run?', in Anshen, M. and Bach, G.L. (Eds) *Management and Corporation 1985: a symposium held on the occasion of the 10th anniversary of the Graduate School of Industrial Administration of the Carnegie Institute of Technology.* New York: McGraw Hill, pp. 99–117.

Held, D., McGrew, A., Goldblatt, D. and Perraton, J. (1999) *Global Transformations. Politics, Economics and Culture.* Stanford, CA: Stanford University Press.

Herzfeld, M. (1992) *The Social Production of Indifference. Exploring the Symbolic Roots of Western Bureaucracy.* Chicago and London: The University of Chicago Press.

Hirschman, A.O. (1970) *Exit, Voice and Loyalty.* Cambridge, MA: Harvard University Press.

Ho, K. (2009) *Liquidated: An Ethnography of Wall Street.* Durham, NC and London: Duke University Press.

Hobsbawm, E.J. (1990) *Nations and Nationalism since 1780: Programme, Myth, Reality.* Cambridge: Cambridge University Press.

Hodgson, G.M. and Knudsen, T. (2008) 'In Search of General Evolutionary Principles: Why Darwinism is too Important to Be Left to the Biologists', *Journal of Bioeconomics*, Vol. 10:1, pp. 51–69.

Hodgson, G.M. and Knudsen, T. (2010) *Darwin's Conjecture. The Search for General Principles of Social and Economic Evolution.* Chicago and London: The University of Chicago Press.

Hogarth, R.H. and Reder, M.W. (1986) *Rational Choice. The Contrast between Economics and Psychology.* Chicago and London: The University of Chicago Press.

Hutto, D.D. and Myin, E. (2013) *Radicalizing Enactivism*. Cambridge, MA: The MIT Press.

Hutto, D.D. and Kirchhoff, M.D. (2015) 'Looking Beyond the Brain: Social Neuroscience Meets Narrative Practice', *Cognitive System Research*, Vol. 34–35, pp. 5–17.

Jakall, R. (1989) *Moral Mazes. The World of Corporate Managers*. New York: Oxford University Press.

Kendal, J., Tehrani, J.J. and Odling-Smee, J. (2011) 'Human Niche Construction in Interdisciplinary Focus', *Philosophical Transactions of the Royal Society B*, Vol. 366:1566, pp. 785–792.

Kirkwood, J.B. and Lande, R.H. (2008) 'The Chicago School's Foundations is Flawed: Antitrust Protects Consumers, not Efficiency', in Pitofsky, R. (Ed) *How the Chicago School Overshot the Mark: The Effect of Conservative Economic Analysis on U.S. Antitrust*. Oxford: Oxford University Press, pp. 89–97.

Kitch, E.W. (1983) 'The Fire of Truth. A Remembrance of Law and Economics at Chicago. 1932–1970', *The Journal of Law & Economics*, Vol. 26:1, pp. 163–234.

Kitcher, P. (1985) *Vaulting Ambition: Sociobiology and the Quest for Human Nature*. Cambridge, MA and London: The MIT Press.

Knorr Cetina, K. and Preda, A. (Eds) (2005) *The Sociology of Financial Markets*. Oxford and New York: Oxford University Press.

Kunda, G. (1992) *Engineering Culture: Control and Commitment in a High-tech Corporation*, Philadelphia, PA: Temple University Press.

Langlois, R.N. (1998) 'Transaction Costs, Production Costs, and the Passage of Time', in Medema, S.G. (Ed.) *Coasean Economics: Law and Economics and the New Institutional Economics*. New York: Springer, pp. 1–21.

Latour, B. (2005) *Reassembling the Social. An Introduction to Actor-Network-Theory*. Oxford: Oxford University Press.

Levy, D.L. and Prakash, A. (2003) 'Bargains Old and New: Multinational Corporations in Global Governance', *Business and Politics*, Vol. 5:2, pp. 131–150.

Maasen, S., Mendelsohn, E. and Weingart, P. (Eds) (1995) *Biology as Society, Society as Biology: Metaphors*. Dordrecht, The Netherlands: Kluwer.

Macpherson, C.B. (1962) *The Political Theory of Possessive Individualism: Hobbes to Locke*. Oxford: Clarendon Press.

Madison, J. (2003) 'The Same Subject Continued: The Utility of the Union as a Safeguard Against Domestic Faction and Insurrection' in Hamilton, A., Madison, J. and Jay, J. *The Federalist*, edited by Carey G. and McClennan, J. Indianapolis: Liberty Fund, pp. 42–49.

March, J.G. (1962) 'The Business Firm as a Political Coalition', *Journal of Politics*, Vol. 24:4, pp. 662–678.

March, J.G. and Olsen, J.P. (1989) *Rediscovering Institutions. The Organisational Basis of Politics*. New York: The Free Press.

March, J. and Simon, H. (1958) *Organizations*. New York: John Wiley & Sons.

Marchand, R. (1998) *Creating the Corporate Soul. The Rise of Public Relations and Corporate Imagery in American Big Business*. Berkeley, CA: University of California Press.

Mayr, E. (2004) *What Makes Biology Unique? Considerations on the Autonomy of a Scientific Discipline*. New York: Cambridge University Press.

Menary, R. (Ed.) (2010) *The Extended Mind*. Cambridge, MA and London: The MIT Press.

Mills, C.W. (1956) *The Power Elite*. London and New York: Oxford University Press.

Mirowski, P. (2002) *Machine Dreams. How Economics Becomes a Cyborg Science.* Cambridge and New York: Cambridge University Press.

Mitchell, S.D. (2003) *Biological Complexity and Integrative Pluralism.* Cambridge and New York: Cambridge University Press.

Miyazaki, H. (2003) 'The Temporalities of the Market', *American Anthropologist,* Vol. 195:2, pp. 255–265.

Nelson, R.R. and Winter, S.G. (1982) *An Evolutionary Theory of Economic Change.* Cambridge, MA: Harvard University Press.

Nord, W.R. and Jermier, J.M. (1992) 'Critical Social Science for Managers? Promising and Perverse Possibilities', in Alvesson, M. and Willmott, H. (Eds) *Critical Management Studies.* London: Sage, pp. 202–222.

North, D.C. (1990) *Institutions, Institutional Change and Economic Performance.* Cambridge: Cambridge University Press.

North, D.C. (2005) *Understanding the Process of Economic Change.* Princeton, NJ and Oxford: Princeton University Press.

Nozick, R. (1993) *The Nature of Rationality.* Princeton, NJ and Oxford: Princeton University Press.

Nussbaum, M.C. (2010) *Not for Profit: Why Democracy Needs the Humanities.* Princeton, NJ: Princeton University Press.

Odling-Smee, F.J., Laland, K.N. and Feldman, M.W. (2003) *Niche Construction. The Neglected Process in Evolution.* Princeton, NJ: Princeton University Press.

Orozco, J.L. (1987) *La revolución corporativa.* México, DF: Editorial Hispánicas.

Orzack, S.H. and Sober, E. (Eds) (2001) *Adaptationism and Optimality.* Cambridge and New York: Cambridge University Press.

Oyama, S. (1998) *Evolution's Eye. A Systems View of the Biology-Culture Divide.* Durham, NC: Duke University Press.

Oyama, S., Griffiths, P.E. and Gray, R.D. (Eds) (2001) *Cycles of Contingency. Developmental Systems and Evolution.* Cambridge, MA and London: The MIT Press.

Penrose, E.T. (1959) *The Theory of the Growth of the Firm.* Oxford: Blackwell.

Perrow, C. (1986) *Complex Organisations: a Critical Essay.* New York: McGraw Hill.

Pfeffer, J. (1981) *Power in Organizations.* Boston: Pitman.

Posner, R.A. (1976) *Antitrust Law: An Economic Perspective.* Chicago and London: University of Chicago Press.

Quartz, S.R. and Sejnowski, T.J. (1997) 'The Neural Basis of Cognitive Development: A Constructivist Manifesto', *Behavioral and Brain Sciences,* Vol. 20:4, pp. 537–596.

Rabinbach, A. (1976) 'The Aesthetics of Production in the Third Reich', *Journal of Contemporary History,* Vol. 11:4, pp. 43–74.

Rose, S., Lewontin, R. and Kamin, L. (1984) *Not in Our Genes: Biology, Ideology and Human Nature.* New York: Pantheon Books.

Rupert, R.D. (2009) *Cognitive Systems and the Extended Mind.* Oxford and New York: Oxford University Press.

Said, E.W. (1978) *Orientalism.* New York: Pantheon Books.

Said, E.W. (1993) *Culture and Imperialism.* New York: Knopf.

Sen, A. (1982) *Choice Welfare and Measurement.* Oxford: Blackwell.

Sen, A. (2002) *Rationality and Freedom.* Cambridge, MA: Harvard University Press.

Simon, H.A. (1955) 'A Behavioral Model of Rational Choice', *Quarterly Journal of Economics,* Vol. 69:1, pp. 99–118.

Simon, H.A. (1956) 'Rational Choice and the Structure of the Environment', *Psychological Review,* Vol. 63:2, pp. 129–138.

Simon, H.A. (1983) *Reason in Human Affairs*. Stanford, CA: Stanford University Press.

Simon, H.A. and March, J.G. (1958) *Organizations*. New York: Wiley & Sons.

Simons, H.C. (1948) *Economic Policy for A Free Society*. Chicago, IL: The University of Chicago Press.

Smail, D.L. (2008) *On Deep History and the Brain*. Berkeley, Los Angeles and London: University of California Press.

Smith, B. (2003) 'The Ecological Approach to Information Processing', in Nyiri, K. (Ed.) *Mobile Learning. Essays on Philosophy, Psychology and Education*. Vienna: Passagen Verlag, pp. 17–24.

Sober, E. and Wilson, D.S. (1998) *Unto Others. The Evolution and Psychology of Unselfish Behavior*. Cambridge, MA and London: Harvard University Press.

Spivak, G.C. (1999) *A Critique of Postcolonial Reason. Toward a History of the Vanishing Present*. Cambridge, MA and London: Harvard University Press.

Stigler, G.J. (1958) 'The Economies of Scale', *Journal of Law and Economics*, Vol. 54:1, pp. 54–71.

Stigler, G.J. and Becker, G.S. (1977) 'De Gustibus Non Est Disputandum', *The American Economic Review*, Vol. 67:2, pp. 76–90.

Stoelhorst, J.W. (2008) 'The Explanatory Logic and Ontological Commitment of Generalized Darwinism', *Journal of Economic Methodology*, Vol. 15:4, pp. 343–363.

Sweezy, P.M. (1956) 'Power Elite or Ruling Class?', *Monthly Review*, Vol. 8:5, pp. 138–149.

Tajfel, H. (1981) *Human Groups and Social Categories. Studies in Social Psychology*. Cambridge: Cambridge University Press.

Tuckett, D. (2011) *Minding the Market. An Emotional Finance View of Financial Instability*. London: Palgrave Macmillan.

Van Horn, R. (2009) 'Reinventing Monopoly and the Role of Corporations: the Roots of Chicago Law and Economics', in Mirowski, P. and Plehwe, D. (Eds) *The Road from Mount Pèlerin. The Making of the Neoliberal Thought Collective*. Cambridge, MA and London: Harvard University Press, pp. 204–237.

Wiarda, H.J. (1997) *Corporatism and Comparative Politics*. Armonk, NY and London: Sharpe.

Williams, G.C. (1966) *Adaptation and Natural Selection*. Princeton, NJ: Princeton University Press.

Williamson, O.E. (1985) *The Economic Institutions of Capitalism. Firms, Markets, Relational Contracting*. New York: Free Press.

Wilson, D.S. (2015) *Does Altruism Exist? Culture, Genes and the Welfare of Others*. New Haven, CT: Yale University Press.

Zaloom, C. (2006) *Out of the Pits. Traders and Technology from Chicago to London*. Chicago: The University of Chicago Press.

Postscript
A new ethics for a new liberalism?

In this book, the two main principles of neoclassical economics (the scientific nature of economics as well as the use of rational choice theory to explain economic behaviour) have been regarded as the pillars of neoliberalism, which has been described as the main outcome of 'economics imperialism'. Economic imperialism has been defined in several ways: 'the economics' capacity to colonize other social sciences' (Fine 2000, 1); 'the imperialist invasive power of [economics'] theoretical categories [which] were increasingly researching non-market interaction' (Grossbard-Shechtman and Clague 2002, 4); 'the imperialism of the discipline of economics in the academic realm and the economy-driven imperialism in international relations and the global economy' (Mäki 2009, 2).

The best definition of economic imperialism, in relation to the way it has been used in this book, is summarized in the following quotations taken from Laezar:

> Economics is not only a social science, it is a genuine science. Like the physical sciences, economics uses a methodology that produces refutable implications and tests these implications using solid statistical techniques. In particular, economics stresses three factors that distinguish it from other social sciences. Economists use the construct of rational individuals who engage in maximizing behavior. Economic models adhere strictly to the importance of equilibrium as part of any theory. Finally, a focus on efficiency leads economists to ask questions that other social sciences ignore. These ingredients have allowed economics to invade intellectual territory that was previously deemed to be outside the discipline's realm.
>
> (Laezar 2000, 99)

In the following passage, the author reminds the reader of the direct link between neoclassical economics, as it has been developed in the United States, and the neopositivist ideal of a unified science:

> The goal of economics is to unify thought and to provide a language that can be used to understand a variety of social phenomena. The most successful economic imperialists have used the theory to shed light on questions that lie far outside those considered traditional. The fact that there

have been so many successful efforts in so many different directions attests to the power of economics.

(Laezar, 2000, 142)

At the very beginning of the new millennium, Colander claimed the death of neoclassical economics; he proposed an 'economist-assisted terminasia' (Colander 2000, 127) because the term 'neoclassical' is useless and misleading to describe modern economics, which has to be intended as the 'economics of the model' (Colander 2000, 138). Moreover, historians of economics especially used to adopt the term in a schizophrenic and inconsistent way: the missing perfect overlap between neoclassical economics and modern economics' attributes emphasizes the necessity to keep them separated.

Contrary to Colander's suggestion, and more importantly despite the persistence of the consequences of the last financial crisis, it seems that neoclassical economics is still in a very good shape, as well as its direct cultural and political consequence, the neoliberal society. A possible way to escape from both neoclassical imperialism and neoliberalism could be by going through a reformulation of the discipline towards a more pluralistic approach which would take great account of ethics and would restore the authentic nature of economics as a political and social science.

As Boulding had explained, a moral proposition is a common value, upon which culture is grounded: 'a moral, or ethical proposition, is a statement about a rank order of preference among alternatives, which is intended to apply to more than one person' (Boulding 1969, 1). The main fault of neoclassical imperialism has been the belief in the 'Immaculate Conception of the Indifference Curve', as Boulding defined it (Boulding 1969, 2), i.e. the naïve idea that preferences are neutral and given: in a dynamic realm, as the one described by economics, this assumption has never been valid. Economics as a moral science is to be intended as a discipline which enables us to solve:

> ethical disputes, especially those which arise out of the continued increase of knowledge (...) [in fact] the process of human learning which is the main dynamic factor in all social systems, (...) is the learning of common values and moral choices, without which no culture and no social system is possible.
>
> (Boulding 1969, 4)

Some famous economists, like Stiglitz and Krugman, who are claiming to fight against the neoliberal agenda, are still far away from a deep critique of economics as a formal science, and their contributions do not radically threaten the theoretical toolbox of dominant economic theory. Other scholars are stressing that the value-free nature of neoliberalism is related to the intrinsic political contradictions of so-called financial capitalism (Crouch 2011; Brown 2015; Fraser 2015).

Following Pareto's description of the role of non-logical actions (actions driven by emotions and instincts) in social phenomena and in the evolution of society as a global system (Pareto [1916] 1963), it is fundamental to study the differences between 'derivations' (quasi-logical explanation able to rationally justify the role of emotions and instincts in human actions) and 'residuals' (permanent elements of human choice theory after having set derivations apart).

Weber's distinction between *zweckrational* (instrumentally rational social action determined by purpose and expectations about a behaviour taken under a condition of scarcity) and *wertrational* (value-rational social action determined by belief in the unconditional intrinsic value of some acts of choice) is also fundamental to understand the pluralism on which individual and social dynamics are grounded (Weber [1921] 1978).

Pareto's distinction as well as Weber's different types of rationality are central in order to understand the partiality of neoliberalism's anthropological interpretation of individual behaviour as well as its sociological explanation of social dynamics. Actually, the logic behind neoliberalism has discarded derivations and residuals, as well as value-rational, affective and traditional social actions. Neoliberalism has neglected the complicated nature of human rationality and the complex dynamics of society as a whole.

Pareto and Weber help us also when the discourse on neoliberalism shifts to the sociological dimension of political power. Pareto's elite theory as well as Weber's *Vorteil der kleinen Zahl* explained the role of elites in governing complex political systems. They are both aware of the fact that in a truly dynamic society, the most virtuous individuals would be involved in elites; but in actual societies, individuals who belong to elites are those able to adopt force and persuasions as well as to strategically use their wealth and family connections, which are often far from virtuous. Neoliberalism has emphasized this distortion, and it has presented it as ineludible.

Along with its theoretical fallacies mentioned above, neoliberalism has released ethical issues from any relevance in decision-making processes, and it has reduced them to a scale of efficiency. The historical development of neoliberalism, as occurred in the past, has fully shown that it has not increased efficiency. Furthermore, it has rather reduced social well-being and individual freedom.

Thus, the scenario is twofold: 1. to accept the great transformation of the twenty-first century, led by neoliberalism, as an irreversible process, by following a Hegelian scheme *à la* Lukács; 2. alternatively, to reject the ineluctability of the neoliberal outcome in order to search for a new theory of justice and freedom, *à la* Rawls or *à la* Sen-Nussbaum's approach.

Following scenario number 1, a Hegelian approach emerges. According to Hegel, the fundamental problem of economics is the relation between freedom (that is twofold: 'the satisfaction of subjective *particularity*' and 'the need and free will of others') and necessity (the manifestation of Reason in human history). In fact, in his *Philosophy of Right* he described the nature of political economy as:

> a science which (...) finds the laws underlying a mass of contingent occurrences. It is an interesting spectacle to observe here how all the interconnections have repercussions on others, how the particular spheres fall into groups, influence others, and are helped or hindered by these.
>
> (Hegel 1991, 228)

Although Hegel correctly posed the question of the idiosyncratic relation between individual freedom and social complexity, his solution, that considers freedom as the appreciation of necessity, can be regarded as the very first form of the logic of rational choice theory. On a related note, this is also one of the most powerful aspects of the ambiguity around the notion of freedom within the tradition of classic liberal philosophy.

Following scenario number 2, the urgency of a new ethic emerges. Setting aside the dispute around virtues and their proper use to build up a just and free society, the present state of neoliberal western society reveals the urgency 'to re-ethicize the social sciences' (McCloskey 2011, 24), and to go toward an effective ecological economics.

It is necessary to go back, at least partially, to the old principles of classical liberalism in a new perspective, based on what can be called virtuous nihilism. Against O'Neill (O'Neill 1996), a virtuous nihilism is possible. It will be restoring an ethics based on the classical virtues into the economic sphere, without any metaphysical implication.

Let's make this point clearer. According to the postmodern vogue, nihilism is, in the field of ethics, what corresponds to the 'anything goes' advocated by enthusiastic readers of Feyerabend's work in the field of epistemology. What is at stake here is not, in fact, the postulation of the non-existence of the truth and the consequent affirmation of the relativism in ethics and pluralism in epistemology. The point is, rather, to acknowledge how reasonable was Nietzsche's claim that individuals can be really free if and only if they have the opportunity to shape their own life according to principles that do not deserve an ultimate foundation (in the sense of a *Letztbegründung*). The narrative about god's death and the following emancipation of mankind from strong metaphysical burdens is essentially focused on this claim. Moreover, Nietzsche's conception of ethics suggests that the principles we need to give some order to our moral life depend on the notion of taste. As it is well known, taste has, traditionally, a bad reputation: Nietzsche's willingness to underscore the importance of taste, as far as ethical issues are concerned, is perhaps a symptom of his penchant for a certain philosophical coquetry. It is common to simply consider flawed any conception of ethics that does not rest on universal principles, which are *per definitionem* different from taste: moral principles remain the same, because they are linked with the metaphysical continuity in time of the subject that refers to them, while taste, as well as any other form of preference, can change over the course of time (Nagel 1970). To say that a strong foundation of value concepts is not strictly necessary, however, amounts simply to say that there must be an arena where the different positions – better, the different conceptions of good – have the opportunity to be tested, discussed, compared to each other, and so forth, as freely as individuals do when they decide to discuss differences concerning their tastes.

In other words, the claim that a virtuous nihilism or, better said, a post foundational ethic has a sufficient degree of plausibility means that a rational discussion about moral values is not aimed at constructing a moral theory: a good psychology of moral conducts would be enough. Strong moral theories, like utilitarianism or Kantism, imply either commitments to metaphysical assumptions or an excessive detachment from the empirical context within which moral subjects really live. To be plausible, however, the ethical discourse must be committed simply to the concreteness of the situation within which the moral subject is called to take decisions. Furthermore, any moral situation is rooted in the body that feels and is affected by emotions (Williams 1973).

Radicalizing the stance Williams has defended since the beginning of his philosophical career, Nussbaum has taken a step further by assuming that taking emotions seriously is a good premise to come to the construction of moral theories. The bodily sphere in which emotions are rooted is not the sphere of unconscious or irrational drives. Emotions have a cognitive significance; they are not simply the rough material upon which moral judgments are constructed. Thus, the philosophical reflection about how human beings should live their lives, how they should behave properly, and how they should interact with their mates, must stem from serious considerations about how human beings build and shape their preferences – even the preferences to which a moral significance is attributed – by listening to their emotions and feelings (Nussbaum 2001).

Nussbaum's aim is, however, to arrive at a substantial conception of good: it is more prudent to maintain a certain caution toward this substantial conception of good, though. It is preferable to observe how human beings conduct their lives in accordance with the importance they confer to their motivations. This formulation might sound pleonastic. Nevertheless, precisely in the case that a certain adherence to real life is felt as necessary, the difference between the simple fact that an individual has a reason for behaving in a specific way and the fact that another individual attributes a specific importance to the reasons that motivate the chosen action must be underscored. This process makes the nihilistic – or post foundational – approach to ethics meaningful: value concepts, as far as they constitute the reason to act, or, more precisely, the reason one would yield if asked to justify the choice to do or not to do something, are chosen for their emotional impact upon the subject, and for the amount of emotion that is connected to them. Emotions are important to individuals as decision makers. Acknowledging their importance means to be ready to observe with respect, and without irony, the intensity of moral conflicts. When disputing about value concepts and different morally relevant courses of action, individuals well know how violent the outcome of the dispute could be. In such a context, where the contrast between moral values reflects a contrast between different conceptions of the world, nobody would mark himself a relativist.

Nonetheless, a post foundational approach to ethics is well disposed toward the methodological relativism that characterizes cultural anthropology. This discipline does not provide examples of human behaviour that always fit into the compact building of moral theory. The set of case studies provided by cultural anthropology refines our insights and our capability to appreciate cultural differences. Deconstructing neoliberalism and its dogmatic efficiency-oriented principle as the only valid principle to handle values and goals, is essential. Neoliberalism tends to reduce the spread of cooperative behaviours and the possibility that cooperation will become the norm in social dynamics. This process would entail, *de facto*, a considerable reduction of the anthropological options disposable for the individuals living in a neoliberal society. This seems to be true with regard to the community composed by students of economics and their teachers (Frank, Gilovich and Regan 1993). On a broader scale, a greater diffusion of cooperation can be noticed in countries or populations that are not totally under the influence of the Western civilization and are closer to the periphery of the empire (Henrich *et al.* 2004). The anthropological perspective helps, in general, to recast how cooperation and competition are both essential components of human associated behaviour and how governmental frames bear upon them (Gintis *et al.* 2005; Bowles and Gintis 2011).

The recourse to data collected by anthropologists or evolutionary biologists is not, however, a simple aid that ethics needs in order to give more substance to its own theoretical framework. Ethics is all about looking at how individuals attempt to behave properly according to some reasons in the presence of some institutional frames that do play an essential role in shaping these reasons – as well as the preferences that mainstream economics considers not subject to any change (Hodgson 2002; 2006). An ethical discourse structured in this way can, then, become the presupposition for a well grounded and strategic critique of neoliberal reason.

In general, it seems difficult just to imagine a critique of given social arrangements that are regarded, no matter for what reason, as unfair, without proposing, at the same time, a modification of the institutional asset within which human action takes place. First, the presence of institutional contexts granting the fairness of the contest about controversial issues or principles is required. This fairness entails at least the implementation of the principle *audi alteram partem*, which is one the minimal requirements for a good society (Hampshire 2000). There are other requirements, however, that must be taken into consideration and are placed in a rather ambiguous position between the claim that procedures are all that we need and the claim that a substantive conception of good is at least desirable.

Drawing attention to the pivotal role played by procedures has always been a concern for the supporters of the classical liberal tradition. This occurred because a clear definition of governmental procedures would have constituted the best way to defend those spaces of liberty within which individuals are supposed to act in the absence of external constraints. Another reason to be concerned about the dangers represented by the shift from negative to positive liberty is related to the anthropological pessimism that pervades a big part of the liberal tradition. Contrary to republicanism *à la* Pettit, which is confident about the possibility that virtuous citizens can build a society where mutual relations based on non-domination can be developed either in institutional practices or in shared habits (Pettit 1997), a considerable part of the tradition of classical liberalism accepts the pessimistic conception of human relations that is impressively grounded in Hobbes' *Leviathan*: a political order governed by institutions aimed at regulating the normal interaction among humans, in order to prevent those who are governed from being governed too much.

What happens, however, when the old liberal order, which was supposed to provide for a clear separation of different realms of action within society, has lost its meaning, as in the case of contemporary neoliberal society? A sort of phantasmatic return of the late medieval and early modern conception of the body politic, as Kantorowicz (1957) described in his masterpiece, affects societies ruled by neoliberalism. Neoliberalism has transformed institutions into incorporated bodies, to be intended as organzations, for the government of individual lives as though they were subject to the rules of an enterprise. The neoclassical model of rationality assumes a mythological feature as soon as it leaves its original domain, i.e. economic theory, to become the discourse that innervates the neoliberal project.

In such a framework a step beyond classical liberalism would be necessary. This shift should embrace at least the possibility to open a discussion on a substantive theory of justice related to freedom. The increasing inequalities spread all around the world provide a topic – even if not everybody agrees with it – for going in this direction (Pogge 2008). Although the impossibility of reaching a universal consensus about the major tenets of this issue can be taken for granted, it can be useful to re-consider the question raised by the classical liberal tradition about a possible connection between virtue and government. In other words: if there are good reasons for being unsatisfied with both a general theory of justice, which could probably never reach a universal consensus, and the management of social issues like inequality based on the calculus of consensus which underpins the political project of neoliberalism, then, the only way out, albeit utopic, seems to refer to the theory of virtue that goes back to the ancients. As Aristotle taught us:

> justice is complete virtue; virtue, however, not unqualified but in relation to somebody else. It is complete virtue in the fullest sense, because it is the active exercise of complete virtue; and it is complete because its possessor can exercise it in relation to another person, and not only by himself.
>
> (Aristotle, *Eth. Nich.* 1129b 30)

And: 'in every kind of knowledge and skill the end which is aimed at is good (…) In the state, the good aimed at is justice; and that means what is for the benefit of the whole community' (Aristotle, *Pol.* 1282b 14).

The coexistence of a virtuous society and individual freedom is the persistent challenge of that post foundation ethic, if it is able to supersede the neoliberal vision.

References

Aristotle (1953) *The Nichomachean Ethics*. London: Penguin Books.
Aristotle (1962) *The Politics*. London: Penguin Books.
Boulding, K. (1969) 'Economics as a Moral Science', *American Economic Review*, Vol. 59:1, pp. 1–12.
Bowles, S. and Gintis, H. (2011) *A Cooperative Species: Human Reciprocity and Its Evolution*. Princeton, NJ: Princeton University Press.

Brown, W. (2015) *Undoing the Demos: Neoliberalism's Stealth Revolution*. New York: Zone.

Colander, D. (2000) 'The Death of Neoclassical Economics', *Journal of the History of Economic Thought*, Vol. 22:2, pp. 127–143.

Crouch, C. (2011) *The Strange Non-Death of Neoliberalism*. Cambridge: Polity.

Fine, B. (2000) 'Economics Imperialism and Intellectual Progress: The Present as History of Economic Thought', *History of Economics Review*, Vol. 32:2, pp. 10–35.

Frank, R.H., Gilovich, T. and Regan, D.T. (1993) 'Does Studying Economics Inhibit Cooperation?', *Journal of Economic Perspectives*, Vol. 7:2, pp. 159–171.

Fraser, N. (2015) 'Legitimation Crisis? On the Political Contradictions of Financialized Capitalism', *Critical Historical Studies*, Vol. 2:2, pp. 157–189.

Gintis, H., Bowles, S., Boyd, R. and Fehr, E. (Eds) (2005) *Moral Sentiments and Material Interests: The Foundations of Cooperation in Economic Life*. Cambridge, MA: The MIT Press.

Grossbard-Shechtman, S. and Clague, K. (2002) 'Introduction' in Grossbard-Shechtman, S. and Clague, K. (Eds) *The Expansion of Economics: Toward a More Inclusive Social Science*. Armonk and London: M.A. Sharpe, pp. 4–20.

Hampshire, S. (2000) *Justice is Conflict*. Princeton, NJ: Princeton University Press.

Hegel, G.W.F. (1991) *Elements of the Philosophy of Right*. Cambridge: Cambridge University Press.

Henrich, J., Boyd, R., Bowles, S., Camerer, C., Fehr, E. and Gintis, H. (2004) *Foundations of Human Sociality: Economic Experiments and Ethnographic Evidence from Fifteen Small-Scale Societies*. Oxford and New York: Oxford University Press.

Hodgson, G.M. (2002) 'The Evolution of Institutions: An Agenda for Future Theoretical Research', *Constitutional Political Economy*, Vol. 13, pp. 111–127.

Hodgson, G.M. (2006) 'What Are Institutions?', *Journal of Economic Issues*, Vol. 40:1, pp. 1–25.

Kantorowicz, E.H. (1957) *The King's Two Bodies. A Study in Mediaeval Political Theology*. Princeton, NJ: Princeton University Press.

Laezar, E. (2000) 'Economic Imperialism', *Quarterly Journal of Economics*, Vol. 115:1, pp. 99–146.

Mäki, U. (2009) 'Economics Imperialism: Concept and Constraints', *Philosophy of the Social Sciences*, Vol. 20:10, pp. 1–30.

McCloskey, D. (2011) 'Hobbes, Rawls, Nussbaum, Buchanan, and All Seven of the Virtues', *Journal des Economistes at des Etudes Humaines*, Vol. 17:1, pp. 1–28.

Nagel, T. (1970) *The Possibility of Altruism*. Princeton, NJ: Princeton University Press.

Nussbaum, M.C. (2001) *Upheavals of Thought. The Intelligence of Emotions*. Cambridge: Cambridge University Press.

O'Neill, O. (1996) *Towards Justice and Virtues: A Constructive Account of Practical Reasoning*. Cambridge: Cambridge University Press.

Pareto, V. [1916] (1963) *The Mind and Society. A Treatise on General Sociology*. New York: Dover Publications.

Pettit, P. (1997) *Republicanism. A Theory of Freedom and Government*. Oxford and New York: Oxford University Press.

Pogge, T. (2008) *World Poverty and Human Rights: Cosmopolitan Responsibilities and Reforms*. Cambridge: Polity.

Weber, M. [1921] (1978) *Economy and Society. An Outline of Interpretive Sociology*. Berkeley and Los Angeles: University of California Press.

Williams, B. (1973) *Problems of the Self*. Cambridge: Cambridge University Press.

Index

Locators in *italic* refer to tables/figures.

For Product Safety Concerns and Information please contact our EU
representative GPSR@taylorandfrancis.com
Taylor & Francis Verlag GmbH, Kaufingerstraße 24, 80331 München, Germany

www.ingramcontent.com/pod-product-compliance
Ingram Content Group UK Ltd.
Pitfield, Milton Keynes, MK11 3LW, UK
UKHW020955180425
457613UK00019B/697